PERGAMON INTERNATIONAL LIBRARY
of Science, Technology, Engineering and Social Studies
*The 1000-volume original paperback library in aid of education,
industrial training and the enjoyment of leisure*
Publisher: Robert Maxwell, M.C.

HABITAT:
Human Settlements in an Urban Age

Other Titles of Interest

BOON, G.
Townlook

DAVIES, R.L.
The Nature of Cities

DEWDNEY, J.C.
A Geography of the Soviet Union, 2nd Edition

HAWKES, L.R.
France: Our Nearest Neighbour

HAWKES, L.R.
Scandinavia

HAWKES, L.R.
West Germany and Benelux

JOHNSON, J.H.
Urban Geography, 2nd Edition

KERR, A.J.C.
The Common Market and How it Works

McINTOSH, I.G. & MARSHALL, C.B.
The Face of Scotland, 3rd Edition

PETRIE, R.
Ghana: Portrait of a West African State (An audio-visual kit)

SCOTT, D.S.
World Resources: Volume 1 Energy
                Volume 2 Metals

SCUDAMORE, C.N.J.
Transport Problems

SCUDAMORE, C.N.J.
Settlement Problems

RUSSELL, D.F.E.
Landforms and Maps

RUSSELL, D.F.E.
North America

WICKS, G.R.L.
Africa

HABITAT:
Human Settlements in an Urban Age

BY

ANGUS M. GUNN

PERGAMON PRESS

OXFORD · NEW YORK · TORONTO · SYDNEY · PARIS · FRANKFURT

U.K.	Pergamon Press Ltd., Headington Hill Hall, Oxford OX3 0BW, England
U.S.A.	Pergamon Press Inc., Maxwell House, Fairview Park, Elmsford, New York 10523, U.S.A.
CANADA	Pergamon of Canada Ltd., 75 The East Mall, Toronto, Ontario, Canada
AUSTRALIA	Pergamon Press (Aust.) Pty. Ltd., 19a Boundary Street, Rushcutters Bay, N.S.W. 2011, Australia
FRANCE	Pergamon Press SARL, 24 rue des Ecoles, 75240 Paris, Cedex 05, France
FEDERAL REPUBLIC OF GERMANY	Pergamon Press GmbH, 6242 Kronberg-Taunus, Pferdstrasse 1, Federal Republic of Germany

First edition 1978

British Library Cataloguing in Publication Data

Gunn, Angus M
Habitat. - (Pergamon international library).
1. Anthropo-geography
I. Title
301.34   GF101   77-30704
ISBN 0-08-021487-8 Hardcover
ISBN 0-08-021486-X Pbk
ISBN 0-08-022998-0 Pbk non-net

In order to make this volume available as economically and as rapidly as possible the author's typescript has been reproduced in its original form. This method unfortunately has its typographical limitations but it is hoped that they in no way distract the reader.

*Printed in Great Britain by William Clowes & Sons Limited
London, Beccles and Colchester*

To HEATHER and ANGUS Jr., potential citizens of the twenty-first century. I hope they will see in their lifetime the fulfilment of the well-known prediction: "They will hammer their swords into plows and their spears into pruning knives. Nations will never again go to war."

Contents

Preface

The purpose of this book is to present in a succinct and readable
form for secondary and tertiary students some of the information
gathered from all parts of the world and published at the time
of the Vancouver United Nations Habitat Conference, 1976.

I am chiefly indebted to the architects of Habitat for background information. They are the people who wrote the national
reports, convened numerous preparatory meetings and made the
proceedings available to the Conference, and prepared a library
of films. Together they have given us a "slice of time" invent-
ory of the condition of humanity in the mid seventies. In particular I am indebted to Maurice Strong for his views on energy,
some of which appear in chapter nine; to the Government of
Bangladesh, extracts from whose report form the fourth chapter;
to Barbara Ward for her historic appeal to the official conference delegates. That appeal is reproduced in chapter twelve.

It is a particular pleasure to be able to use extracts from my
old project, the High School Geography Project of the Association of American Geographers. That project has now moved into
public domain status so it is no longer endorsed by the copy-
right holder. I have quoted from the Urban Unit in chapters
one and two; from the Cultural Unit in chapter six; from the
Manufacturing and Agriculture Unit in chapter seven; from the
Habitat and Resources Unit in chapter eight.

Several people strongly encouraged me to undertake this work,
particularly Enrique Penalosa, Secretary-General of Habitat,
Robert Munro, Head of the Canadian Delegation to Habitat, and
Robert Maxwell, Director of Pergamon Press, official publishers
for Habitat materials. In thinking through the implications of
the Habitat documentation I have been helped by Wilson Garces,
Research Director for the United Nations Centre for Housing,
Building and Planning, and Barry Black and his staff from the
B.C. Provincial Educational Media Centre.

On the difficult task of spelling I have used traditional usage
for the most part, switching to North American for very few
words. Two examples of the latter are "billion" (a thousand
million) and "program".

University of British Columbia, Canada.   Angus M. Gunn

The Issues of Habitat

The issues of Habitat are not new - rapid population growth, urban overcrowding, rural stagnation, poverty, shelter shortage, quality of the environment, use of natural resources, adequate planning with appropriate energy usage and suitable scale technology. These issues have been with us for decades and we will confront them for decades to come.

Habitat, the name given to the 1976 Vancouver United Nations Conference on human settlements, was a moment in time when the world community focussed its attention in a comprehensive way, not just on some of these issues like Stockholm on the Environment in 1972 and Bucharest on Population a few years later, but on the totality of the man-made environment and its physical setting.

The use of the term "human settlements" seems redundant. Are not all settlements human? The term, however, has more subtle meanings. It is far from new. It dates back 30 years to the work of the late Constantinos Doxiadis, founder of the science of Ekistics, the study of rural and urban settlements as a unified whole. As he studied world settlements, he came to the conclusion that as man makes machines do more and more of his work, he pays the price of dehumanized surroundings. Doxiadis spent his life trying to design human environments, that is settlements that are human, providing a certain quality of life for their inhabitants.

The Habitat Conference will be remembered for the vast amounts of information collected on the urban slums of the world, and on the rural hinterlands that caused the slums. For two years prior to the conference this documentation was steadily assembled and now is available in a single place for the use of all the countries of the world. It will also be remembered as the place where the biggest problems facing mankind were faced squarely. They can never again be ignored.

Each chapter of the book deals with a specific issue, and the study of each issue is concluded with three questions - one answerable from the text, a second raising value questions for discussion, and a third extending the study beyond the documentation available in this book. In addition there are numerous maps, statistical charts, photographs, and an end table of facts and figures to further assist in the investigation process.

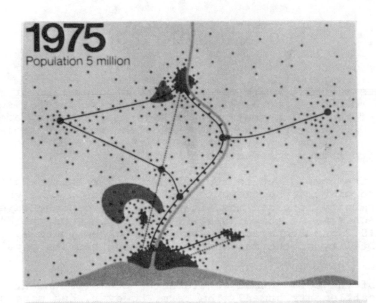

Typical small country

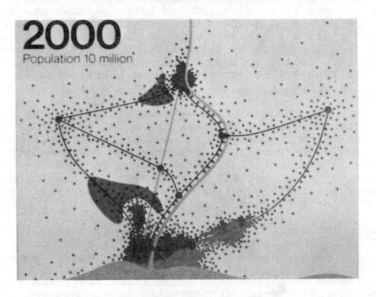

CHAPTER ONE

Rural-Urban System

Improved modes of travel, mass communication - especially television, and interchanges of all kinds of goods and services have profoundly affected our view of the world. No longer can we consider our planet a mosaic of different, largely independent places. Our world has become a single system.

Local cultures, under the influence of such powerful forces as major economic units, ideologies, and military alliances are rapidly evolving into patterns that look remarkably similar from place to place.

Even the familiar distinctions between rural and urban life are becoming blurred. The terms themselves are less and less useful as descriptors of settlements. For centuries towns were widely separated, small enclaves with forms and functions that marked them off from life in the surrounding countryside. Not so any more.

The most dramatic developments have taken place in space travel. The very nature of the vehicles used coupled with the new, remote sightings of the earth from outer space have led naturally to a systems view of the globe and its settlements.

Spaceship Earth

Imagine you are in a spaceship on its way to the moon. The earth gets smaller and smaller until it looks just about as big as the craft in which you are travelling. You begin to make comparisons between your craft and the earth. Both seem to be single, interdependent systems. In ways such as these people have developed the idea of the earth as a spaceship flying at an incredible speed.

There have been simulations developed to spell out this space-craft idea of planet earth. Terra II is the name of one of these. Young people are asked to imagine that they are part of a group of 100 humans far out in space. Like earth the craft has a supply of air, water, energy and food. These supplies can be polluted or used up leaving an environment in which people cannot live. The spaceship continues to support life only if water, air and food are recycled. The simulation goes on to suggest various emergencies that might arise and various ways of coping with these emergencies.

Once that first step was taken of describing the earth as one interdependent system it became easy to show examples of the interconnectedness of various parts. Some of these parts are marked on Fig. 1.1.

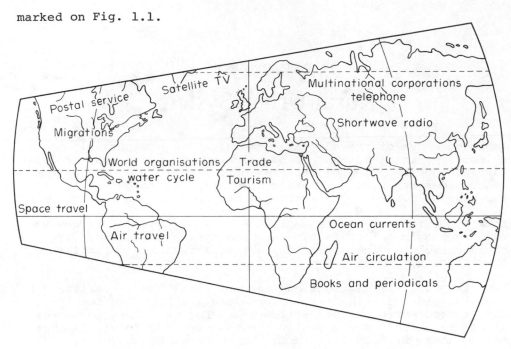

Fig. 1.1 Subsystems of Spaceship Earth

Our small world has become truly interdependent, and the term originally coined by Marshall McLuhan, the global village, has become very much a reality. The efficient functioning of the whole is dependent on the efficient functioning of each part.

Take, for example, the layer of atmosphere that envelops our globe. It is constantly in motion. The world's wind systems make the Canadian atmosphere of today the Russian atmosphere of tomorrow. When China explodes a nuclear device above ground it is not long before planetary winds carry the fallout around the globe. In 1883 the Indonesian island of Krakatau exploded under the pressure of a volcanic eruption and red sunsets were observed worldwide.

It is similar with our social world. Social change keeps accelerating so that traditional systems are disrupted. Over the past 20 years tourism has become the fastest growing industry in the world, growing from a total population of 25 million in 1950 to more than 200 million today. Think of the social effect of large numbers of people from one country with its culture and standard of living coming into contact with large numbers of people in a different country with a different culture and a different standard of living. The effect can be very great, the new demands for changes very strong. These changes are all the more significant when it is remembered that

a great deal of tourist travel takes place from the affluent
countries of the west to the developing countries of Africa,
South America, and Asia.

Still another facet of our interlocking world are the operations
of multinational corporations. Though not well known, they
profoundly affect economic life all over the globe. They have
shifted control from the individual nation to the board rooms of
corporations. Some of these corporations operate in a hundred
countries with head offices in such places as London, New York
and Zurich. Some corporations have the power to ruin the
economy of a country simply by shifting their money reserves
from one currency to another.

The case of Chile in 1973 is a dramatic example of the power of
multinationals. The big bankers of the world objected to the
socialist policies of the man who was President at that time,
so they refused to lend credit. This led to wild inflation and
indirectly caused the overthrow of the government by a military
coup.

There is no indication that multinationals are losing their
power. In fact the opposite seems to be happening. One leading
economist expects that their power will rise from a present
level of 15% of the gross world product to 50% by the year 1985.
At that time it is expected that control of the 50% will rest
with 300 giant corporations.

Some years ago a group of scientists published a book called
Limits to Growth. It was a review of the trends and the
resource consumption in the global system, and it was
devastating in its prediction of doom. By the year 2000, it
predicted, the inevitable doom of mankind would be sealed. By
that time, according to the authors of Limits to Growth, it
would be too late to attempt remedial action.

Although some faults were later found in a computer program
that the authors used, one thing became quite clear. Population
and capital are both increasing at a constantly accelerating
rate. That rate of growth, particularly the acceleration of
that rate, must come to an end before the year 2050. The big
question has to be faced: is mankind prepared for, or willing
to adjust to life in a no growth society.

David Weitzman in his book Communicating across Time and Space
has a chapter entitled "Toward the Global Village". The first
three were speech, ability to write, and printing. The fourth
revolution according to Weitzman was the electronic revolution -
telephone, radio, television and now satellite communications.
In 1965, Earlybird, the first commercial communications
satellite, was launched. Its relay made available 240 voice
circuits and one television channel. Six years later another
satellite, a much bigger one, went aloft with a capacity of
6,000 voice circuits and 12 television channels. Six years
from now the space shuttle will be in operation and anyone can

send up their own private communications satellite for a cost
of something like $3,000.

The day of individual television stations will soon be past. An
unlimited number of voice and picture channels have become
available so that anyone can now have a portable phone and dial
any number on earth. The printed word, in a computerized space
relay world, can be transmitted as easily and as widely as the
voice. Facsimile newspapers, magazines, and books can be
readily available at the press of a button. The earth for the
first time is knit together on a personal instead of a
governmental level.

The story is a similar one for all the other tentacles that link
together the parts of planet earth - trade, air travel,
activities of world organizations like the United Nations, and
so on. And the result, as has already been pointed out is the
collapse of the sharp differences that used to exist between
places. The ways by which the rural-urban system has become a
single unit of human occupance can be traced historically. They
can also be illustrated in some of today's settlements.

Rural - Urban Systems

The percentage of people living in urban areas has been growing
at an alarming rate. See Fig. 1.2. At the same time the sizes
of the larger settlements have been increasing at an even
faster rate, and their nature has been changing. The process
began about a century ago in western Europe. Cities which had
previously been separate began to merge. Groups of cities
behaved as if they were one single city. They shared common
services while retaining their political independence.

A similar pattern has since developed in most countries of the
world. In 1970 there were 174 cities of more than 1 million
inhabitants, 50 of them with at least 2½ million. In 1920 only
20% of the developing world's people lived in cities of more
than 500,000. At that time the corresponding figure of the
developed world was 47%. By 1960, however, it was 43% in the
developing world and 49% in the countries we have come to call
the developed world.

Drastic alterations have accompanied these unequal rates of
growth of big cities and smaller towns. Some urban centres are
highly concentrated, like New York, others are widely dispersed
like Los Angeles. But in both types there is a growing tendency
for the formation of super agglomerations, like Megalopolis
in which the big cities are surrounded by smaller towns and the
spaces in between are being occupied by residential areas.

The three areas of the world in which these super agglomerations
have already developed are: Tokaido, Japan, involving Tokyo,
Osaka, and Nagoya; U.S. Megalopolis, involving Boston, New York,
Philadelphia, and Washington; Northwest Europe, involving
Belgium, Netherlands, and parts of West Germany, France and
Britain. In each of these three areas total population exceeds
50 million.

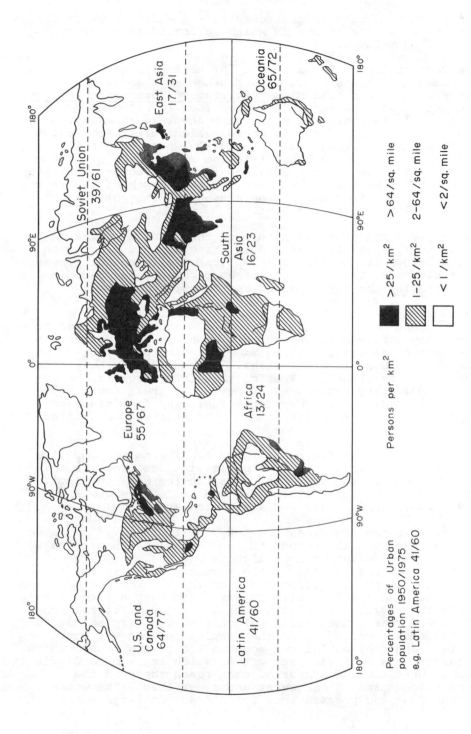

Fig. 1.2 World Population Distribution 1975
and major changes in urban population 1950 – 1975

In less than a century we have come from a world in which cities
of 100,000 were rare to one in which we can identify urban
systems of 50 million.

Pierre Dansereau, of the University of Montreal, has described
the process of collapsing rural and urban settlements into a
single system in his book <u>Man - Environment Interaction at the
Settlement Level</u>. Dansereau outlines four levels of human
occupance. 1. the wild state in which people earn a living by
hunting or fishing; 2. rural, where agriculture is the chief
mode of earning a living;   3. industrial, where things like
mining and manufacturing constitute the main source of income;
4. urban, where the various services to others constitutes the
main function. He goes on to show how the growth of the fourth
category is the main cause of the present merging of human
settlements into a single system.

The widespread and profound nature of the changes overtaking
settlements are well illustrated in three case studies which
correspond roughly to Dansereau's first 3 categories. These
case studies are: The Inuit of northern Canada; the Bedouin of
southwest Asia; the new types of settlements in Israel.

<u>Canadian Inuit</u>
For a thousand years the Inuit, or the Eskimo as they used to be
called, have survived in the north of Canada by adjustment to
the demands of a rigorous climate. They have built their houses
out of snow or out of animal skins. They obtained their food
by hunting or by fishing. They clothed themselves in the furs
of the animals they caught. They developed great sensitivity
to climatic conditions. They found their way from place to
place by windetched landmarks that would scarcely be noticed
by a person from southern Canada.

The sufferings and hardships of their traditional way of life
have been great. In winter time out on the ice floe the only
source of food was the seal, and to catch the seal the Inuit
had to move out over the frozen sea and build snowhouses -
igloos - and live in these for six months at a time.

In summer when the ice floes break up the Inuit moved south to
catch the cariboo. Throughout the summer the cariboo moves
northward, feeding upon summer lichens and the mosses, then
heads south towards the end of the summer. At this time he is
fattest and his fur is at its best condition. The cariboo is a
poor swimmer and so the Inuit can drive him into a lake, over-
take him in a kayak, and kill him with a spear. For the other
third of the year - the fall - salmon trout, or arctic char as
they are usually called, form the staple food for the Inuit.
They are trapped by building a pond in the rivers - into which
the char can easily move - but out of which it is more difficult
to jump. When a large number of char reach the pond the
fisherman can stand in the water and spear them. The women
clean the fish and prepare them for storage in large caches.

This hunting and fishing lifestyle, seal, cariboo or char, is a response to an environment over which the Inuit could exercise little control. Over the centuries the average temperature of his hands and of the muscles of his arms have dropped to a level of 5 degrees lower than that of southern Canadians. It is an adjustment to the environment that permits the Inuit to work with bare hands in temperatures that would cause others to feel a great deal of pain.

Modern conditions have profoundly altered this traditional culture and posed new problems for the Inuit. To begin with, health services from government sources in the post World War II period cut back dramatically on death rates. The result was a very great increase in population. At the same time the introduction of the rifle made it easy to catch the seal or the cariboo. The net result was severe shortages both of seals and cariboo.

The reasons for this shortage are easy to find. A larger population had to be fed because of the cut in death rate. The rifle made it possible to catch seals and cariboo for other purposes than their own immediate needs. Southern demands for sealskins soon led to hunting over and above the local needs. Sealskins were often removed and the meat left for wolves to eat. The wolf packs grew stronger with the extra food supply and so they were able to kill more cariboo, and thus further reduce the cariboo population.

In earlier times when food supplies were low all those who could not be fed died, and the human population kept adjusting in this way to the available supply of food. This kind of adjustment is not necessary today, but the alternatives are not pleasant. They involve the acceptance of an entirely new way of life - either wage earning jobs in the rapidly developing energy industry of northern Canada or government welfare. An age old culture is rapidly disappearing.

There are all kind of additional problems facing the Inuit. In competition with southern Canadians who have moved northwards in the wake of the new development thay are at a disadvantage. The white people are the ones with all the experience, the money, the status, and the greater numbers, and so they get the best jobs and exercise major control in all the new settlements of the north. The urban way of doing things has come to stay, even to the extent of portable plastic igloos.

Kuwait
One day about 70 years ago, a dhow arrived from Bombay with a cargo of timber and gold for a merchant in Kuwait. Dhows do not have strong-rooms, and the gold bars were just stowed on a sack below deck. The crew were some of the poorest men you could find in Arabia. When the dhow reached Kuwait, the captain sent the ship's boy to take the two bars of gold to the merchant. He carried them uncovered on his shoulders, through the crowds in the bazaar to the merchant's house in the main street.

Finding no one at home the boy put the gold on the top step in
front of the door.

An hour later the merchant returned, found the two gold bars,
took them inside and weighed them. There was far too much. The
gold was not meant for him. Then he took the two bars farther
down the street to another merchant, who was expecting some gold
of that weight.

Nowadays that little transaction would be regarded as gold
smuggling, but Kuwait was pretty free of international laws and
regulations at that time and for a thousand years before that
time. In fact, the days when Arab ships sailed from Kuwait to
be pirates in the Persian Gulf are so recent that an older
man can have exciting tales to tell of his experiences as a
pirate. In the recent past Bedouins arrived with herds of
camels which had been captured from another tribe in a
lightning raid made in the hour before sunrise, or under cover
of a howling sand storm.

But enormous wealth has now come to Kuwait and the old ways are
fast disappearing. The dreams of wealth and power foretold in
the Arabian Night's story of Aladdin's lamp have come true for
this country. Aladdin was a young man who had a magic lamp.
Every time he rubbed the lamp a genie appeared to do whatever he
wished. Oil has become the genie of Kuwait.

One man bought a piece of land in Kuwait City in 1940 for 10
dollars. In 1960 he sold it for 20,000 dollars. Someone had
discovered an oil well below it. The per capita wealth that
has come to Kuwait over the past 20 years exceeds that of all
other countries in the world.

Kuwait's educational system in the 1960's called for the
serving of 14,000 free meals every day in the various schools in
the town. These were supplied from a central kitchen, one of
the largest in the world. The food was distributed in thermos
container-cars, and even on holidays the schools' dining rooms
were open so that the children could come and have lunch there,
as on ordinary days.

The poorest Bedouin was able to send his boy straight from his
tent, unwashed, to one of these places, and there, without it
costing him a penny, his son was washed, clothed and stuffed
with knowledge.

The construction boom and other business activities have
attracted large numbers of immigrants to the country. The
social fabric has changed drastically. The old city has changed
too. Water comes from the sea via expensive distilling machines
instead of by barge from the Tigris and Euphrates rivers. Air
conditioners are commonplace as are also the cadillacs. And
the Sheik's summer homes in Europe rival in luxury those of the
medieval lords.

In the short space of one generation the bedouins, the
fishermen, the little merchants of this part of the Persian
Gulf have become world citizens with a lifestyle like that of a
Londoner or a New Yorker.

Israel

About 20 years ago a major resettlement program was launched
in the southern part of Israel to accommodate the many thousands
of Jews who were coming to Israel from Europe, Asia and North
America. The basic unit of the new settlement system was a
compact village organized either as a kibbutz or a moshav.

The design of this settlement brought rural and urban life into
one functioning whole instead of the traditional separate
functions and informal methods of co-operation. Fig. 1.3 shows
the actual and functional arrangements for the region.

The A unit, the village, is a series of 100 family units
focussed on agricultural activities. There is a small store, a
medical clinic, a kindergarten, a synagogue and a secretariat
building. The B unit, the rural centre, is larger and has a
service function for the surrounding A-type units. There are
housing units for the non-agricultural workers, a school, a
technical institute, marketing station, a machinery station, and
some cultural institutions.

The C unit, the urban unit, is a manufacturing centre. The plan
for Qiryat Gat was that it be a marketing and service centre for
three surrounding B-type units, Nehora, Nahala, and Even Shmuel.

Behind the establishment of this novel integrated settlement lay
years of experimentation and difficulty, dating back to the
beginning of the new state in 1948. One feature of this period
was the steady growth of moshav type settlements, and the
decline of the older and more rigorous kibbutz style villages.

	No. of settlements in 1948	No. of settlements in 1974
Moshav	91	352
Kibbutz	151	232

The moshav is a cooperative of farms, each with 100 farm units.
Each farming family is a separate economic and social unit,
tilling its own fields and making its own decisions. All
supplies (fertilizers, seeds, fodder) are purchased by the
cooperative and made available to the farmers on a credit basis,
with repayment from market returns. The produce is marketed by
the cooperative, each farmer being credited according to his
share in the products marketed. Certain other operations and
services are also on a cooperative basis, e.g., collection,
sorting and packing of produce, storage, agricultural machinery.
The elected village committee also handles social services
(education, health, entertainment,) for the farmers.

The kibbutz is quite different. It is a unique form of settlement.

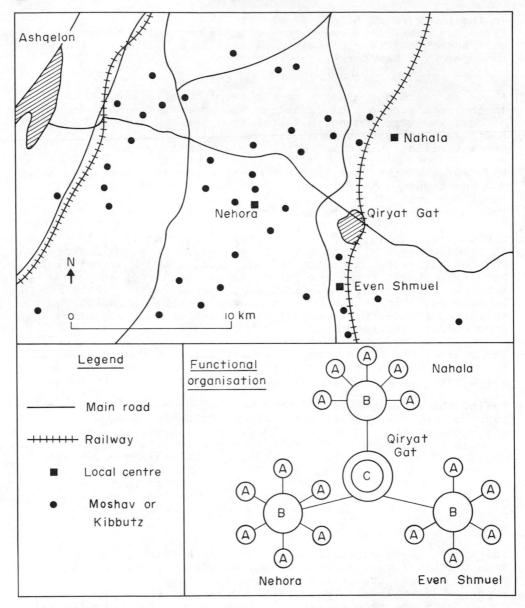

Fig. 1.3   Rural - Urban Systems in Israel

Each family has a separate house, but meals are served in a
communal dining hall and in most kibbutzim the children live in
separate nurseries or houes.   Production is managed and
operated as a single unit, each member working according to a

centralized work-schedule. All personal services are provided
for the members by the collective. Elected committees are in
charge of economic planning and development and decisions on
investments. Matters of major importance, such as decisions on
the budget, the election of committees and branch managers are
submitted to the general meeting of members. The profits are
not distributed among the members, but are re-invested in
production branches or used to raise the standard of living.

The majority of the immigrants to these settlements had not been
employed in agriculture prior to their arrival in Israel. Most
of them came from an urban background and the minority that had
lived in rural areas either did not practice agriculture there
or were engaged in subsistence agriculture. Many came from
developing countries and had cultural backgrounds very different
from those in Israel. Their adjustment to the structure of the
country's settlements, based on cooperative systems, was
especially difficult.

For those immigrants from Afro-Asian countries, adaptation of
the traditional societies even to the moshav pattern was not
simple. The immigrants usually arrived as whole communities,
not as individuals, and they brought with them their own way of
life - the patriarchal, traditional way of life based on the
clan - the stratified family with all its ramifications. At
first an attempt was made to treat this new population just as
the earlier immigrants had been treated. This procedure failed,
and in 1952 - 1953 the whole settlement program which formed
the backbone of development in Israel, seemed to be crumbling.

A new approach was tried in which the methods of development
and of instruction were adapted to the social structure of the
new settlers. Sociological researchers observed and followed-
up the special characteristics of each ethnic group and
adjusted development methods accordingly. To gain the full
cooperation of the population concerned, the new settlers were
trained and encouraged to take matters into their own hands and
to participate in all stages of the development process.

The Qiryat Gat regional structure was a response to the needs
of the new settlers. It had a social aim as well as an economic
one. Experiments until 1954 to settle immigrants from different
countries of origin in one village were not successful, because
of the constant friction between settlers of different backgrounds. The new system allowed each village to remain as one
ethnic unit and integration took place in the centres, at the
central school, at social events, at work, at the clinic and in
the shopping area. Thus constant contact between the settlers
was maintained, while their village remained independent social
units. The main functional design for the region did not work
out as intended, however.

What happened is what has been happening all over the world.
Many of the settlements found their links with other places than
the obvious nearest centre. Many of them went to Ashqelon or

even to the major cities further north. The ease of
communication by road or by rail, and the increasing exchange
of ideas and of people from place to place has the effect of
widening the range of potential contacts, and widening the
interests of the people for exploitation of these contacts.

Another unexpected development was the rapid growth of Qiryat
Gat beyond its expected maximum population. The original target
of 10,000 was designed in relation to a service function for the
surrounding B units. Now, however, with its development as an
independent settlement, over and above any service function for
the other areas, there is scope for a larger settlement. The
population is now 21,000, more than double the original intended
population. It is expected to reach 80,000 within the next 20
years.

Megalopolis and Ecumenopolis

Jean Gottmann, the French geographer, who wrote the book
Megalopolis, was one of the earliest writers to identify the
shift toward a rural-urban system. In his book he described the
large cluster of urban areas extending from Boston to Washington
D.C. on the east coast of the United States. See Fig. 1.4. He
noticed that the very size of this urban area had changed the
whole pattern of land use, and had changed it very rapidly in
the middle of the present century. The development itself was
not seen to be new. It had been observed before in Europe.
The scale and speed however, of the U.S. development marked it
off as unique.

Why did Megalopolis develop where it did?

Three hundred years ago the area now called Megalopolis was but
a small outpost of European settlement. Other parts of the
world had a much longer history of city growth. There were
numerous major cities on other continents from which a
megalopolis might have developed.

If metropolitan growth on a large scale was to occur in the
New World, why did it occur along part of the Atlantic Coast?
Surely other parts of the United States were more favoured with
fertile soil, mineral wealth, and with more amenable climates.
The answer is not simple, but some of the factors that led to
the growth of the area can be identified.

Located in this area were the first major cities to develop in
the United States: Boston, New York, and Philadelphia. Since
they were located on deep natural harbors, ideal for receiving
ocean-going vessels, they were main connecting links in the
trade between Europe and the North American continent. Thus
they had a head start in growth.

The area has maintained its head start to a large degree by
continuing efforts to improve transportation and communication
facilities. The necessary capital, labour, and demand have
been concentrated there to generate further growth and develop-

ment of the area's links with the rest of the world. So a
naturally accessible area has become even more accessible
through the accumulated efforts of generations of workers.

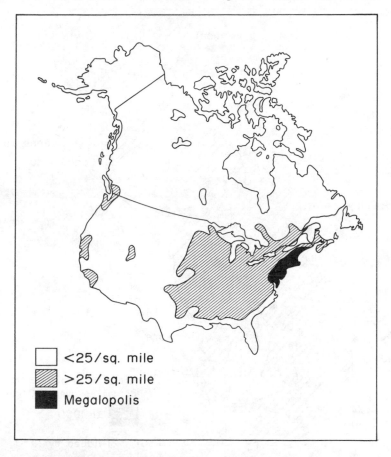

Fig. 1.4 Location of Megalopolis

Megalopolis covers less than 2 percent of the land area of the
continental United States but houses nearly 20 per cent of its
population.

To someone who lives there it may not seem at all like one
great urban mass though the maps of population density might
give this impression. See Fig. 1.5

Nearly half of Megalopolis is wooded, and there are many small
farms scattered throughout the region. Though urban development
is increasing, much land of rural appearance remains.

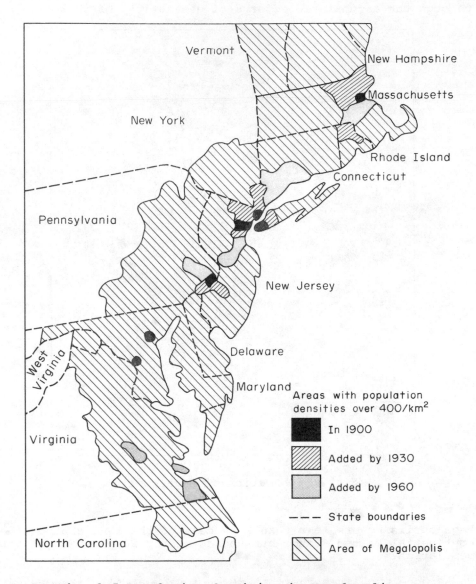

Fig. 1.5 Population densities in Megalopolis

The agricultural and woodland areas, however, are closely linked
with the urbanized areas. Agriculture is geared to supplying
city dwellers with fresh dairy products, poultry products,
fruits, and vegetables. Many of the people living on farms
work at regular jobs in the urban centers and only work their
farms part time. Those who do farm full time do so with

factory-like efficiency. They use space intensively. One dairy
farm is housed on the second floor of a Manhattan building and
rotates part of its herd to a pature in Pennsylvania for some of
the year. In many respects, megalopolitan agriculture is beginning to resemble other urban industrial organizations.

The open space of the region serves an urban function by providing an outlet for city tensions in the form of breathing space
and stretching space. Some people own country homes to which
they can retreat on weekends or in the summer. Countless
others enjoy Sunday drives and picnics in the less crowded outskirts of the cities. Many private and public groups operate
recreational facilities open to large numbers of people.
Scenic areas are within the reach of any urban dweller.

Megalopolis is the political and economic capital of the United
States. Governmental functions are centered in Washington, D.C.
Financial enterprises cluster in New York, as do the headquarters of radio, television, advertising, and magazine
publishing companies. Communications-oriented businesses find
this area particularly attractive since it is the communications
hub of the nation.

Others too have identified patters of human occupance on the
surface of the earth. In 1933 Walter Christaller of Germany
developed a hexagonal theory of settlement based on the effect
of a natural hierarchy of communicating centres. Christaller's
ideas stem from observed patterns in the natural world. He
sought to compare human activities with those of the inorganic
and insect world to see if there were any correspondence in
patterns, and he found that there were.

When a bee wishes to find the maximum amount of space for a
given amount of wax in a limited area under the ground it
instinctively chooses hexagonal shaped cells for the purpose.
This is the most economical way of using wax for cells within a
limited space. When certain minerals deep inside the earth
solidify and form crystals in a limited space they conserve
their texture by adopting hexagonal shapes. Again it's the
same principle of conservation of surface. In a similar way
Christaller observed that if people wanted to maximise their
contacts and minimize their distance of travel within a limited
area the best centres from which to operate would be the centres
of a set of hexagons.

Christaller was not the first person to discover this. He was
the one who systematized it into a theory of human settlement.
But back in 1870, more than 60 years before Christaller's time,
a Turkish general in Iraq had established a centre to coincide
with five existing settlements each of which formed the centre
of a hexagonal grid.

Christaller's theory of hexagons fitted a settlement pattern in
China at the time of the revolution in 1949. For hundreds of
years peasants in that region had walked to market twice or

three times a week to sell their pigs or grain in exchange for
soap, incense, or the services of a fortune teller or a letter
writer. Fig. 1.6 shows both the actual distribution of market
towns and the idealized hexagon pattern which they so closely
resemble.

Walking distance for the basic necessities of life was about 3
kilometres. It was possible for the peasants to travel that
distance frequently, even with their burdens of farm products.
So the basic market towns were found within that range of the
farms. For items that were less in demand, things like cloth
or money, it was possible for the peasant to travel farther
because he did not need these things frequently. So the market
centres which provided these things were bigger and more widely
scattered as the hexagon drawing shows.

Szechwan is one of the largest of the Chinese provinces. High
mountains ring and isolate its heart, the Szechwan or Red Basin
(so named because of the red sandstone bedrock). The Chengtu
(pronounced Jungdu) plain is the largest plains area. Even
that is hilly in parts.

The name Szechwan means "Four Streams"; there are many rivers,
flowing rapidly and cutting deep gorges. One of the main rivers
of Szechwan, the Min, waters the Chengtu plain, which has an
ancient irrigation system. Downstream the rivers join to form
the Yangtze. Most of the rivers are navigable within the basin,
providing water transportation.

Because the mountain ring forms a barrier against the cold winds
the growing season is eleven months long, permitting the growth
of almost every crop found in China. The humidity is high, and
the cloud cover almost constant.

Man has left his mark on the landscape everywhere, from
mountains to plains. The population is dense and rural, and the
agriculture is intensive, with long-terraced hillsides. The
major products are rice, sweet potatoes, sugar cane, silk, tea,
citrus fruit, tobacco, cotton, and tung oil.

The two most important cities are Chengtu and Chungking,
(pronounced Jung-ging) to which the Nationalist Chinese moved
their capital in 1938, to escape the Japanese. These two
cities were joined by rail in 1952. The second rail line of the
province, built in 1958, joins Chengtu to Pao-chi (pronounced
Bao-ji), 400 miles to the north across the Tsinling Mountains.

What has happened to the system since the communist regime
came to power in 1949?

In August 1958, an attempt was made to abolish the traditional
peasant marketing system, including the periodic markets. This
nearly paralyzed distribution and, through lack of supplies and
equipment, agricultural production.

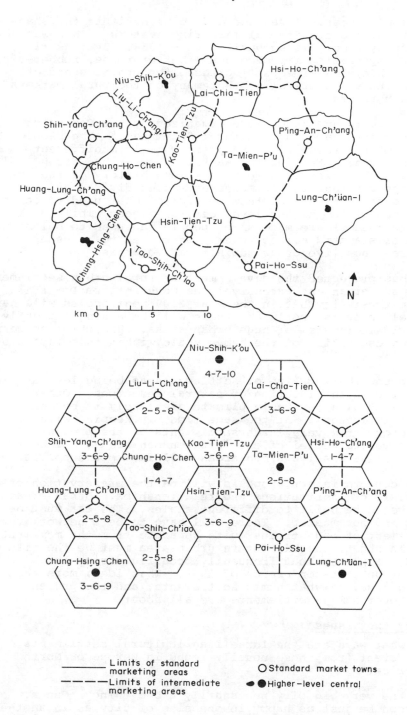

Fig. 1.6 Szechwan, China; patterns of settlement

The following year, it was decided to reinstitute the shape and
structure of the traditional marketing systems. This was not
successfully accomplished until 1962 - 1964. By this time, however, transportation improvements - better roads, rubber-tired
carts and bicycles - had so increased the travel speed of
peasants and suppliers alike that many of the rural markets
were now unnecessary.

Chinese farmers and lands were organized by the Communist
government into large agricultural "communes." The people who
were to work on these communes often came from different
marketing areas. Each of the marketing areas had strong
internal social ties because of the long history of the system.
It now appears that the communes have been divided and re-
organized so that many of them consist of what used to be the
trade areas of the higher level central places, while work
groups (brigades) are made up of people who used to belong to
the former standard market towns. What used to be natural
trade areas now live on as administrative areas.

No-one has projected the development of rural-urban settlement
systems so far and so extensively as Constantinos Doxiadis.
His main thesis is that in the year 2100 megalopoles will have
spread all over the world and there will be a single tightly
knit worldwide system of huge urban areas. His chief concern
was the preservation of the human scale within this vast urban
network.

Doxiadis saw the location of settlements as being less and less
dependent upon the location of natural resources. Other
factors such as a favorable climate are likely to be more
powerful influences. At the same time, in keeping with so much
past history, the very large settlements of the present time
will become the nuclei of the future urban areas. Linked
together these massive urban areas will form ecumenopolis.

The big concern in ecumenopolis will be the preservation of a
human scale of institutions and relationships. Urban areas
will have to be built to different scales. The car must be
servant and not master. There will have to be a network for
the movement of pedestrians quite separate from the movement of
cars. In short, the big future urban area must be the city of
mankind - a phrase that frequently occurred during the
Vancouver Habitat conference of 1976. This idea, more than
anything else, is what human settlements, and the present
concern over human settlements are all about.

Identify the issues

1.   In what ways are the Israeli agricultural settlements
     different from those usually found in Europe or North
     America?

2.   Is the very big city necessarily a bad thing? Can a
     person be just as happy in one size of city as in another?

3. To what extent is your community a part of the worldwide
   system which has been described as "spaceship earth"?
   Make a list of the world "tenacles" that are found in the
   place in which you live.

"Urbanization is worldwide, but is is most rapid in the developing countries where most towns and cities have more than
doubled their populations in the past decade. Municipal governments in these countries are being overwhelmed by the problems
facing them. They cannot control their growth, nor can they
provide adequate housing, public services, or amenities.
Industry and commerce expand, but not fast enough to keep pace
with the demand for jobs. Without money to pay rent, urban
newcomers cluster in every available empty space, living in
makeshift shacks. The squatter settlements often hold a third
or more of total urban populations, and continue to spread. The
squatters and their families are urban pioneers. They work hard
to improve their small homes, adding a window, a door or an
extra room whenever they find material. Their communities
quickly build a social organization with leaders, mutual
protection and small businesses. Earlier government policies
of forced evacuation and bulldozing have given way to a
realization that the squatter settlements fulfil a social
function." From Habitat Preparatory Paper.

CHAPTER TWO

Urban Frontier

The urban frontier, the dilapidated settlement sector of urban
areas, is today's biggest challenge to mankind. Huts and
hovels, sometimes no shelter at all - only a bit of space - are
accumulating on these urban fringes as multitudes flock in from
the countryside in search of a better life.

The settlements are known by different names in different
places: gecekondu in Turkey, shantytown in Manila, bustee in
India, favela in Brazil, barriadas in Peru, colonias
proletarias in Mexico, bidonville in Morocco and sharifa in
southwest Asia. The general term "slums and squatter settlements" has been adopted to describe the many kinds of human
clusters in this frontier all over the world.

Urban areas in the lesser developed countries now accommodate
about 760 million people. In 10 years it is expected that
another 411 million will be added. By the year 2000 the figure
will have tripled. In Africa it will have increased fivefold.
Altogether these developing countries will continue to urbanize
at a rate that is 2½ times that of the developed countries.
See Fig. 2.1.

In the year 1950 there were only 70 cities in the world with a
population of 1 million or more. Today the developed countries
have 84 of these "millionaire" cities, and developing countries
have an additional 74. By the year 2000, at present rates of
growth, it is expected that there will be 276 of these very big
cities. See Fig. 2.2. And the majority of this new urban
population is likely to be very poor.

One result of these trends is that by the year 2000, 23 other
metropolitan areas will join New York and Tokyo in the super-
city class with more than 12.5 million inhabitants each. See
Fig. 2.3 and 2.4. Of these no fewer than 18 will be in developing countries. Mexico City, Sao Paulo and Shanghai will be
first to arrive at super-city size, followed by Peking, Bombay,
Calcutta, Seoul, Buenos Aires, Rio de Janeiro, Cairo, Karachi,
Teheran, New Delhi, Bangkok, Manila, Lima, Bogota and Jakarta.

About 40 percent of the present population of urban areas in
the developing world live in slums and squatter settlements.
In Africa the figures run like this: 90 percent of the
population in Addis Adaba; 61 percent in Accra; 33 percent in
Nairobi. In Asia, 67 percent in Calcutta; that amounts to a
total of 6 million people, and of these 2 million live in the
worst kind of slum.

23

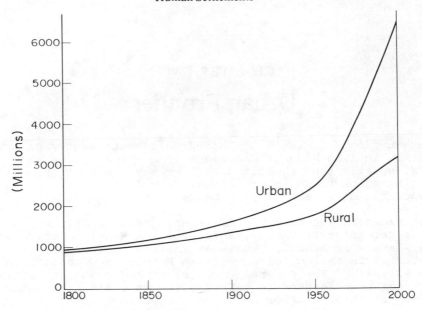

Fig. 2.1 Growth of world's rural and
urban populations, 1800 - 2000

In Latin America the story is similar to that of the other two
developing world continents: 46 percent in Mexico City; 40 percent in Lima; 42 percent in Caracas. And those slums and
squatter settlements are growing at a rate that is double that
for the urban areas as a whole.

Traditionally urbanization has been high in the wealthier parts
of the world. See Fig. 2.5. The present pace of urbanization
in poorer countries is therefore a new and unexpected phenomenon.

Conditions vary greatly from place to place around the world.
Physically they differ in size, location, density, terrain
conditions and services generally. But of greater importance
are the social and psychological conditions - the degree of
cohesion among groups, people's backgrounds, what their
aspirations are, and what opportunities for economic and social
improvement exist.

Statistics gathered for the United Nations World Housing Survey
suggest the following: a large number of the migrants were born
in rural areas; their average age is very young; household
sizes are bigger than others in the urban areas; incomes are
invariably lower than others in the urban agglomeration.

Biggest attraction is often the capital city. It is usually a
well-known centre, the biggest place, and a former colonial
capital. The economic bases of these former colonial centres
are frequently in some combination of export-import trade, and

this trade is often in the hands of a multinational corporation
or government. The jobs which go with this kind of business are
similar all over the world. They are the mails, other kinds of
communication systems, highways, department stores, and so on.
And the proportion of urban dwellers in a developing country
which can pay for these services or which can secure jobs in
such a sector is small.

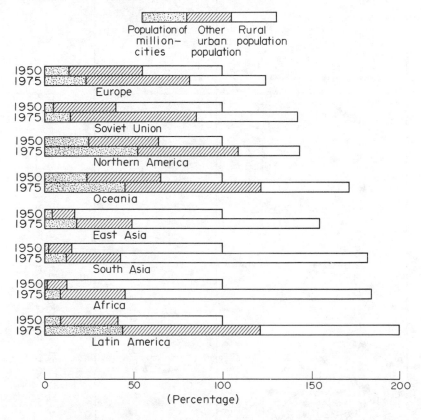

Fig. 2.2 Populations in 1975 as
percentages of 1950 populations

The slum and squatter settler has to step outside this international consumer-oriented society and find a livelihood in
what has come to be known as "the informal sector" - menial
tasks and enterprises which keep the city going but which
provide the barest of incomes, just sufficient to stay alive.

While the cost of living in the consumer-oriented society of the
developing world is just the same as in North America or Europe,
sometimes even more, the informal sector pays a worker less than
$100 per month. For him there are no mass-produced
refrigerators, automobiles, or processed foods. But neither are
there any hopes of conventional housing.

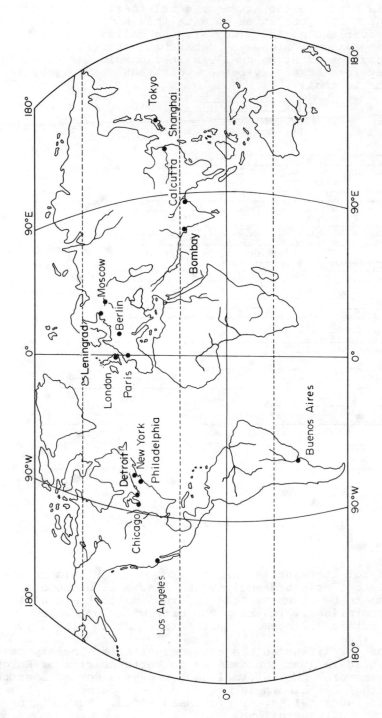

Fig. 2.3 Big city areas, 1950: urban clusters
with populations over 2½ million

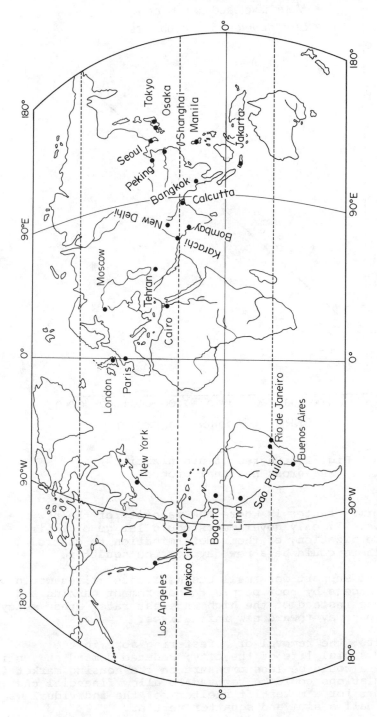

Fig. 2.4 Super cities of the year 2000: urban clusters with projected populations over 12½ million

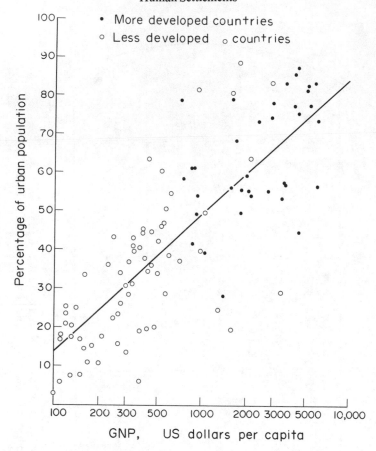

Fig. 2.5 Degree of urbanization
and gross national product

Yet this informal sector is where the majority of the new
urbanites live. If only governments could let go of their
dreams of modernization, of their determination to control
everything, there could be a new day for the squatter.

A little bit of support for small business enterprises would go
a long way. Access by poor people to government banking and
credit services instead of the high interest rates urban money-
lender go a long way toward new initiatives.

And the results: the removal of a festering sore in the
political and social life of the city; reduced demand on public
welfare. There would be less pressure on the housing market if
outdated regulations could be removed to allow financial and
service support for a makeshift shelter for the individual we
have come to call a slum and squatter settler.

The cheapest possible types of accommodation that can be secured
in the consumer society are beyond him. So the squatter settlements have to make do with something local, some self-produced
shelter.

So we see people settling where they can, moving in with
relatives, crowding into subdivided spaces of already overcrowded neighbourhoods, renting unserviced space in vacant lots
(all of the serviced city land is already in the high-priced
bracket), or simply commandeering rooftops and sidewalks. Some
take over institutional and private premises or just band together to establish a new peripheral settlement or unoccupied
land.

Why People become Squatters

The people who organize and live in squatter settlements are not
all recent arrivals from rural areas. A common pattern is for
rural families to migrate into the centre city slums for a
number of years while they learn the ways of the city close to
regular, though poorly paid, employment, and a source of food
and drinking water.

It is in these inner city, landlord-owned slums that the former
rural family develops a desire for something better. The
migrant also becomes aware that should he lose his job through
no fault of his own then his family would be in a very difficult
position. With the housing market closed to him the slum
dweller is prepared to exchange the convenience of his central
location for security of tenure by joining with others, at no
small risk, to become a squatter and fight for title for a small
piece of land.

Establishing a settlement can be a dramatic event. One report
says that land "invasions" that are fairly common in Latin
America and parts of Africa and Asia are the result of a
collective decision involving voluntary participation and group
solidarity. The site to be settled, the timing of the invasion
and preparations for settling and avoiding possible eviction
are well planned.

Whether public or privately-owned land is seized will depend on
the attitude of the government. In many countries vacant
public lands are favoured because of the more tolerant attitude
of the government.

When resistance occurs the leaders of the invasion will seek the
support of prominent political groups or appeal to the media to
dramatize the plight of the settlers. Holidays are preferred
for the move because politicians are often reluctant to
confront squatters when the mood of the day is celebration.

The fact that the settlement is established illegally often
exposes the settlers to harassment by the police and this
threat makes people organize in order to resist efforts to oust
them. This threat to their tenure serves as the single most

important unifying force in the community; it becomes the
major preoccupation of local organizations.

The success in establishing a community is the evidence of the
benefits that can come as a result of their collective efforts.
"It gives them a sense of being able to control their fate", is
how one writer described their condition. This sense is further
reinforced by building and improving their shelters. The sense
of independence which comes with the establishment of the
settlement contrasts with the dependent position of those who
move into government-provided high-rise dwellings and have to
look to the official authorities for improvements in their
dwellings.

Thus the urban poor, using techniques of popular participation
in an effort to solve their individual housing problems, are
helping solve the larger problems of urbanization.

Trends in Government Approaches
Officials traditionally treat these "invaders" as undesirables,
liable to cause health problems, not entitled to live in the
city unless they can afford the prices of the international
consumer society. They want them eliminated. Repressive acts
of slum clearance have often been adopted in line with this
kind of thinking, and these have left the poor still poorer.

They have been outstanding examples of the opposite kind of
thinking but in the main the "get-rid-of-them" philosophy has
prevailed. The big change did not occur in the minds of most
planners until the sheer volume of the problem forced a different approach.

During the 1960's, several professional people who had lived in
squatter settlements wrote books and articles which pointed out
some of the positive aspects of life in these settlements. They
pointed to the resourcefulness of the people in adapting to
their circumstances, and in providing for themselves what
government and industry were quite unable to provide.

A new trend in planning began to appear, pressured into acceptance by the vast numbers of people who were making their way
into the cities. Self-help became an acceptable way of development. The do-it-yourself philiosphy, which has become a fad in
wealthier societies, increased in popularity as the only way of
survival for the new urban immigrants.

So today three dominant attitudes are evident in government
approaches. There is first of all the laissez-faire approach,
an old "technique" in western planning, in which governments
pretend the problem does not exist. It is a bit more tolerant
than the "get-them-out-of-here" approach. Nothing is done for
the newcomers, and governments go on spending money on the same
things as they did before there was a squatter problem.

A second approach is the forced movement of the city-bound

migrant back to the countryside, a method which is productive
even if it is harsh. Several of the communist countries of
Asia have adopted this approach.

Thirdly there are supportive policies, various attempts to
improve the conditions in the settlements. This sometimes
involves legalizing the occupation of land and providing some of
the city services such as water and sanitation. The legal-
ization process is often a matter of security of tenure rather
than outright ownership. In this way the ownership of the land
remains where it was before, but the new occupant knows that he
cannot be evicted and is therefore willing to do a lot of things
to improve his habitat.

There is a fourth possible approach, an untried proposal that is
now gaining more and more acceptance. It resembles a method
that evolved haphazardly in Chicago in the early years of this
century when immigration rates were high. The first generation
of a particular immigrant group would occupy the oldest central
city premises then, as they gathered some money, moved out step
by step to the better and newer suburbs. This lifestyle is
seen as both economically and socially advantageous for developing countries. The deteriorating areas at the centres of these
former colonial cities can be utilized, even renewed for
permanent residence, provided the government is willing to
underwrite the cost. It is certainly less expensive than
starting with completely unserviced land in the outlying areas.

Almost every city in the world now faces the problems of overcrowded, inadequately serviced, slum and squatter settlements.
The following are a few examples from four major regions.

Metropolitan Manila
Like so many other big cities in the post World War Two era
Manila's urbanites have spilled out into the suburbs, rendering
meaningless the neat political boundaries of the old colonial
capital. Now we do not talk about the city of Manila as an
independent entity. Instead we focus on Metropolitan Manila -
the cluster of four cities and 13 municipalities.

Manila was a settlement over 400 years ago, long before the
European powers began to colonize east Asia. It had one of the
world's best natural harbours, a 30 mile square area of water
that was almost completely landlocked. It provided a safe
anchorage and its small tidal range simplified the problems of
entering or leaving at low tide. A 6 mile channel allowed
entrance south of Corregidor Island. Northwards of this Island
there was the more popular and safer 2 mile channel.

Chinese and Arab merchants had established a settlement in the
area now known as the Tondo foreshore close to downtown Manila.
The immediate hinterland was suitable for agriculture, and the
Pasig River, which entered Manila Bay at this point both
provided fresh water and gave interior access for small boats.
Then came the Spanish conquerors and after them the United

States colonialists. Trade expanded and Manila flourished.

World War Two was a devastating experience. The Japanese
destroyed much of the city. Four years after the end of that
war the total urban population was slightly over 1 million.

By 1960 the urbanization crisis had begun. A 100 percent jump
in population occurred between 1950 and 1960. An additional
60 percent hike followed in the 1960-70 decade. By 1975 the
metropolitan area's total population was 7 million. Manila
was replaced by Quezon City as the national capital in 1948.
The original settlement of Tondo was flooded with squatter
settlements.

The area of Tondo, with its 30,000 squatter families, represents
a political powder keg. It is the only slum area with strong
community organizations capable of getting the people into
action. Since the martial law of 1972, Tondo slum-dwellers
have taken to the streets many times, demonstrating against re-
locations, the right to strike, or for restoration of other
civil liberties.

Typical of Tondo residents is 44 year old Anna. She squats in a
vacant lot next to a restaurant on Roxas Boulevard in the heart
of the tourist area. Her neighbours are well-dressed businessmen in nearby offices and foreign diplomats in embassies. Anna
and her family, however, wear threadbare remnants of some
happier time.

For all that, they are clean and healthy-looking, except for
the insect bites and sores. Anna says this is because they have
no mosquito net when she and her busband, Bert, and their two
children, bed down on a piece of plywood. They share the lot
with 20 other families.

They have houses, but do not live in them, because they are in
one of the government's relocation sites outside Manila to
which Anna, her family and friends were taken soon after the
declaration of martial law. They built wooden shanties at the
site but then returned to Manila because there were no jobs
there.

In the relocation areas, the government gives squatters 200
square metres of land on which to build a house and plant a
vegetable garden. According to officials, 40 percent of
relocated squatters return to Manila.

The majority of those who stick it out in the sites are unemployed. A number of government agencies provide training,
day care and supplemental feeding in the schools, but one
official admitted in private that the programme is a failure
because there are no jobs near the sites.

Anna and her neighbours make their living by catching crabs and
shellfish in Manila Bay. They float around the bay in inflated

inner tubes and sell their catches from the polluted water to
restaurants and private householders in the tourist area.

The government is caught between trying to help the country's
poor like Anna and wanting to turn Manila into an attractive
metropolis.

About 80 percent of the nation's industry is located in or
around Metro-Manila, where the country's construction boom is
also centred. Even Department of Tourism technocrats complain
that their regional development programme is being sacrificed
for the sake of Manila. These factors all combine to draw more
rural folk to the capital.

One Cabinet secretary sought to justify the concentration of
government projects in the capital, pointing out that Manila
had to be a symbol of the nation, not only to foreign countries,
but to Filipinos throughout the archipelago. He argued that in
nation-building this lead was of vast importance. Asked how
much relevance a cultural centre or a big hotel had in the life
of the average Manilan or provincial peasant, he argued that
although they might not use these facilities, they could look
on them with pride.

Aside from the economic and social problems posed by the growing
incidence of slums, there is also the political problem of
squatter disenchantment. Anna and her friends in the vacant lot
pose no real problem, but in other areas of the city huge
tracts of land have become not only eyesores but also breeding
grounds for political dissent.

Because of the government's interest in resettlement programmes,
the UN has selected the Philippines for the study of low-cost
housing projects. The government has been developing one area
adjacent to Tondo, called Dagat-Dagatan, at a cost of 103
million pesos. The low-cost housing scheme is aided by the
International Bank for Reconstruction and Development (World
Bank).

The scheme, however, has come under fire from Tondo
organizations because of government reluctance to allow the relocated squatters to own the land. But the fact that the
government is developing a relocation site next to the present
slum indicates that officials realize that Manila's squatters
do perform an economic function in the city - whether working
on the docks or scavenging scrap metal and glass from rubbish
dumps.

Sao Paulo and Rio de Janeiro

These two cities are the main collection points for the slum and
squatter settlers of Brazil, Latin America's biggest country.
Only two thirds of the people of Sao Paulo are supplied with
clean water. Only one third are connected to the sewers. Three
million people drink from wells sunk into soil which is heavily
polluted with sewage. One Sao Paulo health expert believes

these conditions are responsible for 50 percent of the unnecessary deaths among the poor. He estimates that 10 percent
of poor children die in their first year of life. In the richer
parts of the city, the rate is only three percent.

Between 1 and 2 million people live in slums in rotten housing,
as if mocking the soaring skyscrapers of the main part of the
city. Land prices have made it impossible for people to have
any hope of permanent housing. A great deal of work is being
done by the authorities. They hope to get safe water to more
than 20 percent of the entire city within three years. They are
working on public transportation arrangements and discouraging
the use of private cars. But the job is made virtually
impossible by the yearly addition of half a million people to
a city that is already bursting at the seams.

The story around Rio de Janeiro is similar. One the hillsides
and in the valleys behind the downtown waterfront are hundreds
of shantytowns. These places are on steep slopes, little used
for other purposes and therefore available for this kind of
occupation. But a tropical rainstorm can quickly create
disaster and trigger mudslides.

Early in 1977 a sudden thunderstorm accompanied by 12 hours of
steady rainfall triggered just such a mudslide in the squatter
settlements. 27 people were killed and 60 others injured. To
make matters worse mudslides partially blocked the roads into
the area, making assistance from neighbouring towns almost
impossible.

Sao Paulo is as good a symbol as any of the world situation. It
combines the crises of the cities of both the developed and developing nations. Sao Paulo is twentieth century Tokyo imposed
on nineteenth century Manchester.

Sao Paulo has nearly as many cars per person as New York - without the freeways and other facilities.

So every day the city centre becomes jammed for hours. The
hooting of frustrated drivers is one reason why Sao Paulo is
reckoned to be the second noisiest city in the world - the
noisiest of all is nearby Rio de Janeiro.

The fumes from car exhausts mingle with air pollution from
factories: 47 percent of Brazil's industry is crammed into this
one city. In winter, climatic conditions often prevent these
pollutants blowing away. Photochemical smog and sulphur
dioxide - both more often associated with cities of the developed world - build up to crisis levels.

Air pollution in Sao Paulo is now becoming a serious threat to
health, and last winter 60 percent of its people told a public
opinion toll that it was the city's worst problem. This winter,
industry may have to be shut down and people and traffic banned
from parts of the city when things get really bad.

But for millions of the people of this wealthy city, air
pollution is only an added insult. Like the vast majority of
the citizens of the Third World, their main concern is the
pollution of poverty.

Nairobi

On hillsides and in valleys, Nairobi's slum and squatter settlements continue to grow. They provide a sort of home for all
sorts of people, all ages, from elderly landless peasants to
young criminals. Ken Yago village is the name of one of these
settlements. It is just 20 minutes from downtown Nairobi. The
common experiences of all the residents are poverty, poor
living conditions and crime. One resident has been in squatter
settlements of this kind for 16 years, moving whenever the city
council of Nairobi takes over the land for other uses. The
absence of any firm land tenure or any other kind of security of
tenure is one of the main reasons for the dilapidated state of
the dwellings. No-one knows how long he will be in a particular
place.

Mathare Valley is another squatter settlement on the outskirts
of Nairobi. It is probably the dirtiest and poorest of the
city's squatter settlements, densely populated with every kind
of illegal activity. Crime abounds. Most of the children are
barefoot and shirtless. Only a handful go to school.

The children are often the saddest part of the story of these
settlements. Often they have to leave home as early as five
years of age, walk into the nearby city to beg for change, or to
earn a few pennies protecting cars for their owners. At night
the "parking boys" as they are sometimes called will just sleep
in the open, wrapped in whatever material they can find to cover
themselves - discarded pieces of plastic or cardboard. Most of
the adult males in the settlement are unemployed and either
single or separated from their wives. Their houses, such as
they are, are made of mud and wattle or patchwork arrangements
of bits of wood and cardboard. Chickens and goats try to eke
out a living on the garbage piles. The city council is supposed
to collect the garbage, but they rarely do.

In these slums and squatter settlements of Kenya's capital there
is no hope of planning for the future. The Nairobi city
government wants to move people from these settlements to safer
and more sanitary premises. But one requirement is that the
people be able to prove that they have a monthly income of at
least $25.00. Since most of the earnings are illicit and there
is no record of income it is virtually impossible for them to
show that they have a guaranteed income. So the round of misery
continues.

The American Ghetto

There are millions of non-whites living in the downtown areas
of the bigger U.S. cities, most of them negroes. About half of
these ghetto residents have incomes below the national poverty
level. Although the total number of ghetto residents is a small

fraction of the total population - less than 10 percent - they
are a very serious problem in the urban life of America,
comparable to the slum and squatter settlements of the developing world.

Peter is a six-year-old negro who lives with his mother, brother
and 3 sisters in a two room rental accommodation in Boston. His
father died a few years back. His mother makes just about
enough income to keep the family alive. Peter sleeps with his
brother in one bedroom. The three girls sleep in the living
room, which is a bedroom. And there is a small kitchen. There
is practically no furniture. The kitchen has a table with four
chairs, and there is a television set which is constantly on.
The girls sleep in one big bed. Peter shares his bed with his
brother, and his mother sleeps on a couch.

Peter, so young, has already developed a distaste for school.
He sees it as totally irrelevant, and longs for the day when he
can get right away from it and do other things. Peter sees rats
all the time. He has been bitten by them. He has a big stick
by his bed to use against them. They also roam the alley, even
in daytime. It is hard to understand why authorities don't
attempt to get rid of these rats, or for that matter the cock-
roaches, mosquitoes, the flies, the maggots, the ants and the
garbage that lies around everywhere. Peter and his mother and
the rest of the family have no illusions. The future for them
is "more of the same".

City Origins
Many of the earlier cities grew out of villages. A village was
seen as a group of homes of peasants who were mainly engaged in
cultivating the fields around about them. The town that grew
out of such a village had a different set of functions - a
commercial or industrial or administrative one. So the
essential difference between village and town was functional
rather than size. You could have a large village and a small
town.

This view of the emergence of towns sees them as late arrivals
in the long history of mankind. But there are other views of
the origin of towns and cities that place them much further back
in time. In fact most cities originated in the alternative way -
as places of worship for religious orders. From the beginnings
of agriculture there was a certain amount of leisure, and this
gave rise to institutional structures which provided leisure
occupations. At the same time the hierarchy within the
religious order was concentrated in the city.

At a later point in time, cities emerged as points for military
fortifications. In particular the expansion of empires required
points of defence on the frontier. Examples from the areas we
now know as France, Britain, and Tokyo illustrate this kind of
city formation. The cities concerned are Paris, London and
Tokyo, three of the biggest urban areas of today's world. In
these early days of settlement two considerations were of prime

importance, the site and the situation of each location.

The site of Paris is the immediate area of the first settlement. This was on an island in the River Seine, now called the Ile de la Cite. Two wooden bridges linked the island with the banks of the river. On either side there were marshes and this was an extra protection for the people who occupied the island. The Romans occupied the island at the time of their conquest of Gaul and named it Lutetia. Surrounding the island on either side of the river were members of the Gallic tribe called the Parisii. In later years the name of this tribe was given to the city.

The situation in Paris is its relationship to the larger surrounding area. In the case of the Ile de la Cite this part of the River Seine marked the intersection of the water route and land route which joined the mouth of the Rhine river with the southwest of France. It therefore was an important point of trade. The Romans therefore employed the advantageous position with regard to the country as a whole as well as the site characteristics in order to establish a suitable centre for the conquest of the whole area.

In the case of London the site was called Londinium - hence the present name. It was located on some high ground on the north side of the river near the present London Bridge. It was free from the periodic flooding that occurred and it was north of the River Thames so the river protected them from any attacks from the south. A city wall was built on the north side of this raised piece of ground and this served to protect the settlement from any attacks from the north. At the spot on the river where this Roman fortification was established, the river could be bridged. This situation therefore provided ready access to the rest of the country from France.

Like Paris and London, Tokyo was originally a suitable military site, and later a suitable place for trade and capital city functions. About 500 years ago, more than 1500 years after the establishment of Paris and London, a Japanese warlord moved northwards from the old capital of Kyoto, and established a castle on the right bank of the river Yedo at the point where the river enters Tokyo Bay. He calculated that any enemy from the north would have to cross the river, or else approach his castle from the sea, to attack him, and he considered himself to be in a strong position to repel either attack. Later the big situational advantages became evident as the surrounding kanto plain became the main agricultural region of the country.

About the same time as Tokyo had its first beginnings there was emerging in Europe a series of pre-industrial cities focussed on trade rather than defence. While these cities normally occupied important locations, and could be defended, their main growth was due to the development of trade. They were less and less dependent on their immediate hinterlands for food and raw materials. Instead, because of extensive trade systems and increasingly more sophisticated transportation systems, the

cities expanded their hinterlands until they included distant
places overseas. These cities were the forerunners of the type
of urban development we see today.

Industrial Revolution

About 200 years ago there began in England a series of changes
that altered the whole life of the country within a very short
period of time. Land that for centuries had been cultivated as
open fields was fenced; villages became towns with factory
chimney stacks dominating the skyline in place of the church
spires; new highways were built; canals were dug linking the
rivers of the east and west coasts with those of the south of
the country; railways appeared; the total population grew
rapidly.

Accompanying these changes there was steady movement of people
away from the countryside into the towns and cities. Within the
short space of 50 years the changes that had taken place were so
great and so widespread that they have come to be described as a
revolution - the industrial revolution.

The fencing of the open fields was part of an enormous improvement in agricultural productivity. New inventions and new ways
of rotating crops had greatly improved both the quantity and
quality of agricultural production, and in the process had done
many people out of work or caused them to lose their traditional
use of land. The loss of land was the direct result of a
tradition that had been indifferent to legal title. As land
became fenced, and as new levels and scales of production
appeared, those who could not prove ownership lost all claim
to the land.

About the same time as the land improvement was taking place new
inventions were changing the pattern of industrial production.
Instead of home crafts and very small scale operations, factory
towns began to appear, absorbing the surplus labour from the
countryside, and moving into very large scale machine production.
Power looms were set up in large factories where they could be
driven by steam power. Coal was the chief source of power for
making steam, and most of these new factories were set up near
coal fields.

Between the years 1700 and 1800 the population of England
doubled. The reason for this rapid increase was the reduction
in the death rate, just as it is today in the developing
countries. The same number of births took place but now fewer
people died from starvation. Fewer also died from disease.

Manchester in 1840 looked very much like many of the developing
cities of 1977. One writer described it as an overgrown
village, built with no plan. Every owner just built where he
pleased. Cholera epidemics were common because of the lack of
any drainage system. The demand for housing and the general
speed of growth made it impossible for the authorities to cope
with the demand for drains and streets. Cellar residents became

common - a hole in the ground about 12 by 15 feet in floor area, with no windows and no ventilation. Throughout the 19th century the city doubled in population every generation.

In spite of the difficulties attending the first years of industrialization the movement spread across the channel to France, Belgium, Germany, then to European Russia and thence by stages to all parts of the world. Industrialization became the model by which growth and economic power and improvement in standards of living could be obtained. Right up to the last few years this was the way by which all the countries of the world intended to go. The sudden awareness of diminishing earth resources and the very rapid rise in population have made people rethink this whole direction of development.

The Modern Phase
The modern phase dates from the spread of industrialization from Europe to other parts of the world. First came North America, then Japan, and now most countries of the world. In North America there was first the rapid opening up of the interior of the continent in the 19th century. Urban settlements appeared almost everywhere. Then, in the present century came profound changes in the internal structure of these new cities. These developments can be illustrated by means of three predictive exercises, two concerned with the 19th century and one with today's problems.

Imagine that all you had available for information was the map shown in Fig. 2.6 and the following letter from a pioneer resident who lived in the area we now know as Ohio before there was any European settlement in that place. Choose 4 or 5 interior U.S. locations at which you would expect to see settlements of 20,000 or more people develop within the 40 years following the writing of the letter. After you have made your prediction, do two other things before reading on: (1) repeat the prediction for 4 or 5 interior U.S. locations that you would expect to reach 200,000 or more between 1840 and 1890; (2) make a list of the kinds of additional information you would like to have had available to improve your predictions.

In a simple cabin on the frontier, Thad Williams, a young lawyer from Philadelphia, sat looking out through a cabin chink at a world of swirling white. Snowbound in eastern Ohio in the early spring of 1805, he was writing the following letter to his brother in Philadelphia:

Sometimes I wonder why I came. Not that I'm unhappy, but it wasn't so bad in Philadelphia. At least my family was there and I had a roof over my head and there was no wind blowing through cracks in the walls. Last night was the first night I've slept in a house since I began crossing the mountains two weeks ago. Quite a home this is, too. You can see daylight between the logs any direction you look. But who am I to complain - with all that snow out there I'm pleased to be here inside. How many families would take a stranger in - even in a snowstorm?

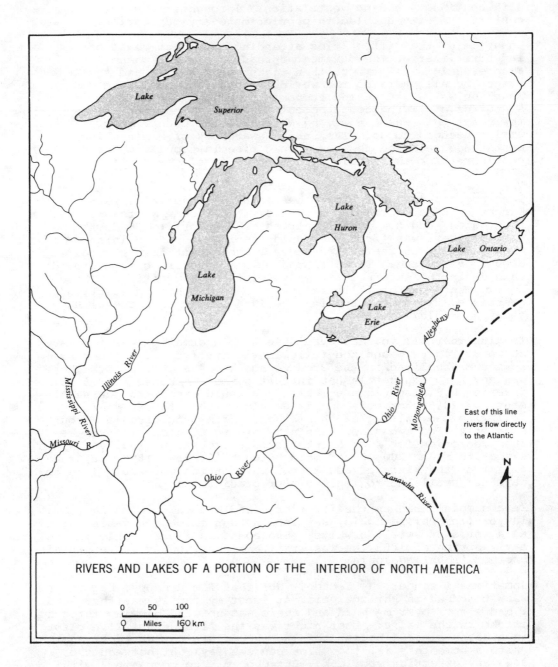

RIVERS AND LAKES OF A PORTION OF THE INTERIOR OF NORTH AMERICA

Fig. 2.6 Rivers and lakes
of Interior North America

Not many back east. I suspect a few more would out here.
Folks do seem friendlier here in the Ohio country.

Philadelphia seems a long way behind me now. I was making
pretty good time on the road till the storm hit. Two and a half
weeks to Pittsburgh, another three days to Wheeling, then a day
and a half more on into Ohio - and then the snow began to fall.
It's been falling for a whole day now. Hard to tell when it
will quit.

I hadn't intended to leave so early this spring. Some of my
friends who had been out here in the Ohio country said it was
better to travel before the spring thaw. They claimed that it's
easier to ride over packed snow than over what roads there are.
They were probably right. All that the road builders did was to
cut a strip about ten feet wide through the underbrush. I could
hardly believe my eyes at first when I saw stumps eighteen
inches high right in the middle of the road. Can you imagine
roping a couple of logs together over a stream and saying it is
a bridge? That's what they've done any number of places along
the Forbes Road east of Pittsburgh. But I don't imagine the
route through Albany and Utica would have been any better.
About the only other way I could have reached this country was
to have gone down through the Cumberland Gap and then back north
through Kentucky, but the distance would have been several
hundreds of miles longer.

Of course I admit I came pretty close to boarding a keelboat or
a flatboat at Pittsburgh and continuing my trip west by floating
down the Ohio River. River traffic, I hear, is increasing every
year. Certainly I saw lots of settlers loading all their world-
ly goods on board and setting off. But I don't like to take big
risks, and I'm probably better off sticking to the roads. Spring
floods on the Ohio River have a bad reputation, and I wouldn't
be surprised if one of those boats I saw at Pittsburgh was ship-
wrecked before it reached its destination down river. I also
thought of heading north from Pittsburgh to Lake Erie where I
could maybe book passage west on a sailing ship, but I heard
that one often had to wait many days before getting any kind of
a passage.

This area may not look like much today, but it has got a real
future now that we've settled things with the Indians. Coming
through western Pennsylvania the woods were full of new settlers.
You could hear axes echoing and trees falling around us as we
passed. There are sizeable towns all through this area that
aren't even on my map. Sure, most of these settlements are
crude. The log cabins are rough and the families will be eating
nothing but corn meal and game for a while, but give them a year
or two. When they've cleared those rich bottom lands, they'll
be getting 75 to 100 bushels of corn an acre. With good land
there are going to be some prosperous towns developing in this
part of the country. There ought to be plenty of room in one
of these places for a man like me with legal training.

The problem is in finding the place where many people are going
to settle sooner or later. While there is going to be money
all through this area, certain places are going to have a better
future than others and are going to grow into large cities. I
want to find a place where a large city is going to grow. I
don't want to settle in a place that will stop growing after a
few years.

My map is getting tattered from all my folding and unfolding
and pencil marking. Trying to figure out the most likely place
to visit where cities might spring up is pretty tricky business
at best.

In Canada the development of interior cities was slower. In the
year 1800 no city was bigger than 20,000. By 1825 Montreal and
Quebec had passed the 20,000 mark and by 1850 three additional
cities had reached this level - Toronto, Halifax and Saint John.
West of Lake Ontario there was no settlement as big as these.

Now check your predictions. Of the three major routes of
United States migration into the interior plains the two
southern routes (the Pennsylvania route and the Cumberland Gap
route into Kentucky) were much more important at this time than
the Mohawk route through New York State. There was not therefore much settlement along the shore of the Great Lakes and in
the northern part of the Middle West in the years immediately
following 1805.

Information that might have been helpful in making predictions
include some or all of the following:

Location of waterfalls and other factors affecting navigation
on rivers.

Location of the minerals where mining might become important.

Location of the areas with the best potential for prosperous
farming.

Location of places where land promoters might be planning to
establish towns.

Settlement of the area west of the Great Lakes did not begin
until the Indian threat was virtually eliminated around 1830.
This factor, combined with the completion of the Erie Canal in
1825 making water transport from eastern New York State possible,
opened the Lakes region to extensive settlement.

Growth of cities in the Middle West by 1840 was primarily in the
areas of earlier settlement. Buffalo grew rapidly when it
became the terminus of the Erie Canal and a gateway to the West.
The era of western migration along the Lake routes was just
beginning about the year 1840. Cleveland, a village in 1796,
was starting to grow. Detroit, originally a garrison outpost,
began to enlarge in the 1830's as a result of lake traffic and

and the subduing of Indians.

City growth was most apparent along the Ohio River. Pittsburgh, Cincinnati, and Louisville had populations of 20,000 by 1840. So had St. Louis and Buffalo. Louisville started at a point where rapids on the Ohio River forced freight to be portaged around them. (Later a by-pass canal was built.) Lousiville also became a point of embarkation for pioneers from Kentucky and Tennessee who were settling the wooded areas of southern Indiana and Illinois. St. Louis had been established by the French fur traders in the 1760's and had long funnelled cargo down the Mississippi River to New Orleans.

By 1890 the Great Lakes waterway was in full swing and 5 of the 8 interior cities of 200,000 or more population were on the lakes: Chicago, Milwaukee, St. Louis, Cincinnati, Detroit, Cleveland, Pittsburgh, Buffalo.

In 1830 there was no trace of Chicago on the western shore of Lake Michigan. The first wave of migrants traveling the Lake route landed at the tiny settlement some five years later. Thus, Chicago grew first as a jumping off place for settlers going to establish homes in northern Illinois. Its natural advantages for water transport on the lower lake were enhanced when the Illinois and Michigan Canal that joined Lake Michigan with the Illinois River was opened in 1848. This linked the Great Lakes with the Mississippi River system, with Chicago at the juncture. Chicago became an early rail centre; by 1855 it was a hub for long-distance railroads from the south and east. Short lines fanned westward to the lead-mining districts. People and goods were routed through Chicago, which grew as a commercial centre. By 1890 it was the largest city in the region.

Now consider a completely different type of prediction, one that relates to a contemporary situation of urban transportation and the location of the central business district. See Fig. 2.7.

Travel routes in a city are limited by the layout of the city's streets and sidewalks. Many things influence people's choice of routes other than simple distance. One of these factors is travel time.

Fig. 2.7 Map 1 shows a hypothetical American city with a population of nearly 60,000. A river flows from northeast to southwest through the city. Each letter represents the middle of a district in the city. The lines connecting the lettered points are important streets. Not all the streets in the city are shown. At each lettered point there is a small black number representing the population of that district in thousands. Point C, therefore, represents a district with 20,000 people. The time it takes to drive from one point to another is shown with each street.

Which lettered place could be reached most quickly by all the people of the city?

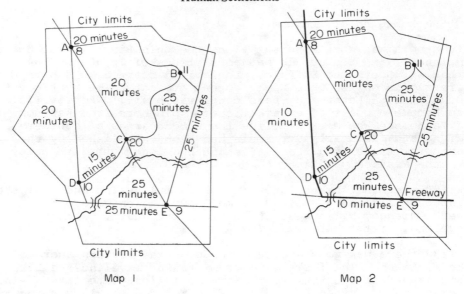

Fig. 2.7 Time distance city maps

Consider the question and try to answer it before reading on.

Suppose all the poeple went to point A. It would take 0 minutes
for the people of A to get to A. Since it would take 20 minutes
for one person to get to A from B, hypothetically it would take
20 minutes times the population of B, or 220,000 minutes, for
all the people of B to get to A. By the same method it would
take 20 minutes times 20,000 people, or 400,000 minutes for all
the people of C to get to A. If we add the minutes it takes to
get all the people of the city to point A then we know how much
time is involved in moving all the people of the city to A -
1,225,000 minutes.

By repeating this process of calculation the most accessible
location can be found.

Point C has the fewest number of minutes associated with it and
is probably the most accessible place.

The CBD (Central Business District) is probably in the vicinity
of point C, since this place is well connected with other parts
of the city.

In Fig. 2.7 Map 2 a freeway has been added and time distances
have changed. Point D has become slightly more accessible than
point C.

We might expect an intensification of land development near the
freeway exits now that they are more quickly reached by more
people. Development is likely to be most extensive near D. New

houses, apartment buildings, stores, and industries might now
be built near these exits.

It appears likely that new suburbs might be built near the freeway just outside the city limits near D. Also, there is a
possibility that some new housing might be developed near the
freeway in the vicinity of A or near E.

Normally, of course, all the people of a city would not move to
one place, as in the hypothetical situation in the activity.
Efficiency of transportation is important to businessmen who
need efficient ways to get their products from factories and to
disseminate the goods and services they sell to their market.
Time-distance and cost-distance are therefore often important
measures to businessmen and strong determiners in their choice
of route and mode of transport. Other considerations, however,
may have a stronger influence when monetary profit is not the
primary concern.

Time-distance, road-distance, and cost-distance are all easily
measured. Perceived distance, however, may be a strong
motivator but is not so readily measurable.

Microclimates

Location and transportation are important characteristics of
urban areas but for the slum and squatter settler the physical
environment is often critical. The flimsy shelters are highly
sensitive to heat, humidity, wind, and pollution of all kinds.

In large settlements the shape of the buildings, their heat-
retaining properties and the heat-generating activities which
take place within them combine to create a micro-climate which
is quite distinct from that of the surrounding area. Strong
winds are slowed down and light winds are accelerated as they
move into towns, the chemical composition of the air is changed,
radiation gains and losses are reduced, temperatures are
raised, fogs are thicker, more frequent and more persistent,
visibility is reduced, and rainfall is increased.

There is a complex relationship between the local climate of a
settlement and the various forms of air pollution produced by
the settlement. The waste heat, gases and other pollutants
released into the air help to shape the climate, while the
climate in turn influences the extent to which these pollutants
remain concentrated over the city. The shroud of pollution over
a city affects the way the sun's rays reach the ground. In
badly polluted areas half the visible radiation and four-fifths
of the ultra-violet radiation can be lost. London's campaign
to stop smoke pollution has not only resulted in cleaner air
but has also increased the average amount of winter sunshine by
50 percent compared with the situation before the passing of the
Clean Air Act in 1956. This increase in sunshine is not only
welcome in itself. By increasing surface temperatures it has
strengthened air turbulence and helped to reduce the concentration of sulphur dioxide.

High temperatures are not always welcome. Throughout much of
the central and eastern United States prolonged periods of hot
and humid weather during the summer are associated with higher-
than-average death rates, particularly among the elderly and the
infirm. These 'heat deaths' are the most common in large urban
areas, where night-time temperatures are several degrees higher
than in nearby rural areas.

The blanket of warm air over cities also tends to increase
rainfall - by about 10 percent compared with nearby open
country.

Air flow is another important element in this complex system
of interrelationships between settlements and their local
climate. Good air flows help to disperse pollution. On the
other hand air turbulence caused by large tall buildings can be
dangerous to the buildings and can make life very difficult for
people on the ground.

The severity of air pollution in urban areas depends, of course,
not only on the local climate but also on the number, kind and
concentration of pollution sources - domestic fires and central-
heating furnaces, power stations, industrial processes, modes of
transportation. The pollutants arising from these sources
include sulphur oxides, nitrogen oxides, carbon monoxide, soot,
metals, dust and grit. They damage vegetation and buildings
and they are known to have bad effects on human health.

Smoke and sulphur dioxide from burning coal have been associated
with an above-average number of deaths in large cities on
occasions when freak weather has prevented these pollutants from
dispersing. Those who die are generally the very young, the old
and people suffering from cardiac and respiratory diseases.

In hilly or mountainous terrain, topography is a governing
factor in the creation of microclimates. It may determine land
uses. It may cause temperature inversions that, in turn, create
'frost holes' which are traps for pollution. Ridges have the
highest wind velocities, and this is a desirable feature for
smoke stacks but less pleasant for dwellings. Equator-facing
slopes have the best exposures to sun. This is good for cold
regions but in hot areas the pole-facing slopes are better.
Mid-slope locations usually have warmer temperatures, especially
at night, because they lie above the valley inversions. They
have been the favourite spots.

Removal of vegetation creates extremes in daily maximum and
minimum temperatures. The process can be reversed by planting
shade trees.

Street widths and building heights can have the same effects as
topography on the incidence of solar radiation. In cold
climates ground floors in narrow streets may never get a ray
of sunshine. In areas of abundant sunshine mutual shading of
houses is a time-honoured practice for creating more tolerable

conditions in homes and streets.

Microclimatic manipulation can be practiced in such ways as
these in the overall design of settlements. In smaller ways too,
as with plantings around houses. Deciduous vines can protect
walls from excessive radiation. Shrubbery can act as a
pollutant screen.

In chapter seven the physical environment of human settlements
will be studied in greater detail.

Identify the Issues

1. What distinguishes a slum and squatter settlement from
    a poor area of a city?

2. What is the single biggest problem that the slum and
    squatter settler has to face in the city?

3. Compare the climate of the city nearest to where you
    live with the climate of the surrounding area. What
    differences can you find?

"As population rises in the countryside, the traditional balance
between man and land is broken. Young people growing up in
rural villages without opportunity choose the only road open to
them - migration to the cities. But overpopulation isn't the
only reason for the rural exodus. In schools, through better
communications, and by word from those who have gone before,
people learn of a way of life that is more vital and interesting. More often than not it is the most ambitious who reject
the old ways of dawn-to-dusk work in the fields, homes without
light, and social isolation. And added to those who leave in
pursuit of a better life are the victims of natural disasters
such as floods and drought. Nearly 300 million people in Africa,
Asia and Latin America have left their rural homes in the past
25 years, creating the largest human migration in history."
From Habitat Preparatory Paper.

CHAPTER THREE

Rural Stagnation

Sixty percent of the world's population live in rural areas. In
the developing countries, it is seventy percent; most of them
are engaged in agriculture, forestry and fisheries,
concentrated mainly in the fertile irrigated districts of Asia,
Africa, and in the high mountain areas of the Andes. See Fig.
3.1. 500 million live in absolute poverty. In spite of
increasing migration to cities, their numbers will continue to
grow so that by the end of this century there will be more than
two billion people in the developing countries struggling to
make a living from the soil. See Fig. 3.2. And these people
who work in agriculture have but a small fraction of the income
of those engaged in other occupations.

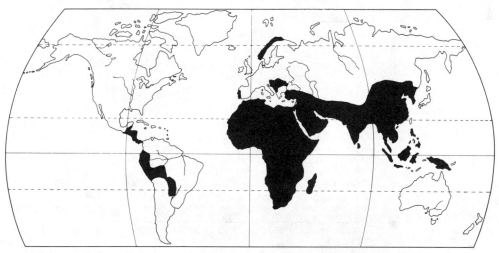

Fig. 3.1 Countries with more than 50% of
their populations in rural settlements

The real difference between urban and rural levels of living is
even greater than it appears because services such as hospitals,
schools, water supplies and electricity are overwhelmingly
concentrated in the urban areas where the main decision-makers
of the country live. Rural people, dependent as they are upon
climatic conditions, are the most vulnerable with little or no
reserve stocks of food and no savings.

Their low income, usually based on tenancy rather than ownership
of land, the fluctuating natural conditions, and the lack of

alternative employment in the off-season, all tend to keep them
in poverty. Because their income is low, the productivity is
low, and so new investment in agriculture is almost nil. So the
general condition of the rural dweller gets worse rather than
better.

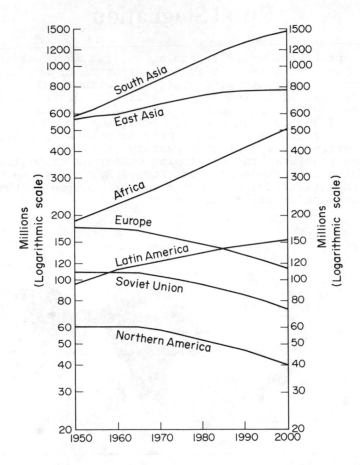

Fig. 3.2 Rural population trends in 7 major areas

Unless drastic measures are taken to improve their lot, and
taken soon, the future prospects for the rural population in
developing countries will not improve. A continuation of
production trends would require net imports of food grains of
85 million tons or more in 1985. The over-riding need, therefore, is for a massive acceleration in food production. This
will require, among other things, vast amounts of capital, not
easily available to governments of developing countries and
well beyond the reach of poor farmers. Added to this is the
problem of land distribution, in some countries as few as 3
percent of farmers holding 80 percent of the arable land.

A key focus must be rural market towns. These places are the
service centres for villages, and they can become "growth
centres". They are the ideal locations for marketing, banking,
credit, storage, processing, provision of inputs, repair and
maintenance facilities and other services vital to the modernization of agriculture. If they can be sufficiently up-graded,
they can help in attracting the essential trained staff to work
in the rural areas. By providing urban amenities near at hand,
they can slow down the migration that is choking the large
cities. The up-grading of market towns can provide much-needed
additional employment opportunities.

The heart of the rural problem, however, lies in the villages
themselves. And within the villages the biggest problem is
the rural women, most of whom live in conditions of appalling
drudgery. They must be the most oppressed class in the whole
world. Much can be done to ease their lot, not only by improving their dwellings but also through rural electrification and,
most urgent of all, through the provision of safe and accessible
water supplies.

Water

The consensus of the delegates at the time of the Habitat
conference was that water was the most urgent need of rural
people. Safe water was considered the single biggest
contribution to improved health.

An improvement of water supply makes possible the processing of
food produce, fish freezing, or dyeing of wool. In ways such as
these a plentiful supply of safe water makes for generally
improved social conditions. But probably the absence of decent
drinking water is the most common and crucial problem. Lacking
centralised water-supply systems, most villages depend upon
wells, tanks, ponds, rivers and lakes as sources of drinking
water. In rural India about 99 percent of households depend
on a water source of doubtful quality. Similar conditions
prevail in several countries of Africa and Asia.

The World Health Organization of the United Nations has placed a
high priority on the provision of safe water for rural settlements. The following interim report from that organization
illustrates the importance of water in a Philippino village
(barrio).

Mr. Jesus B. Tutor, 37 years old, is a member of the barrio
assembly of Abaca, an out-of-the-way barrio with a population of
995 persons. Farmer Tutor lists the following main problems of
his barrio:

Water. Barrio Abaca's 177 families fetch water from five open
dug wells at the foothills. Some families, like that of farmer
Jesus Tutor, have tanks for storing rainwater. Artesian well
drillers sent by the government were unsuccessful - the barrio
is on a high ridge. The only plentiful source is a spring some
three kilometres from the centre of the village. A survey of

the spring had actually been made and an impounding area had
been walled in. But the villagers could not afford the pipes;
they had offered the labour, if the government would provide the
material.

A Road. The barrio nestles on a ridge about eight kilometres
from the town proper. A four-kilometre feeder road connects
Abaca to the provincial road but, like most feeder roads, this
one too had been swept away by the rains. Cargo trucks which
had visited the community earlier had cut deep furrows which
became muddy trenches during rainy days and sharp-edged
crevasses in summer. Now the road is usable only by buffalo-
drawn sleds and people on foot.

Irrigation canals. The ricefields of Abaca are totally dependent on the rains for water. Long dry spells had resulted in a
very poor harvest although 1975 was a particularly good year.
Farmers like Jesus Tutor have a weary experience of parched
summers and they want irrigation canals to water the rice
paddies when the rains are long in coming.

Market day for Abaca's barrio folks is once a week at the
junction of the feeder and provincial roads. They bring their
products and purchase their household needs for the week. It is
also during this day - Tuesday - that they are able to consult
the rural health doctor about their ailments.

In October of 1975 the government's health officer, Dr. Nestor
C. Ayag launched a "toilet campaign" in the barrio, and
achieved 100 percent coverage. All houses now have water-seal
toilets. Jessie, as farmer Tutor is called, had a hand in this.
He was taught how to make toilet bowls by the sanitary inspector
and during the toilet campaign he built 50 bowls which he sold
to the villagers for six pesos (80 US cents) each.

Dr. Ayag says that Abaca's main problem is water supply.
Gastrointestinal diseases are prevalent in the barrio and that
was why they concentrated on a toilet campaign. Dr. Ayag noted
that the 1962 outbreak of cholera was in this barrio. During
the off season, farmers from Abaca go to the seashore to catch
shrimps. They eat them raw, and Dr. Ayag thought this practice
could have triggered off that first epidemic.

The problems of inadequate or polluted water supplies have
plagued rural people for a long time. At the 1977 United
Nations water conference in Argentina these problems were again
aired. Two thirds of the world's people do not have access to
an adequate and safe water supply.

Most of these people live in rural areas. They live short,
stunted lives, always hungering for more food than their dry
lands can produce; or they die of water-bred diseases like
typhoid or cholera, or live weakened, shadowy existences, their
strength sapped by bilharzia. Children are especially
vulnerable. Even when they survive the hazardous childhood

years they may be permanently less intelligent because of the
effects of water-borne illnesses.

Rural - Urban Migration

When health and sanitation standards began to improve in the
1950's, so that the death rate dropped markedly, the greatly
increased population - tired of the long history of poverty -
began to look elsewhere for a living. Thus began the massive
rural-to-urban migrations. But worst of all was the fact that
the best qualified, the youngest and the most ambitious were the
ones who left the countryside for the city. Instead of a
traditional resource of young people who would take over when
the older generation passed on, the countryside began to inherit
an aging population. See Fig. 3.3 and Fig. 3.4. This happened
at the very time that agriculture production had to be stepped
up in order to feed the burgeoning urban populations.

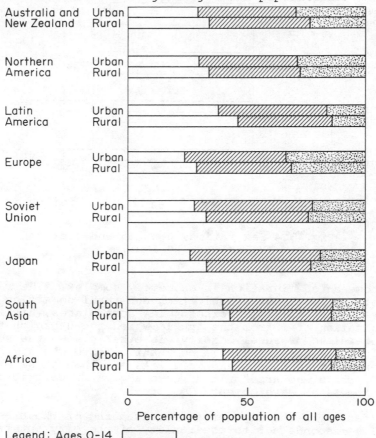

Fig. 3.3 Age structures in 8 major areas

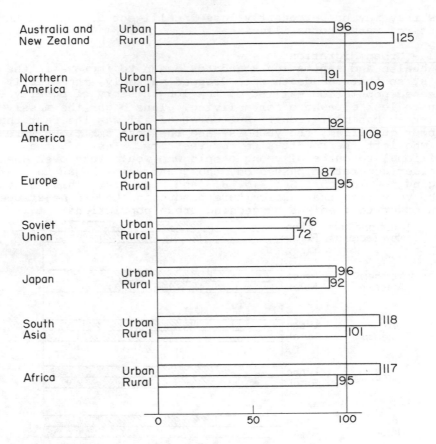

Fig. 3.4 Sex ratios, ages 15 and over.
Males per 100 females

The phenomenon of migration is extremely complex. The relationships between levels of urbanization and rural densities reflect
the operation of multiple forces. In some places, high levels
of urbanization stem from the "pull" which the urban centres
exert regardless of rural density; in other places the so-called
"push" from the rural areas is dominant. Those who are "pulled"
are generally more modern and more literate than those who are
"pushed"; those who are "pulled" make a greater contribution
to the process of development.

Another factor is the migrant's understanding of the urban areas.
He usually responds not to the reality of the city but rather to
his conception or image of it. His motives are diffuse ("seeking a better life"). If certain amenities that he is seeking,
such as better education, are brought to him in the village, his
migratory tendency may increase. A small taste of modernization
may create a demand for more.

Even within the planned economy of the Soviet Union the migrations to the urban areas are just as serious as they are in countries with a much lower standard of living.

In his book titled The Russians, Hedrick Smith described some of the problems of rural life. He gives some statistics for the exodus that has taken place from the land to the cities - more than 20 million in the period 1950 to 1970. He reinforces these statistics with the interesting item of information that workers on collective farms do not get the passports needed for travel within the Soviet Union (the domestic passports) that are provided for urban dwellers. This presumably is because many more would move to the cities if they could. By 1975 the demand for these domestic passports became so strong that the government finally promised to issue them to all citizens. It is now in the process of issuing them.

Smith points out that the contrast between life on the farm and life in the cities is much more marked in the Soviet Union than it is in western counties. Income is lower. Provision of education, health care, consumer goods, leisure outlets, and transportation are all much worse. Worst of all is the sense of isolation. In winter the roads are impassable. Children cannot get to school. A state farm of 3000 people may have only 6 telephones. A small village may have none. They are cut off from the life streams of the big cities, doomed to sit and watch an occasional truck pass by as their principal source of entertainment.

Some of the "push" and "pull" factors affecting rural-urban migrations are listed in the following charts. See Pages 56 & 57.

The drift to the cities seems destined to continue for many years to come. For two out of every five peasants in the world their land holdings are about two acres, not sufficient to provide a living for a household. Furthermore many of those who have two acres do not own the land. They are tenant farmers or sharecroppers, so they have to pay a certain amount of the land's produce to the land owner.

The very poor who do not even have tenant rights number one third of the rural population in Asia and about the same in Latin America. For them life is extremely impoverished. They depend on seasonal employment for their total annual income.

Governments have occasionally made efforts to redistribute agricultural land, but this rarely constitutes a once-and-for-all change that will relieve the rural population from want. Other conditions in the national and world economy influence the viability of small farms. Without investment to raise the small farmers' output, the redistribution of land is not more than a temporary palliative. Where the quantity of soil makes it uneconomic to invest, non-agricultural employment is the only method available for sustaning or raising rural incomes.

RURAL–URBAN MIGRATION: PULL FORCES

ECONOMIC

1. Prospects of material welfare.

2. Improved standard of living.

3. Higher wages in urban occupations.

4. Lot of job opportunities.

5. More profit in industrial sector than in agriculture.

6. Less interest on loans than the interest on loans from private money lenders in villages.

SOCIAL

1. Educated & trained villagers seek intellectually satisfying occupations available in cities.

2. Information media, newspapers, radio, T.V. available in cities.

3. Satisfaction of social and cultural aspirations.

4. To join families already migrated to cities.

5. Recreational facilities, shopping centres in cities.

6. Medical facilities available in cities.

7. Proper housing, electricity, water system & sewerage in cities.

8. Transportation & communication facilities in cities.

9. Social mobility.

10. Migration due to war & refugee problems.

RURAL-URBAN MIGRATION: PUSH FORCES

ECONOMIC

1. Growing pressure of population on land.

2. Increase in rural debt.

3. Unemployment or under-employment.

4. Small holdings of agri-cultural land due to divided inheritance.

5. Lack of alternative sources of income.

6. Joblessness after harvest.

SOCIAL

1. Insufficient social amenities like recreation & shopping centres.

2. Poor state of medical facilities.

3. Lack of educational institutions.

4. Ineffective maintenance of law & order.

5. No proper family planning in villages.

6. Rivalries in villages.

7. Desire to live near the centres of administration.

8. Lack of proper housing, electricity, water supply & sewerage.

9. Insufficient transportation & communication facilities.

10. Information media, such as newspapers, radio & T.V. are seldom found in villages.

When the smallholders suffer a sudden decline in their incomes
or increase in their costs, they may be forced to sell their
land and even their animals and crop reserves, reversing the
effects of previous redistribution. The combination of low
prices for jute, Bangladesh's main export, and high world prices
for grain set off just such a regressive redistribution of the
agricultural wealth in Bangladesh in 1974.

Even in a country like Brazil, with substantial amounts of
potential new areas for cultivation, the position of large land-
owners appears to have limited the landless to the most remote
and least promising new areas.

Some of the innovations to increase productivity introduced into
agriculture in recent years have not helped many of the rural
poor. New seeds, fertilizers, pesticides, proper grain storing
facilities and transportation to ship the marketable surplus are
certainly available but, since these require credit, they are
only available to the large-scale farmers. Similarly, the
benefits of government production incentives such as tractor
subsidies, price support programs, relief from taxation,
institutional credit services, research and preferential terms
for inputs accrue mainly to a small minority of the rural
population.

There is one thing that can always be done to improve the
situation of people in the rural areas: let farm prices find a
higher level - something close to their natural level - and put
more investment resources into agriculture.

The vast majority of poor people in developing countries are
helped when food prices rise. It is a myth that the poor in
poor countries are harmed by food price rises, because most of
them grow food either as farmers or as farm workers.

The brightest prospect on today's horizon is the self-help type
of rural development. Where rural dwellers - characteristically
individualistic in their lifestyles - are able to band together
and determine their own destiny, often through political
pressure on the central authorities, there is a reversal of the
trend toward deterioration. Experience in places like Tanzania,
China and parts of the Indian Subcontinent are beginning to show
evidence of the value of this kind of approach.

Tanzania
95 percent of the people of Tanzania are rural dwellers and so
the main thrust of the country's settlement development has been
in the rural areas. In 1967 President Julius Nyerere launched
his famous Ujamaa Villages project - a network of socialist
villages to cover the entire country. It was a bold venture and
it has attracted international attention. Here was one of the
25 poorest nations in the world breaking boldly with the colonial
era with clearly defined aims.

In 1973 Nyerere announced that all peasants had to resettle in

villages before the end of 1975. Between 1967 and 1973 various
experimental projects had been carried through to demonstrate
the viability of the new Ujamaa Villages. In one or two places
large settlement schemes had been established but now the whole
thing was to be placed on a national footing involving most of
the 15 million people of the country.

National organizations cleared land, transported great
quantities of bush poles and other materials, and moved families,
household goods and cattle. Schools, community centres, beer
houses, cooperative shops and sometimes workshops and chicken
farms were built with very little outside assistance. Rural
construction units coordinated the construction work and
introduced the peasants to some new building techniques.

At first both carrot and stick were used with varying degrees of
success, but the increased construction program soon indicated
mounting self confidence in the villages and growing support
for the self-reliance construction work. In one region alone
over a million people were resettled within a year. This was
stretching the planning capacity too much.

The accelerated villagization program started at a difficult
time for the country. The decision to move the capital from Dar
Es Salaam at the coast to Dodoma in the centre of the country
disrupted a great deal of the country during the 1973-75 period,
and the oil crisis that hit the entire world was added to all of
that.

News reports of the time showed that many villagers were
unwilling to move quickly to new communal settlements, and give
up their traditional way of life. These accounts spoke of
peasants facing court action, members of the militia arresting
people and forcing them to go to their villages, and so on.

One incident described peasants in Inchugu as being taken by
surprise to see armed militiamen climbing on top of their homes
taking away the thatch, ripping off iron sheets, and then
removing doors and windows and smashing them. Having destroyed
the homes, the militiamen then forced the people to move
immediately to the new villages that same day, complete with
chickens, children, cattle, goats, sheep, beds and bedding, etc.
Some of them had to settle for a day or two under trees when
they arrived at the village.

This massive transformation of rural Tanzania within such a
short span of time seems to be one of the great historical
events of post-Colonial Africa. It is too soon to predict the
final value of the popular participation implied by the entire
Ujamaa program. In the eyes of Nyerere and the other leaders of
the country there seems to be no doubt that the program is
achieving its objectives. They are committed to what they have
launched and they have recently added a series of slogans that
go something like this, "farming for life or death". At its own
scale the Tanzania development is similar to the much larger

experiment now fully underway in the People's Republic of China.

China

Development planning in China is motivated by social criteria.
Rural development and a reduction of the differences in living
standards between town and country are primary goals.
Industries are being dispersed as much as possible throughout
the countryside and urban dwellers are encouraged to move with
them. In some cases, entire enterprises with their equipment
and staffs have been transferred out of the very big cities, to
the benefit both of the city and the countryside. This integration of town and country, industry and agriculture, is
consistently pursued. Together with programs for the social and
cultural development of the individual, the family and the
community, it has already begun to create innovative patterns of
settlement and new forms of social relations.

China's rural development policy is directed to the village as a
part of a commune of several villages, the basic unit for the
implementation of national agricultural policy. The land in the
commune is owned collectively by its members, but a small amount
is privately owned. The annual and long term production goals
for the commune are set by the central government, but day-to-
day operations are locally controlled.

The produce of the commune proper is distributed among its
members, after determining the share of the members according to
their work and productivity (the "work point" system). The rest
of the produce is exported to the cities and towns. These
exports provide the capital out of which most agricultural
development has been financed. This economic self-reliance has
been a major feature of Chinese agricultural development policy.

Traditionally, animal labour was used to drive irrigation
mechanisms and, in years of drought, it was common for the
cattle population to decline from overwork and undernourishment.
Today, most of the irrigation and drainage is mechanized and
ponds and tube-wells generally provide an ample supply of water.
Farm machinery supplements human and animal labour in the
fields.

Most of the nitrogen, phosphorous and potassium fertilizers come
from organic sources, principally animal dung and night soil.
The total of organic based fertilizers is quite high compared
with most industrialized countries. It reflects an age-old
tradition of Chinese agriculture.

Indian Subcontinent

Throughout this vast area of 800 million people many innovative
forms of rural development are appearing. In Nepal there is
the anti-malarial and settlement projects on the low-lying
Terai; in India large-scale land reform is underway; Sri Lanka
boasts its now world famous self-reliance scheme; Pakistan has
its agrovilles; and in Bangladesh there is BRAC, the Bangladesh
Rural Advancement Committee. See Fig. 3.5.

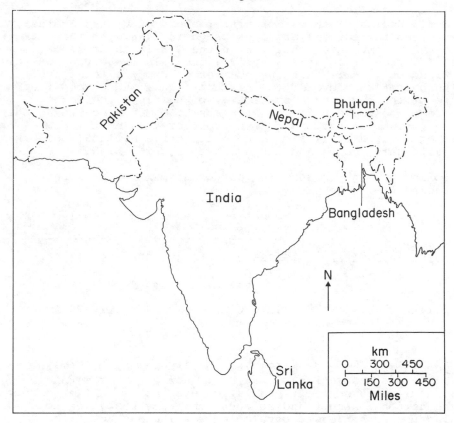

Fig. 3.5 The Indian Subcontinent

Nepal is always perceived as a mountainous country because of
its associations with Mt. Everest and because the capital and
most of the population have been concentrated in the mountain
area. But there is a large section of the country 20 or more
miles wide and running the whole 525 mile length of the border
with India, where the ground is comparatively flat, where the
land is only 600 feet above sea level, and where all kinds of
agricultural crops can be grown on a large scale.

Why then have these areas of potential mango orchards, sugar
cane, and paddy fields not been more developed? In a word the
answer is mosquito. An attempt at settlement was made in 1889
but, like all previous attempts to occupy this region, it ended
in defeat. The only use it seems that people could find for the
area was a penal colony in which criminals were sent to serve
out their sentences while engaging in agriculture. It was not
until 1966, with the eradication of malaria, that settlers
began to move into this rich agricultural area.

The World Health Organization with the aid of United States
money began its anti-malarial campaign in 1958. At that time
two out of every three children in the Terai, as it is called,
were afflicted by malaria. By 1971 the malaria scourge was all
but wiped out. More than one quarter of Nepal's total public
health budget was devoted to this campaign. And beyond the
period of the campaign a small army of nearly 4,000 workers
were required to keep the malaria mosquito under control. This
army has now been reduced but the cost of keeping the place
clear of malaria until a much more effective national network
of health services is available is still quite high.

The following figures show the effect of making the Terai
habitable.

	Mountains & Hills	Terai	Nepal
Population 1961	5,985,000	3,425,000	9,410,000
%	63.6	36.4	100
Population 1971	7,046,000	4,293,000	11,339,000
%	62.1	37.9	100

The population shift from 1961 to 1971 shows that the Terai had
increased its population by 868,000. However, the mountain
areas had increased their population even more. While so much
of the national budget and so much publicity was given to the
opening up of the Terai, population was increasing in the
traditional areas higher up the mountain sides. With this
increase in population there has been a worsening of the bad
conditions that have always prevailed there. There is a clear
limit to the number of acres that can safely be terraced in the
hill forests. A few more people in a home or a few dozen more
people in a village can alter the available food supply.

The development of the Terai clearly attracts the youngest and
best qualified of the young people from the villages. The
result, the rural to rural migration can cause the same kind of
stagnation in the older rural areas as the rural to urban
migrations have caused. The national government is now trying
to correct the imbalance by a series of development corridors
extending north to south across the different levels of terrain.
These transportation routes make possible interchange of
commodities and provision of services to all parts of the
country.

India's population is expected to increase from 548 million in
1971 to 945 million in the year 2001. These figures are based
on the assumptions that birth rates will drop from 39 per
thousand to 26 per thousand and that death rates will drop from
17 per thousand to 10 per thousand. These same trends make it

clear that the rural population will be a very large proportion
of the total in the year 2001. While the urban population
increases by 200 million in these 30 years, the rural
population will increase by 300 million. It is clear that the
problems of human settlements in India will be mainly concerned
with rural settlements for the remainder of the 20th century.

Plans for improving conditions in rural areas focus on land
reforms. The surplus land is being distributed among landless
peasants and consolidation of land holdings is being arranged
wherever possible. Land consolidation means bringing scattered
bits of land together into one larger section of land. The
scattered bits are the result of inheritance laws which permit
farmers to subdivide farms and give the smaller fields to their
sons. By the year 1974, for example, an additional 20 million
tenants had been brought into possession of land. Other plans
include regulation of rent and provision of security of tenure
for tenants. To date about 25 percent of the total agricultural
land has been colsolidated. That amounts to about 36 million
hectares of land or 90 million acres.

The major migrations that have been taking place in India have
been from rural area to rural area. One reason for this high
rate of rural migration is the marriage custom. A girl will
normally marry outside of her own village.

In 1977 India's new government increased its popularity
by keeping its promise to shift the country's economic thrust
to the rural villages.

The plan, outlined in the first budget, aimed at stimulating
food production, rural employment, and development of the
nation's village industries.

The budget's most important aspects provided a new thrust to
government spending for irrigation, electrical power, and
development of village industries. It also provided new tax
concessions for the handloom and powerloom sections of India's
textile industry.

One of the most powerful expressions of the third world's self-
help movements is in Sri Lanka. It can be seen in the proud
face of a peasant farmer as he shows a visitor from a far-off
country his heat, airy mud-walled house, surrounded by a trim
kitchen garden. Or it can be seen in the extensive training
programs for on-going work in the villages.

The Peradeniya Training Centre is a rambling old house which
serves as the headquarters for 18 regional training centres.
Each year, some 40 girls between the ages of 18 and 20 graduate
after a year-long study program in which they learn how to help
women on the small farms.

They will return to their home villages and form a club, mainly
with girls who have completed school at 15 but are not yet

married.   Daily classes in good nutrition and health habits
are organized for girls of the village, and the girls are then
encouraged to persuade their families to adopt better farming
techniques and improved hygiene.

At the training centre a half-acre demonstration kitchen garden
is laid out, in which many of the elements of a balanced diet
may be grown: soybeans for protein, yams, maize and bread fruit
as "energy foods" and mangos, chillies, onions and leafy
vegetables to supply other elements.

Sugarcane provides treacle as a substitute for sugar.   Keeping
of poultry is encouraged, and girls are told to persuade their
farmers to dig an improved latrine and well, and to be careful
of where the waste goes.

Most peasant houses have only a fire on the kitchen floor for
cooking, a constant danger for small children.   One of the
most successful projects has been the building of simple mud
brick and tin stoves, raised from the floor on legs and
connected to a few lengths of stove pipe.   The sheet tin and
pipe is the only investment needed.   Another simple improvement
is a food storage bin placed outdoors in a cool place and raised
off the ground, away from rodents and insects.

Better sanitation around the home cuts down on illness.   Building new stoves reduces accidents and encourages better food
preparation.   More than that, there is a spirit of co-operation
among all the villagers.   The girls and young women feel they
have accomplished something at home, and there is much less
desire to head for the cities.

Pakistan's agrovilles are the most recent development in a long
history of rural development extending back to 1954.   In that
year a major thrust into community development was launched
to cope with a series of disastrous droughts and floods which
hit the country in 1953.   Certain villages were selected as
centres for small-scale industries, adult education, family
planning, and improved transportation.   The agrovilles date
from 1972.   They are building on the experience of the previous
18 years.

They bring urban facilities to the small towns in the rural
areas so as to relieve big cities of the continuing
population pressure.   These agrovilles offer a maximum of
urban amenities and opportunities for participation in civic
life.   An existing town is selected or a new urban settlement
is established to function as a market place, offer employment
to the surrounding rural areas, and contain establishments for
the storage and processing of agricultural produce.   It will
also have small manufacturing industries and repair workshops
for agricultural machinery.   Industries like cotton ginning
factories, rice husking mills, flour mills, and workshops for
servicing tractors are important features of the agrovilles.

Agroville sites are selected by the provinces in consultation with the Federal Government. Once a site is approved, a team of technical staff produces a feasibility study. This includes the analysis of present population trends, available communications, health, education, sewerage and drainage facilities, water resources, potentials for mineral and industrial development and the level of commercial activity. The study also gives details of the cropping pattern in the surrounding agricultural areas and the possibilities of locating agro-based industries.

The proposed agrovilles are central places or potential growth poles within the framework of a region. In the planning and development of these new settlements, the direct focus is on the farmer, and the main impact of the agroville must be on the development of agriculture and of agro-based industries, increased employment, higher living standards, and improved educational facilities.

Bangladesh
Rural development means much more than better homes and healthier environments. A whole new structure is needed if people are to be persuaded to stay in the countryside. The following story from the Canadian International Development Agency tells of one such new structure undertaken by a self-help organization in Bangladesh:

The Bangladesh Rural Advancement Committee (BRAC) was formed in February, 1972 following the widespread devastation of the 1971 civil war. By October, BRAC's rehabilitation program had replaced 10,200 war-destroyed houses and repaired 3,900 others; 169 fishing boats were built and 4,500 pounds of nylon twine imported for distribution to fishing co-operatives. Seeds, fertilizer and cash loans were given to refugees returning to their land, and medical care and child feeding programs were launched.

The emergency relief effort was changed into an integrated development program in October, 1972. The Sulla region was singled out because it had suffered severe devastation and was unlikely to receive assistance due to its inaccessibility.

Sulla is an agricultural and fishing area covering 160 square miles of lowlands, with a population of approximately 120,000 scattered throughout 200 villages. During monsoon season, 90 percent of the land is under water.

BRAC began by building community centres in the larger villages for use by co-operative societies, youth and women's organizations, and adult education classes. Villagers provided land, labour and part of the cost of materials. The centres helped to foster a new sense of community spirit in many villages.

Agriculture is the livelihood of 82 percent of the population of

Bangladesh. In the Sulla region, rice was the only major crop
under cultivation. New crops were introduced by CRAC to
increase yield and improve nutritional value.

Blocks of land were leased. Farmers received advice on
financing, seed purchase, fertilizers and insecticides.

After three years of intensive promotion by field staff, vegetable cultivation has achieved wide acceptance. During the
first year, seeds were distributed free of charge.

Vegetable seeds imported by the Menonite Central Committee were
distributed to more than 10,000 families in the area and to all
primary and secondary schools. Vegetables were grown on 500-
800 acres of land.

During the floods of April, 1974, workers mobilized villagers to
build dams to fight rising waters. As a result, while neigh-
boring areas suffered total destruction of crops, the BRAC area
suffered only a 40 percent loss.

One of the most innovative and important aspects of the BRAC
program is use of paramedics who function as "barefoot doctors".
Each of 30 paramedics visits 5,000 people in five villages.
They are trained to diagnose and treat the 12 most common
diseases, which account for 96 percent of all disease in the
area.

Bangladesh, the second most populous on the Indian Subcontinent
is an outstanding example of the problems of rural life. For
that reason it is being singled out as a detailed case study in
the chapter that follows. It is also exceptional in relation
to population and poverty. Of the 10 most populous countries
of the world Bangladesh, Brazil and Indonesia are the 3 fastest
growing. Bangladesh's rural population alone will double by
the year 2000. In terms of poverty the country is among the
world's poorest. Chapter 4 will therefore serve both as a
summary of this chapter and an introduction to Chapters 5 and 6.

Identify the issues

1.   What are two of the main reasons for the huge exodus of
     people from the rural areas to the cities?

2.   Should rural areas receive the same financial support from
     governments as do urban areas? Would you consider the
     benefits of a rural lifestyle to be worth a certain amount
     of money in itself?

3.   Why cannot rural areas absorb increasing numbers of people
     just like the cities? Some countries seem to be able to
     keep their people down on the farm no matter how many
     there are.

CHAPTER FOUR

Bangladesh

The countries of the world submitted national reports to the
Habitat Conference. In all more than a hundred countries
contributed. Of these the report of the People's Republic of
Bangladesh was one of the most detailed and objective. The
following material has been taken from that report.

Bangladesh, though a new nation, has a very old culture. The
writings of the Greek, Chinese and the Arab historians show that
it had early commercial transactions with the countries of Asia,
Africa and Europe. During the medieval period, Dacca 'muslin'
was famous throughout western Europe.

The country is located 90°E at the Tropic of Cancer. To the
north are the Himalayas. To the south lies the Bay of Bengal.

The land frontier is almost totally shared with the Republic of
India. A small portion in the south-east borders the Republic
of Burma.

The soil is formed of old and new alluvium, carried by three
rivers - The Ganges, Brahmaputra and Meghna. These rivers carry
enormous quantity of silt and sediment which is spread over the
vast deltaic plain. These sediments gradually build up the
land and add to its fertility. The country as a whole is a
complex of intricate rivers and canals, and these are the
principal means of inland transportation.

Physiographically the country can be divided into six regions:
(i) the Piedmont alluvial plain in the north-eastern part and
the Barind and Madhupur tracts formed of old alluvium; (ii) the
central valley flat formed of new alluvium; (iii) the South-
Western region or the Moribund delta area; (iv) the coastal area
and the off-shore islands (the active delta region) formed
of saline soil; (v) the Haor region (the area of low depression)
in the north-east and (vi) the hilly region to the east of the
country.

The climate is wet tropical monsoon during the summer, heavy
rainfall during the monsoon and short winter. The high
Himalayan range exerts a very great influence on the climate of
the country. In the winter Bangladesh is protected from the
biting cold from the north winds and during the rainy season
the relief rain floods it. The rainfall is 56" in the mid-west
central part, over 200" in the north-east, over 100" in the
southern and eastern regions, and 80" in the central part.

The alluvial soil which is renewed every year by freshly laden silt is exceptionally fertile and produces high quality jute. Water is a great natural resource and it could be better harnessed to improve agriculture through irrigation.

Forest resources are enormous. Sixteen percent of the land is under tropical and mangrove forests.

The Bay of Bengal is an excellent fishing ground. Shrimps, shells and sharks abound in this sea.

The country is primarily agricultural. There are 65,000 village settlements, and in each settlement you can find a farmer, fisherman, weaver, potter, carpenter, milkman, grocer, boatman, barber, medical practitioner and teacher.

Industrial development is still in its initial stage. Jute is the main cash crop. Jute and tea are the main exports.

There are two ports: Chittagong and Khulna. The capital is Dacca.

The country is faced with an alarming population explosion, which overshadows all other problems.

Total population was 29 million in 1901. It rose to 42 million in 1951 and 51 million in 1961. It is now over 75 million with one of the highest densities in the world.

92 percent of the population are scattered in the rural areas. Only 8 percent can be described as inhabitants of urban centres.

The urban centres have a high concentration of population in the age group 20 to 29 years. The rural areas have a high concentration of population in the age groups 44 years and above and children under 16.

Rural Settlement Patterns
Bangladesh is a flat land intersected by a network of rivers and rimmed by hilly tracts and swampy depressions. Six different types of settlements have developed.

In the high flat land on the northern Piedmont and Barind regions, settlements cluster along the main thoroughfares. These high flat lands are safe from the danger of floods. The rainfall is low (60"), but it increases as one goes eastward. The northern part is irrigated by sub-soil water, but the southern part depends entirely upon monsoon rainfall. The south-eastern margin is irrigated by surface water and shallow tube-wells. Houses are built with mud and straw, and have been arranged in a regular village shape, giving a nucleated pattern to the settlement. Villages usually have 400 families each.

Most of the deltaic plain is exceptionally fertile, and is under heavy innundation during the monsoon.

Every year the soil is renewed by silt, which greatly increases
fertility. People on these areas, establish scattered homesteads by raising the level of the land with earth. Surface
communication is extremely difficult and costly. It is only
during the flood season that movement by boat is possible.

The rivers flow sluggishly over the flat land depositing silt
as they go. When in spate, the banks overflow, and the silt is
deposited on the banks, raising them high. The sediment also
spreads far out into the surrounding areas. These high river
banks, or levees as they are called, are linear in pattern, and
offer good opportunities for establishing settlements. They are
normally protected from floods, they provide ready access to
water for domestic purposes, and transportation is readily
available. As the river courses change, the settlements which
once grew along the levees continue to remain there.

The islands of the Bay of Bengal, formed at the mouth of the
Ganges - Bhahmaputra delta, are extremely fertile. Settlements
flourish on them. The off-shore islands are, however, subject
to destructive cyclones. A typical story of such settlements
is as follows. After the island appears above sea level, a few
years pass before the soil is ready for cultivation. The first
family then arrives on the island, digs a pond for fresh water,
and erects a dwelling on the raised bank. As time passes more
families move in, and build their houses in a similar fashion.
The whole island finally becomes inhabited with dispersed and
isolated clusters.

The eastern part of the country is composed of low hills, with
luxuriant evergreen vegetation. The settlement pattern that
has developed here is unique, influenced almost entirely by
topography.

Agriculture is difficult, and the availability of land is
severely limited. The farmers can only prepare the hill slopes
for cultivation after terracing. On the flat surface of the
hills and also on the gentle slopes they practice a shifting
method of cultivation.

In the north-eastern region, and in part of the south-central
zone, homesteads are built on artifically raised mounds,
resulting in the formation of clusters of high density. In
these patterns of settlements, as in other areas, it is
extremely costly to provide socio-cultural and health facilities.

The settlement problems of Bangladesh are staggering. There is
the enormous and ever increasing population in the rural areas
and there are the special physical hazards, the cyclones and
floods.

Urban Centres
Urbanization in the modern industrial-commercial sense has just
started and the country is still at an elementary level of
urbanization. Only 8 percent of 75 million people live in the
119 settlements defined as urban.

These urban centres offer direct or daily urban services to about half of the territorial area of Bangladesh. The rest of the country is served by 5,000 rural market places, spread all over the country, within walking distances of one another. There are nearly 65,000 villages in the whole country. Distinction is made between the 119 urban centres on the one hand and the rural markets and the villages on the other.

Although no full scale study of the extent and nature of urban-rural interaction has yet been undertaken in Bangladesh, the geographers and physical planners of the country have made some progress in the delimitation and study of the nature of the hinterlands of a number of urban centres. The criteria selected include distances covered by perishable items, commuting distance, hospital, educational and other professional distances, newspaper circulation, daily travel distance for recreation, and social distance.

Relationships between urban centres and their hinterlands may be studied in terms of the hierarchies of the centres. It is well known from studies in central place theory that both the size of the hinterlands and the variety and quality of services offered, vary according to the populations of the urban centres.

The rural markets form the lowest or 1st order in the hierarchy of central places in Bangladesh. The markets serve as exchange or collecting centres for rural primary products and distribution centres for urban-industrial products and services. The hinterland of the rural market is the village and for the small markets the radius of influence is usually 3 miles. The larger periodic rural markets may command service areas 15 miles in radius. The average population of a rural village is 1,000.

The second order in the hierarchy of central places is one of the urban centres. These centres each have an average population of 27,500. There are 25 centres of this order. The centres possess a few urban characteristics interwoven with many rural features. Common services include one commercial bank, an agricultural bank, a post and telegraph office, a few professional medical practitioners, a number of retail and wholesale establishments, secondary schools, a college, and a cinema. These centres usually command hinterlands of 30 square miles.

The 3rd order centres have populations averaging 15,000. These centres enjoy most of the basic urban amenities and they usually have colleges, hospitals and movie houses. A very few may even have weekly newspapers. There are 34 centres in this order and thay have a significant role to play in the diffusion of urban services to rural hinterlands which, for each centre, covers approximately 50 square miles of territory.

The 4th order with populations averaging 35,000 are the most numerous. There are 40 of them. They offer all the services of the centres of the previous order and many of them have become

important trading, educational, and cultural centres. The area
covered may be well over 100 square miles.

Most of the 5th order urban centres averaging 75,000 are
district headquarters. In addition to all the fundamental
characteristics of the preceding orders, these centres are
distinguished by growing industrial and commercial activities.
Higher technical education, and higher order administrative
services differentiate them from lesser order towns. Many of
these centres have weekly newspapers, and at least one, Bogra,
has a daily newspaper. Local buses, trains, motor-launches
and country boats compose the major transportation links between
the urban centres and the rural hinterlands. The hinterland
covers 200 square miles.

The 6th order with populations well over 100,000, include 5
centres. Rajshahi, Khulna, Chittagong, Mymensingh, and
Narayanganj. The two port towns, Chittagong and Khulna, have
vast hinterlands each covering half of Bangladesh. Their
zones of daily urban influence cover 2,000 square miles for each.

The 7th and highest order in the hierarchies of urban centres
has only one centre, Dacca, the National Capital with a
population of just over 1.6 million in 1974.

The three largest urban centres, Dacca, Chittagong and Khulna,
are all rapidly growing cities. They act as forces of attraction over vast rural as well as smaller urban areas throughout
the country. This has resulted in large scale squatting and
serious problems in the provision of basic urban amenities like
housing, transportation, employment, health, education, and
recreation.

Environmental Conditions
The law of inheritance permits division of property amongst
all the children of the deceased person. Fragmentation of
agricultural holdings and farms has been the result. Out of
6.87 million farms 38 percent are less than 1.5 acres each.
Farms of 2.5 acres each constituted 56.63 percent of the total,
and 83 percent of the farms were under 5 acres each. An average
family needs at least 1.5 acres of good agricultural land to
maintain itself. Farm acreage includes homestead land, ponds,
courtyard, family graveyard, farm road, current fallow, and
orchard. Of the farms under 0.5 acre, about 34 percent is
not available for cultivation; and of the farms between 0.5
acre and 2.5 acres, 12 percent of the land is not available
for cultivation.

Rural settlements are characterised by scattered clusters of
homesteads surrounded by agricultural fields. A few fruit-
bearing trees, a bamboo grove, and some other trees that
provide firewood are found within the compound of a homestead.
In most cases, each cluster has a pond, which is the ready
source of drinking water, one or two ditches that provide water
for washing, for bathing cattle, and for other domestic and

agricultural purposes. The pond, as well as the ditches are
also used for rearing fish. In almost every village there are
one or two shallow tube-wells often provided by the government.

Houses in the rural areas are made of bamboo, thatch, and
corrugated iron sheets, and are vulnerable to storms, hurricanes
and floods. Brick built structures are rare. Sanitation
conditions in the settlements on high land is good. Settlements
in the low lying areas are surrounded by stagnant water for many
months of the year and decomposed vegetable matter leads to
pollution of this water. Disposal of human excreta in the low
lying areas is a serious problem, as this often finds its way
into the water.

To improve sanitation the government has introduced water-seal
latrines in 620 villages and 700 selected schools. The program
is being implemented slowly as public acceptance and sustained
care of the facilities are necessary for the success of the
scheme.

For potable water supply, the rural settlements depend on river
water, hand pump tube-wells and pond water. To provide a safe
water supply system, the government, with assistance from UNICEF,
has undertaken an ambitious program of sinking shallow hand-pump
tube-wells as a source of drinking water.

Tube-well water cannot meet all the requirements for drinking and
agricultural purposes, and so the people have to use river water.
Prevention of pollution of the river water is, therefore, of
great importance. Of all the various factors responsible for
pollution of river water, discharge of untreated industrial
affluents is a major one. The government has created an
organization with statutory powers to look after this problem.

Malaria is another menace. The government, with the assistance
of the World Health Organization, has launched a new program
for malaria eradication. The disease is first tackled by
intensive D.D.T. spraying inside each and every home during the
attack phase, and strict surveillance in the late attack and
consolidation phase, in order to detect, treat, and eliminate
the malaria parasites not the mosquitos.

Cholera and smallpox eradication measures have also been taken
by the government with the assistance of WHO. These measures
have provided considerable protection to the population against
the menace of these two normally fatal diseases.

In the urban areas the demand for houses and urban services has
been steadily increasing. The resources available to the
government were inadequate to cope with this escalating demand.
A modest attempt was made to expand the basic resources of
Dacca city by providing land for houses, commercial buildings,
industries, schools, colleges, hospitals, roads, and sanitation.
But the population expansion far exceeded the planned
enlargement of the city. As a result, surrounding agricultural

fields were built upon without adequate provision of roads,
drains, schools, shopping centres or other public services.
These areas have turned into slums of the worst kind. Serious
housing shortages, traffic congestion, overcrowded transportation services, inadequate drainage and water supply, shortage of schools for children, and virtually no playgrounds,
have become features of the major cities.

During the last few years, the major urban centres have been
receiving new waves of migrants from the rural area. They are
mostly landless labourers who have been forced by circumstances
to migrate to urban centres in search of employment. In the
cities, they pick up some sort of casual work, and get rice and
wheat through ration shops, at a price much cheaper than they
would have paid in the village markets. In the urban areas they
squat on vacant government land, on public roads and pavements,
and on vacant properties of absentee landlords.

These squatter settlements have no drainage, no water supply,
and no proper latrines. The squatters build hovels with anything they can find, as shelter against sun and rain. They live
under sub-human conditions. The squatter settlements are a
social threat to public health, and are breeding grounds for
anti-social elements, and criminals. The squatter population
has now increased so much that it constitutes a substantial
portion of the total population of the three major cities of
Bangladesh.

Natural Hazards
Bangladesh has many natural hazards, floods, cyclones, storms,
river erosion, drought, landslides. Of these, floods and
cyclones have been a regular annual feature since 1950. Prior
to this period a lull in weather problems had existed for quite
a long time.

Bangladesh lies directly in the path of tropical cyclones.
When storms coincide with high-tide, the surge height may rise
24 feet above sea level as happened in November, 1970.
Cyclones occurring during the retreating monsoon are more
devastating than those that hit at the beginning of the monsoon
season.

Areas that are most seriously affected are the south-central and
eastern coastal districts (Patuakhali, Barisal, Noakhali and
Chittagong).

The four severe cyclones of 1584, 1737, 1876 and 1897 took a
toll of a hundred thousand lives, while the nine cyclones of the
decade 1960-70 caused 400,000 deaths, 300,000 in 1970 alone.
The total monetary value of all the loss (1960-1970) amounted
to 2,500 million taka, out of which 1,000 million taka
(approximately U.S. $ 80 million) was lost because of the 1970
cyclone alone (3% of the gross national product). It is
evident that the cyclones of 1960-70 have caused greater damage
to life and property than have all the earlier cyclones put

together.

The cyclones have a further effect on soil and agricultural
lands by the onrush of sea water. The whole economic infrastructure of the region is paralysed. Not only is this true
but, in addition, social structures of the community collapse
because of diseases in epidemic form. The government comes
forward with all available resources, but the magnitude of the
disaster makes it practically impossible to handle the problems.
The settlement pattern is dispersed and isolated without
adequate communication links, so it is all the more difficult to
rush help and relief at the time of the emergency.

The flat nature of the country, the high rainfall in the region
and in the catchment areas of the main rivers, siltation of the
river beds, and obstruction in the flow of water by high tides
are the major causes of floods.

Extensive floods occur every year. About 1,100 million acre
feet of run-off is brought from outside the country, while about
100 million acre feet is obtained from rainfall within the
country. The three major rivers, the Ganges, the Brahmaputra,
and the Meghna, drain a total catchment of more than 600,000
square miles, of which only about 7.5 percent lies in
Bangladesh. These rivers also carry a huge quantity of silt
and sediment. By gradually depositing silt and sediment the
river channels are choked up, and the flood situation worsens.

During the last 15 years, ten devastating floods have occurred.
The increase of population, and the expansion of settlements
in previously uninhabited areas, are further accelerating soil
erosion. Debris from this erosion brought down and deposited
in the river channels and flood plains are increasing the danger
of flooding daily. The potential loss and damage are thus
gradually increasing due to expansion of settlements.

In a normal year, more than 18 percent of the country (about
10,000 square miles) is flooded, but in a year of abnormally
high floods as in 1954 and 1974, more than 36 percent of the
land (20,000 square miles) is affected.

In contrast to the rural settlements, the urban areas are in a
favourable position with respect to flood hazards, for they are
situated on comparatively high land. Only in exceptional cases
are the urban areas affected, as happened in 1954 and 1974, when
Dacca and many other urban centres were badly flooded.

Coping with the Urban Immigrants
The urban population of Bangladesh has increased 138 percent
from 1961 to 1974 and a significant proportion (39 percent) of
this increase was due to the shift of population from rural to
urban regions. Immigrants are concentrated in the major cities.
The reasons for their moving into urban regions were mainly
economic, i.e., in search of jobs. Migrants from rural areas
tend to move into the nearest urban centres and they usually

originate from densely populated areas. The squatters are
usually landless. They are not satisfied with their present
occupations and income, and a majority of them are in debt.
They are less educated than the urban population. They demand
training and skilled jobs and they ask for community facilities
from the government. A majority (80 percent) of the squatters
say that they are willing to go back to their places of origin,
i.e., rural areas, if some cultivable lands are made available
to them.

To cope with the needs of these urban immigrants, the government
plans to increase the housing units, employment opportunities,
transportation, health and education facilities. To encourage
potential rural migrants to stay where they are the government
proposes to increase employment opportunities in the rural
regions.

For the long term management of urban immigrants, the following
general policies are recommended.

1. Decentralization of urban areas. To minimize the pressure
    of immigrants on a few very big cities, we should de-
    centralize the urban areas by moving industries, government
    offices, colleges and hospitals to smaller urban centres.

2. Creation of job opportunities in the rural areas. To prevent
    the urban services from further deteriorating, potential
    rural to urban immigrants should be settled at their places
    of origin. We will have to generate economic activities in
    the rural areas. We will have to revitalize the agricultural
    and non-agricultural sector of the rural economy. We should
    put emphasis on high yielding varieties of crops through co-
    operative farming systems. High yielding varieties are
    labour intensive and evidence suggests that they generate
    considerable agricultural employment.

    Non-farm activities should be created in the rural areas,
    e.g., introduction of rural works program in the form of
    digging canals, building roads, bridges and constructing
    embankments; setting up cottage industries, dairy and
    poultry farms, development of fisheries; creation of
    opportunities for marketing and processing of agricultural
    products; setting up small scale secondary industries.

3. Narrowing the gap between rural and urban wages. We will
    have to minimize the present wage disparities between rural
    and urban areas. Various studies have shown that
    individuals base their decisions to migrate on the income
    potential in the urban regions. This may explain the drift
    of people from rural to urban areas despite high unemploy-
    ment in the urban areas.

4. Rural development. We will have to make rural life
    attractive. For this, we should concentrate not only on
    generating economic activities in the rural areas but also

introduce some modern amenities. At present, most of the
modern amenities of life are in the urban areas.

Here is how some of these measures will work out.

The First Five-Year Plan proposes to increase the housing
service faster than the population growth. Since 1972, the
government has constructed about 4,500 semi-permanent housing
units in Dacca city for the low income groups.

In Dacca the squatters have been taken to Tongi (Duttapara),
Demra and Mirpur on the outskirts of the city for resettlement.
Detailed plans have been drawn up to provide housing and other
service utilities. There are about 12,000 plots (measuring
either 13' x 25' or 14' x 26'), which are distributed more or
less equally among Tongi, Demra and Mirpur. Services to be
provided include primary schools, high schools, vocational
schools, maternity-cum-health clinics, parks and play grounds,
shopping and community centres, cinemas, piped water supply
and sanitation facilities. A police station, a fire station
and a social welfare office will also be set up in these areas.
There will be direct bus connections with Dacca city. Arrangements have also been made for plots where small scale industries
will be set up.

In the same five year plan (1973 - 78), the urban labour force
is being substantially increased. Textile industries will
generate the largest increase in employment, followed by
engineering and jute industries. The textile units are
concentrated in the two big cities of Dacca and Chittagong. The
new textile units will be widely dispersed, so as to reduce the
pressure on these cities.

In the development of rural areas emphasis will be placed on
various small scale industries like weaving, leather and metal
goods. An additional employment of 50,000 is expected to be
created. This employment will be additional to the main agricultural occupations. The government proposes to set up
compulsory multi-purpose cooperatives in each village. This
scheme is expected to provide jobs for landless peasants.

THE PLACE OR ORIGIN BY URBAN AND RURAL STATUS OF
THE SQUATTERS OF DACCA, CHITTAGONG OR KHULNA CITIES

Place of origin	Dacca 1974	Chittagong 1974	Khulna 1974
Urban	7.63%		
Rural	92.37%	100%	100%

LAND OWNERSHIP, AVERAGE MONTHLY FAMILY INCOME,
FINANCIAL DEBT, AND INCOME SATISFACTION OF THE
HEADS OF THE HOUSEHOLDS OF SQUATTERS IN DACCA

	Dacca 1974
Agricultural land holding	
None	80.77%
1 acre	12.31%
2 acres	0.77%
Not known	6.15%
Average monthly family income (in taka).	300.00
Financial debt	
Yes	64.06%
No	35.94%
Income satisfaction	
Yes	10%
No	90%

5. Need for a national survey. Last, but not least, to chalk
    out a comprehensive plan for management of the urban
    immigrants, we need the following information about the
    immigrants: demographic characteristics; reasons for
    migration; demands and needs; past and present occupations
    and incomes; perceptions of living in urban and rural areas.

Identify the Issues

1. Compare Bangladesh with your country in relation to
    population density, location, climate, and major
    natural hazards.

2. What controls should donor countries exercies over
    money or other assistance given to needy countries
    such as Bangladesh?

3. Find out all you can about the Pakistan Civil War in
    which the two halves of the country became separate
    nations. What were the main causes of that war?

"For every man, woman and child alive in the year 1900, there
are three today and there will be six early in the next century.
This explosion in human numbers underlies the urgency of better
human settlement planning. But nearly as important as growth in
numbers is the change in where people live. At the beginning of
the century, four out of every five people lived in rural areas,
in small villages or isolated farms. By the year 2000, more
than half of all people will live in urban areas. One way to
see this change vividly is to count the number of cities with
one million or more inhabitants: 11 in 1900; 191 in 1975; an
estimated 309 in 2000. Most of these "million plus" cities will
be in developing countries. Yet, while the urban populations
will increase dramatically, the number of people in rural areas
will continue to rise." From Habitat Preparatory Paper.

CHAPTER FIVE

Population

At the root of both the urban and rural crises is the story of world population growth over the past twenty years. During most of human history, world population grew very slowly. Birth rates were high; death rates too were high. Famine, disease and wars kept the population down. The result: from 1 AD to 1700 AD the world population just about doubled, with a final total well under one billion.

Even after 1700 the loss of life due to famine, disease and wars remained very high. In the Taiping rebellion in China in the 1850's, the loss may have been as high as 30 million. In Ireland, during the great famine of the 19th Century, close to 1 million deaths occurred in a population of 8 million. And the influenza epidemic of 1918 caused 15 million deaths in India alone.

Throughout the 1800's, the death of one out of every four infants in the first year of life was a common experience. Life expectancy was 35, about half of what it is now in developed countries. Cancers and heart diseases - things that usually affect older people - have replaced tuberculosis, cholera, diptheria, and typhoid as the main causes of death in low death rate regions.

In spite of these losses, the world's population more than doubled between 1700 and 1950. In that period the industrial revolution produced an enormous increase in scientific knowledge. Man acquired new abilities to control, even eliminate diseases. Better sanitation and better medical practices contributed to the cutting back of death rates.

The really big increase in the world's population, the growth that has come to be known as the "population explosion" has occurred since 1950. From that date to the present time, the world's population has increased from 2.5 billion to 4 billion. See Fig. 5.1. Medical services throughout the world have caused a dramatic cut in death rates. Birth rates, however, have remained high.

The rate of population increase is even more startling than the total numbers. It took 135 years for the world to go from 1 to 2 billion. It took only 30 years to go from 2 to 3, and only 15 years more were needed to reach the 4 billion mark. In the time it takes you to read this far in this chapter, 500 babies will have been born.

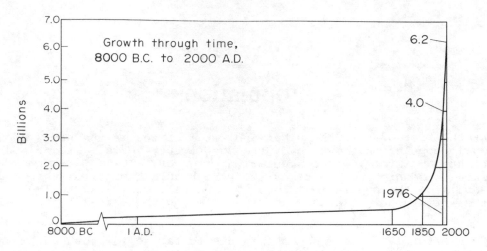

Fig. 5.1 World Population Growth through time

At the current rate of growth of 1.9 percent, the population will double in less than 40 years. This rapid increase is a new phenomenon in terms of man's history on earth.

Population growth increases exponentially. A familiar story, said to have originated in Persia, offers a classic example of exponential growth. It is a story of a clever courtier who presented a beautiful chess set to his king and in return asked only that the king give one grain of rice for the first square, two grains for the second square, four grains for the third, and so forth. The king, not being mathematically inclined agreed and ordered the rice brought forth. The eighth square required 128 grains, and the twelfth took more than one pound. Long before reaching the 64th square, the king's coffers were depleted. Even today the world's richest king could not produce enough rice to fill the final square. It would require more than 200 billion tons or the equivalent of the total world production of rice for 653 years.

As long ago as 1798, Thomas Malthus recognized that populations increase at an exponential rate of growth. Malthus felt that the ultimate check on world population growth would be the lack of food. He claimed that food production would increase at an arithmetic rate which means growth by a constant rather than an increasing amount. Of course Malthus' scheme did not take account of the impact of modern technology on agricultural production.

The current growth rate of 1.9 percent may not seem high in itself, but when it is applied to the world's large population, it represents an increase of 204,932 people per day.

Four areas of the world stand out as centres of very large
population clusters: eastern Asia, southern Asia, western Europe
and east-central North America. All of these places are in the
northern hemisphere where the largest portion of the earth's
land is located. Of the 15 or so most populous nations of the
world, only Brazil and Nigeria are not within these four broad
areas.

Fastest growing of the ten countries with biggest populations
are Bangladesh, Brazil and Indonesia. These three will have
doubled their already big populations by the year 2,000. Fastest growing among 7 major regions are Asia, Africa, and Latin
America. See Fig. 5.2.

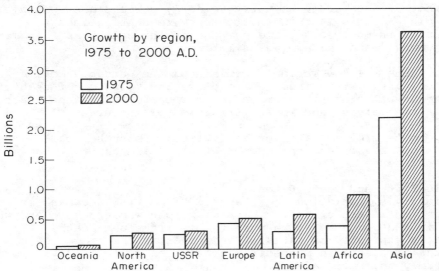

Fig. 5.2 World Population Growth by region

Counting People
The statistics we use, and the ways in which they have been
obtained are far from precise. At best they are rough approx-
imations. A time difference of 10 months between two counts in
the same year in taking the populations of say, India and Japan,
could mean an error of 12 million people in the published
statistics.

When Nigeria's one-week national population census is held there
are several traditional prejudices to be surmounted. Nigeria is
a vast country of over 200 ethnic groups with distinctive
cultural heritages, languages and life-styles.

Hundreds of thousands of posters, leaflets and booklets are
distributed at the time of the census. Newspaper space is used
for advertising materials. Many languages are used for the
printed word. Special souvenir buttons - BE COUNTED - are

distributed to schools; illiterate parents take an interest in
their children's buttons, and the boy or girl explains what is
taught about the census in school. The core of the campaign is
focused in radio, television, and mobile vans.

A jingle in calypso (lilting, entertaining and good for dancing)
is broadcast by radio, calling on "brother, sissie, baba and
mama" to rise in the census week and be counted.

"Won't my children die, if they are counted?" a section of the
population thinks, so the census promotion teams explain that no
disease will come to them as a result of the count.

In another area of the country, elderly persons are spoken of in
the plural! This is being overcome by requesting them to
describe themselves for the purpose of the census as "big man
(or woman)" and the ego is satisfied.

Then there are the serious problems of the purdah. Moslem men
seclude their wives from public view, and males other than their
husbands cannot reach them in their rooms. Female enumerators
visit the harems, and Moslem tradition is honoured.

Polygamous families are not so difficult, but the head of the
household may forget the number of his children if he has
several wives.

World Birth and Death Rates

A country's population and its rate of natural increase is
largely a result of the numbers of people who are born and who
die in that country. The numbers of births and deaths are
usually expressed as rates. Rates measure the frequency of
births or deaths in a specific population during a given period
of time, generally a year.

$$\text{Crude birth rate} = \frac{\text{births per year}}{\text{population}} \times 1,000$$

$$\text{Crude death rate} = \frac{\text{deaths per year}}{\text{population}} \times 1,000$$

The rate of natural increase is the difference between birth and
death rates. Since birth and death rates are measured per 1,000
population, the birth minus death difference is divided by 10 to
convert to a percentage.

$$\text{Rate of natural increase} = \frac{(\text{birth rate} - \text{death rate})}{10}$$

The annual growth rate of a country is calculated by subtracting
crude death rate from crude birth rate, then adding net
immigration (immigrants - emigrants per 1,000 population) and
dividing by 10 to obtain a percentage.

Throughout most of man's history, until the industrial
revolution was well underway, birth rates were high, averaging
40 per thousand. Hunger and disease meant that death rates were
also high, around 36 per thousand. Thus societies needed high
birth rates just to maintain their numbers; this resulted in
very low levels of population growth. This is shown by the
narrow difference between birth and death rates in 1775 for
both the developed and the less developed countries. See Fig.
5.3 and Fig. 5.4.

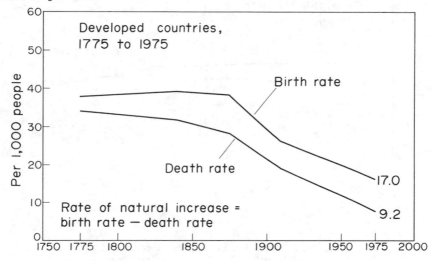

Fig. 5.3 World birth and death rates
(developed countries)

In the 200 years since 1775 Western European countries, the
United States, Canada, Japan, and Australia and New Zealand
have developed from traditional, agricultural economies to
industrial, urban ones.

During that time the high levels of fertility and mortality
slowly declined to the low levels that characterize these
countries today. Whatever population growth occurred was easily
absorbed by expanding industrial economies.

Demographers refer to the gradual shift of birth and death rates
from high to low levels as the demographic transition. This
demographic transition has tended to follow a pattern with three
distinct stages. During the first stage death rates fall from
relatively high levels due to the introduction of modern medical
practices and improved sanitation. The second stage is
characterized by high birth rates and relatively low death rates;
this is a period of very rapid population growth. The third
stage of the transition process occurs when fertility decreases
to close the gap between birth and death rates, resulting in
slower rates of population growth.

In the developing nations of Asia, Africa, and Latin America,
industrialization is a recent development. The demographic
transition has not yet happened. Effective public health and
sanitation measures have decreased mortality. But there has
not yet been any significant decline in fertility. The result
is a rapid increase in population.

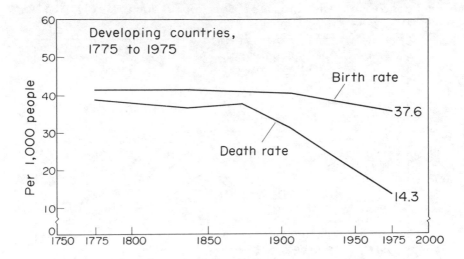

Fig. 5.4 World birth and death rates
(developing countries)

Attaining lower levels of fertility appears to be closely
associated with a country's degree of development. Attitudes
about family size change slowly as a country becomes more
urbanized and industrialized. The traditional role of the
family as the centre of employment, economic security, education,
and recreation is altered drastically in urban areas. Increasing costs of feeding and educating children, as well as changing
attitudes toward work and the education of both men and women,
seem to foster attitudes that favour small families. Because of
the long-term nature of these changes, the developing nations
will be saddled with rapid population growth for an extended
period - at least until the overall level of development
improves.

In reports prepared for the U.N. World Population Conference in
Bucharest in 1974 Algeria estimated that its population would
stop growing in the year 2090 if an average of 2 children per
family were achieved by the year 2000. That in itself is a tall
order for a country that now averages 7 children per family.

Under the same conditions as those proposed for Algeria Rwanda
would not be able to stop its steady increase in population
growth until the year 2115. The reason for the longer period is

the larger proportion (compared with Algeria) of young people.
Again, the change to 2 children per family is a difficult task
for a country which, like Algeria, has a present average of 7
children per family.

The differences in total world population by the year 2000 for
4 major regions under conditions of present fertility rates and
2 children per family rates are shown in Fig. 5.5.

Age-Sex Graphs
The age-sex structure of population is the proportion of people
at each age by sex. Information about a country's age structure
is basic to determining the needs of people. A population with
a large proportion of young people will have needs that are not
the same as a population with a large proportion of old people.
As people age, their needs change - from schools and recreation
facilities to jobs, housing, and medical care.

The "age" of a country is easily studied through the use of age-
sex graphs. Each one of these provides a visual image of age-
sex structure. On the vertical axis are the different age
groups. The horizontal bars and numbers show the percentages of
people in each age group by sex.

The age-sex graphs shown in Fig. 5.6 are generalized versions of
the different kinds of graphs found throughout the world. No.1
represents countries with high birth rates and high death rates.
Most countries had this kind of appearance 100 years ago. No.2
represents countries where death rates have begun to fall while
birth rates remain high. Mexico is like this. No. 3 is a
picture of low birth rates and low death rates. No. 4 describes
countries that traditionally have had low birth rates and low
death rates but have recently experienced an increased birth
rate. Usually found in wealthier developed countries. No. 5
represents countries where there has been a dramatic shift in
birth rates. Japan is a good recent example.

The numbers on the bases of these graphs are percentages - males
to the left of 0 and females to the right. To read off the
percentage of either males or females in a given age range you
just draw lines vertically down to the base from the sloping
edges that correspond to the ages you want.

During the 20th century, the population of the United States has
changed from a situation of rapid growth and a large excess of
births over deaths to one of little growth and less difference
between births and deaths. The age-sex graphs illustrate these
shifts.

The pyramid for 1900 shows that death rates at that time were
considerably lower than birth rates. The difference between
the birth rate of 32 per 1,000 and the death rate of 17 per
1,000 coupled with high immigration kept the population growing
till the 1930s.

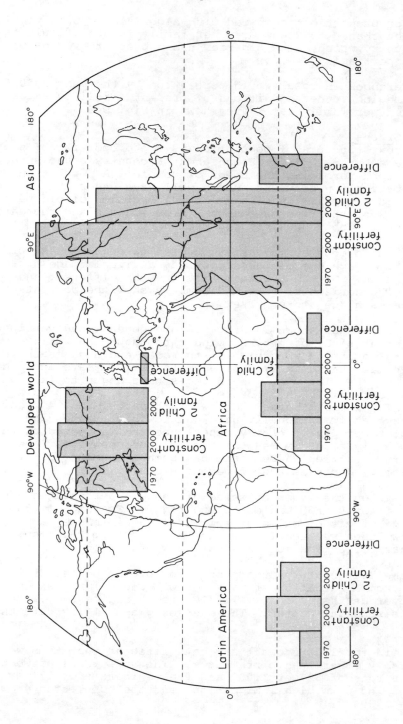

Fig. 5.5 Trends and alternatives in population growth

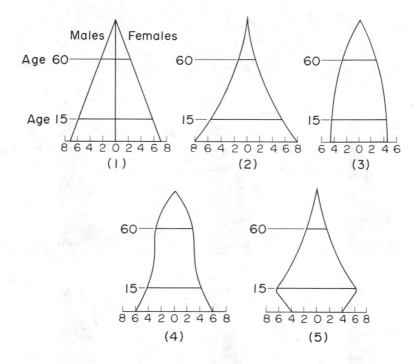

Fig. 5.6 Types of age-sex graphs

Both births and immigration dropped off during the depression years. The low birth rate is reflected in the narrow based 1940 pyramid. After World War 2, the birth rate surged upward, finally peaking off in 1958. This postwar period of high fertility, the baby boom era, disrupted the progress toward low birth and death rates.

Since the 1960s, the birth rate has fallen steadily and is now at its lowest level in U.S. history (under 15 per 1,000). The bases of the 1970 and 1975 pyramids show this progressive decline. With the current death rate of 8.9 per 1,000 and legal immigration of 400,000 per year, the population continues to grow slightly at an annual rate of 0.7 percent. If an equilibrium of low birth and death rates could be reached (assuming no immigration), the U.S. population would eventually stop growing.

The most significant impact on the U.S. age structure during this century was the baby boom which lasted from 1946 to 1958. This period of rapidly rising fertility was initially attributed to the return of soldiers from overseas assignments. But the baby boom lasted for over a decade and was the result of numerous factors including larger family-size norms; "the bigger, the better" ethic; the large number of post World War One babies

reaching their child-bearing years; and an increasing marriage
rate. The combination of these factors culminating between 1955
and 1959, the peak of the baby boom, gives the very wide base to
the 1960 pyramid. As this group of babies ages, the bulge moves
up the pyramid, as seen in both the 1975 and 2000 pyramids.
See Fig. 5.7.

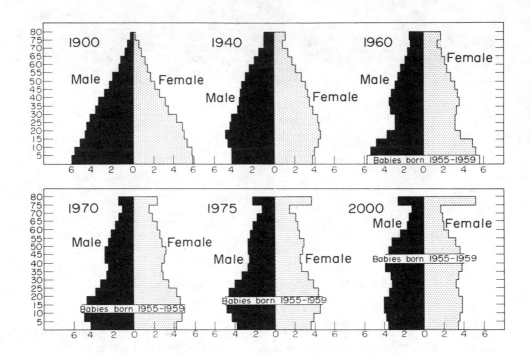

Fig. 5.7 Age structure of the U.S. population

The problems associated with the baby boom babies change as
they pass through the life cycle. In the 1950s and early 1960s,
elementary schools were forced to conduct double sessions and
were often seriously understaffed. Later in the 1960s, college
enrolments swelled, and today jobs and housing are at a premium
given the increased demands from this extra large generation.
By 2020, the United States will be adjusting to an "elderly
boom."

The dependency ratio is another indicator of the age structure
of a population. This ratio indicates how many people are
dependent on the "economically active" sector. People aged 15
through 64 are economically active, while those under 15 and
those who are 65 or more are classed as dependent.

$$\text{Dependency Ratio} = \frac{\text{People aged 0 through 14 + 65 \& over}}{\text{People aged 15 through 64}} \times 100$$

The sex ratio is yet another measure of population structure. It is defined as the number of males per 100 females, and its equation is as follows.

$$\text{Sex ratio} \quad = \quad \frac{\text{Males}}{\text{Females}} \quad x \quad 100$$

U.S. experience demonstrates the fact that it is the "quality" of a population - the age structures and the economic levels - not just the total numbers that matters most.

Age distribution for example affects a host of social and economic conditions. In Canada, for the first 50 years of this century the population was growing "older". The median age increased each decade from 23 years in 1901 to 28 in 1951. The aging was due to longer life expectancy - particularly through the control of diseases - and to declining fertility. Shortly after the Second World War there was a rapid increase in fertility (the "baby boom") which peaked in 1959.

Fertility is now in steep decline. The Canadian population has once more begun to grow "old". The median age is forecast to increase from 26 years in 1971 to 30 by 1986 and 35 by 2001. The median age of voters is expected to be 39 in 1986 and 46 in 2001. At that time society will be more "democratic". In 1971 just over 60 percent of the population was eligible to vote. It will be 76 percent in 2001.

If trends are maintained into the next century, a quarter of the population will be over 60 in 2030 while about a fifth will be under 20. Several consequences follow:

1. A steady increase in cost of health care is inevitable.
    About three-fourths of those over 65 have some chronic
    illness. Due to the aging process alone, demand for
    hospital services will increase 40 percent more than
    percentage growth in population.

2. A decline in violent crime can be expected as those in
    the most crime-prone age bracket (15-25) form a smaller
    and smaller proportion of the population.

3. The dependency ratio will decline from .60 in 1971 to
    .46 in 2001. While the old-age dependency increases,
    the youth dependency is reduced. This will help to
    balance costs. Increased health care costs are balanced
    by lower education expenses.

4. There will be a concentration in the work force between
    the ages of 30 and 45, quite unlike anything Canada has
    experienced before. The millions who fill this age range
    will find promotion difficult. There could be a generation
    of middle-aged drop-outs or intense pressure for the early
    retirement of upper management.

Population Control
Three ways of controlling population have been tried at different times and in different places:

1. Move surplus populations to new areas and open up new
    agricultural land for them. The Indonesians and their
    former colonial overlords, the Dutch, frequently em-
    ployed this method. Large areas of Sumatra were
    developed to accommodate people from overcrowded Java.

2. Develop industrial-urban centres which can provide a
    livelihood for much bigger populations than agricultural
    pursuits could ever do. This has been the typical
    approach in Western Europe, North America and Japan.
    Unfortunately it can only work for limited numbers of
    people. It cannot cope with the explosive situation in
    today's developing world.

3. The most immediate, the most obvious solution is the
    control of population by limiting births. In 1974 at
    the World Population Conference of the United Nations
    in Bucharest, a declaration was adopted by 136 govern-
    ments. It stated that family planning is a basic human
    right and that governments had a duty to provide people
    with the means to enjoy this right.

This last approach is more easily described than implemented.
People readily accept improved health and sanitation measures
that cut down death rates. It is not so easy to cut down birth
rates. Children, especially sons, are insurance policies for
many parents. The more they have, the better the policy. That
kind of thinking changes very very slowly in developing
countries.

In a recent world survey people were asked whether or not they
wanted an increase in the size of their communities. The
following responses were received:

	Would Like Increase	Would Not	No Opinion
Canada	25%	72%	3%
U.S.A.	14%	83%	3%
Western Europe	26%	65%	9%
Latin America	53%	45%	2%
Far East	60%	34%	6%
Africa	69%	26%	5%

Chinese methods of population control may seem strange to
westerners in the 1970s yet their methods are entirely in keep-

ing with western traditions. The key is self-control. Late
marriages are encouraged; usually couples do not marry until
their combined age is fifty. Premarital intercourse is both
socially unacceptable and almost unknown, and practical
contraceptive information is only given after marriage.

There is an interesting brand new development in population
control that might well upset many of the predictions of the
present time. It came to light for the first time in 1977. It
could profoundly change those developing countries where
preference for male offspring is rooted in the culture. This is
how it was first reported.

Fertility specialists are awaiting the births of a special group
of babies with up to a 90 percent chance of being male because
of the use of a new sperm separation method.

The technique holds no promise for parents of sons who long for
a baby daughter, as only the male-producing Y sperm are isolated
in the process. Clinics that have been accepting applications
for the procedure asked couples to sign consent forms which
included an acknowledgement "that any baby that is conceived is
likely to be a male".

The technique involves placing a sample in a glass tube containing a solution that enables the "strongest swimmers" among the
sperm - also the ones most likely to bear the male producing
Y chromosome - to make their way to the bottom of the tube.

If this new technique is successful and inexpensive, male
chauvinism will no longer be identified by words. Actions -
especially the actions of the poorer segments of society - will
tell the truth much louder and much more accurately than words.

Singapore
The example of Singapore points out some of the problems of
population control by limiting births.

Family planning activities in Singapore began in 1949 with the
formation of the Singapore Family Planning Association, a voluntary agency concerned with the health and welfare of mothers and
children.

In December 1965, Parliament passed the Family Planning and
Population Board Act establishing the Singapore Family Planning
and Population Board, a statutory authority charged with the
responsibility for implementing the National Family Planning
Program. The aim was to provide family planning services to 60
percent of all married women aged 15 - 44 years. The remaining
40 percent was assumed to be either practicing family planning
with private medical practitioners, or using contraceptive
methods which do not require clinic attendance, or for some
reason not practicing family planning at all.

The Family Planning Clinical Services are fully integrated into

the existing widespread network of maternal and child health
clinics. A full range of modern contraceptives, at nominal
charges, is provided, including eight brands of oral contraceptives, the intra-uterine device, condoms, an injectable
contraceptive, diaphragms and spermicidal creams.

When the program began in January 1966, the first concern was
to provide a good clinical service to the women who had already
accepted family planning. However, it was realized from the
beginning that for the program to expand, educational input was
necessary. Three massive national family planning campaigns
have been held since 1967. Radio, television and the press
have been fully utilized to convey the family planning message
to the masses.

Two pieces of legislation which reflect policy on family and
population planning in Singapore are the Abortion Act and the
Voluntary Sterilization Act, which came into effect in March
1972. The Abortion Act permits abortions on socio-economic
indications while the Voluntary Sterilization Act regularizes
the position on sterilization.

By the end of 1972, 60 percent of all married women aged 15 - 44
were using the family planning clinical services provided by
the board. Another five percent had been surgically sterilized.
Surveys have shown an additional 15 to 20 percent are practising
family planning by going to private medical practitioners or
using contraceptive methods which do not require attendance at a
clinic.

From 1966 to 1969, the crude birth rate dropped from 28.3 per
thousand to 21.8 per thousand. However, from 1969 onwards,
the crude birth rate began to rise until it reached 23.1 per
thousand in 1972. The main reason for the reversal was the high
birth rate in the immediate post-war years. The large numbers
of men and women born in the 1950s are now reaching reproductive
age.

Besides the impact of the post-war baby boom, which is largely
beyond the control of population planners, the main problem
today is still the relatively large average family size desired
by Singapore couples - 3.6 children. The actual completed
family size is 4.3 children.

The Singapore experience has clearly demonstrated that it is not
enough to leave families to plan the number of children they
want - they want too many. Even if almost all eligible couples
have access to modern contraceptive services, the population
problem remains, though perhaps in a less acute state. In this
respect it should be noted that most national family planning
programs have reached less than 25 percent of the target
population even though they planned to reach as many couples as
possible.

It is often stated that the success of family planning programs

is limited by the lack of social and economic development. It is
widely accepted that low fertility levels are associated with
certain factors such as urbanization and industrialization, a
high level of literacy, a high status of women reflected in
education and employment outside the home, good housing, a high
GNP and a high age of marriage. In Singapore today, most of
these factors already exist. Yet Singapore is facing a rising
population trend and the existing fertility rate is still too
high.

Indonesia
In countries like Indonesia where distances are great, where
communications are poor, and where nurses and doctors are few,
it is a slow process getting birth control information to the
villages. The most difficult hurdle of all is illiteracy. The
information must be conveyed by visual images (posters and
pictures) rather than by conventional literature, and this takes
more time. See Fig. 5.8.

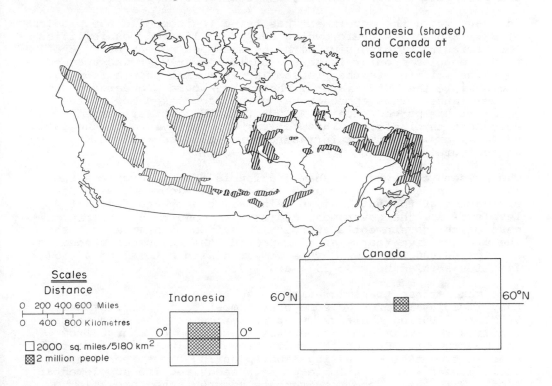

Fig. 5.8 Indonesia compared with Canada

Indonesia's population problem was made worse by President
Sukarno's insistence, right up to the time when he was removed
from the presidency in 1966, that Indonesia needed more people,
not less. He was arguing in the old military tradition that

counted the strength of an army by the number of men in it.

Indonesia is a widespread country made up of some 3000 islands.
The distance from east to west is about the same as it is in
Canada. In this vast area live some 130 million people and,
with a net population increase of 2.5 percent per annum, more
than 3 million are added to the population each year.

At first glance the over-all population density does not appear
to be a problem - about 70 persons to a square kilometre. But
this figure is misleading, as huge areas are covered with
jungle or are undeveloped. As a result there have been huge
concentrations of people living on the fertile soil of Java and
Bali. On these two islands, whose combined area is only 137,735
square kilometres, the present population is about 90 million,
equal to a density of 650 per square kilometre. This presssure
of population has had serious effects on land utilization,
unemployment, underemployment, and standards of living.

For many years the government has tried to reconcile the problem
of Bali and Java's overcrowding and their limited possibilities
for agricultural expansion with the untapped resources of the
thinly populated outer islands. Until recently it was assumed
that the solution to the problem lay in moving people from Java
and Bali to the outer islands where they would pioneer and open
up new lands. This approach has often been taken but on the
whole it has proved such a failure that the settlers ended up
worse off than before. This failure was mainly due to the lack
of necessary government infrastructure, plus social and
agricultural services.

The present concept of transmigration is that it provides the
manpower needed for integrated regional development, with co-
ordination at the national, provincial, county and district
levels of all the government departments concerned. The serious-
ness of the government's approach is evidenced by the fact that
the present Five-Year Plan will provide the resources needed to
settle 250,000 families. This compares with a total of 40,667
families settled between 1971 and 1975.

What makes these transmigration projects so successful is that
they immediately provide some of the most basic needs of the
settlers. During the first year of settlement the transmigrant
families receive minimum food assistance free of charge from
the government. But as they have back-breaking work to do from
sunrise to sunset - clearing land, planting crops, working on
their houses - their calorie-protein needs require supplementary
food. With their food requirements assured, they are able to
carry on until their first crops are harvested.

Most of the new settlers come from villages in Java where they
either owned no land, or had so little that they were unable to
grow enough food to support their families. The chance to have
their own land with a decent house and the possibility of growing enough food for their own needs, and even with some left

over to sell, is a dream come true. They are proud of their new
farms and willing to work hard both to establish themselves and
to help improve the new communities. In Java there was no
future for a man nor for his sons. They could never hope to
have their own land. But now when a son marries he in turn will
be given land and the opportunity to change it from wilderness
into lush crops.

Education
Educational levels affect many aspects of a nation's life - e.g.
the ability to utilize health and family planning literature
and the know how to cope with all kinds of modernization.

The number of students in the more developed regions has become
an important factor in the well-being of these regions. In the
United States of America and Canada, there were more than 400
students per 10,000 population in 1970. Furthermore, there is
an important proportion of young adults in higher education.
More than 20 percent of Europeans and 50 percent of Americans
between the ages of 20 and 24 are students at the university
level.

Number of students per 10,000 inhabitants

Regions	1960	1965	1970
WORLD TOTAL	55	73	97
Africa	7	9	12
Latin America	27	37	57
North America	190	275	402
Asia	27	34	48
Europe	73	109	135
Oceania	98	134	159
Developed Countries	99	146	197
Developing Countries	19	25	35

Health
Dr. A.E. Martin, A consultant to the World Health organization
was interviewed at the time of the Habitat Conference. Here
are some of his comments on the world health situation.

Which types of settlement would offer the healthiest and least
healthy conditions?

Ideally a person would wish to bring up a family where people
were not subjected to any health hazard, whether communicable
diseases, diseases spread by poor sanitary and environmental
conditions, chemical hazards such as air pollution, adulterated
or contaminated foods, or physical hazards such as earthquakes
or hurricanes. There would be efficient preventive health

services (including vaccination and immunization facilities,
maternity and child welfare services, health education
facilities, occupational health services), good medical care
services, good social welfare services, and good social services
(including care for the physically or mentally handicapped, home
help services to provide domestic help in case of sickness or
old age, and geriatric services). There would also be a
satisfactory standard of living and quality of life to ensure
sufficient quantity and variety of food, satisfactory housing
and satisfying employment together with pleasant surroundings,
facilities for recreation and social intercourse.

An environment which is detrimental to health would be the
opposite of the above. The poorness in quality of any given
combination of harmful factors becomes a matter of a value
judgment, in which individuals would differ markedly in what
they accepted.

What sort of health differences are to be expected between
human settlements in different parts of the world?

The differences between developed and developing areas are very
great. A study of mortality in children under five, carried out
by the Pan American Health Organization during 1968-71 in ten
countries of the Americas, showed large differences in deaths
between the ages of one month and one year, and in deaths from
communicable diseases. In one area, deaths in children under
five were approximately 1,000 times greater than in a healthy
suburban area in North America.

Nutritional deficiency proved to be the dominant cause of death
in developing countries, making children more susceptible to
the effects of disease. In some areas two-thirds of the
children who died had shown evidence of malnutrition. Nutrition
of the mother was also an important factor since it led to
infants of low birth weight, among whom there was excessive
mortality during the first month of life.

The provision of piped water and adequate sanitation was shown
to be an important factor. There is a greater likelihood of
children dying in houses without these facilities.

An inverse relationship existed between the deaths and the
educational status of the mother, presumably reflecting the
effects of socio-economic status. More children died in
crowded houses, again largely as a result of socio-economic
and cultural factors.

Are health conditions invariably worse in rural than in urban
areas?

In most parts of the world, yes. The American study of deaths
in childhood showed higher mortality rates in the rural areas.
This pattern is likely in most developing countries with scarce
water supplies, inadequate sanitary facilities, poor health care

services and frequently higher communicable disease rates.

In developed countries the cities often have higher mortality
rates than rural areas, where there are good health care
services, good water supplies, sanitation, and housing.
Frequently there are important differences in socio-economic
class distribution, with a larger proportion of people of low
socio-economic class living in the towns, particularly in slum
areas.

Deficient water supplies and poor sanitation contribute to ill-
health and excess mortality. How important are they?

A World Health Organization survey has shown that a high proportion in developing countries, particularly in rural areas,
have no piped water supply, and have inadequate sanitary
facilities. Lack of safe water and sanitation is associated
with an increased incidence of communicable disease. As a group
the gastrointestinal infections - cholera, enteric diseases,
salmonellosis, dysentery and parasitic intestinal infections
are responsible for a large proportion of the world's communicable disease. Apart from the more direct routes of infection,
the lack of water for washing and the fly infestation associated with bad sanitation result in contamination of food and, in
consequence, food-borne infections.

What other aspects of housing may affect health?

In certain areas, housing may actually encourage the breeding of
specific vectors of disease, such as the tritomid bug responsible for the spread of Chagas' disease in Central and South
America, mosquitos which carry malaria, or rats capable of
carrying plague, typhus, and jaundice.

Overcrowding can contribute to the spread of airborne infections.
Old and dilapidated property often cause higher accident rates.

How may human settlements affect mental health and well-being?

Mental ill-health is difficult to measure. Conditions which
cause stress are known to affect mental, as well as physical
health. Excessive noise, crowded housing, particularly where
members of different families share accommodation, or oppressive
landlords all may increase stress. Overcrowded slum areas are
frequently associated with serious behavioural difficulties.
Life at the top of high-rise tenement buildings may cause stress
in the mother, since she has difficulty in supervising her
children, and it may also be associated with a feeling of lone-
liness. Badly planned new housing schemes, in which there are
inadequate opportunities for social intercourse may harm the
psychological and social development of the younger members of
the family.

What other harmful effects of new settlements have been
observed?

The creation of artificial lakes or reservoirs has at times
caused schistosomiasis (bilharziasis). This is a parasitic
disease, spread in damp conditions by freshwater snails. It is
a serious chronic debilitating ailment and may affect 50 percent
or more of a population. In similar situations onchocerciasis
(river blindness) occurs and leads to a high incidence of
blindness. The unplanned growth of new settlements such as
squatter settlements in towns may present communicable disease
hazards because of the lack of pure water, poor sanitation and
the breeding of disease vectors. Malnutrition due to poverty
increases susceptibility to these diseases.

Governments in Canada spend 8 billion dollars a year on health
care. Nearly 12 percent of all government expenditures go to
health care. And, at the present rate of increase, by 1981,
the bill for health will be 20 percent of the federal budget.

What are Canadians getting for this money?

One traditional measure of health is life expectancy, and,
since 1941, there has been a significant increase, from 63 to
69.4 years for males, and 66.3 to 76.5 years for females. We
have greatly reduced infant mortality rates, and we have also
learned to treat childhood diseases much more effectively.

Fifty years ago, infectious diseases like pneumonia, influenza
and tuberculosis were major causes of death. We have learned
to protect ourselves against these diseases, but fall victim
instead to chronic disease and accidents. A major factor in
these causes of death is the way we live. We drive cars, we
smoke, we consume alcohol, we worry too much, eat too much,
and exercise too little. Despite the billions that annually go
into health care in Canada, we still have many serious health
problems, because our costly health care system cannot always
protect us from the destructive aspects of our way of life.

A look at the medical system in China suggests that there are
other ways to provide competent, inexpensive health care.

In the twenty-six years since the Revolution, China has developed a health care system that reaches all of the Chinese people,
in every part of the country. What, in the Chinese context,
are great advances may not seem impressive to us, but relative
to conditions before the Revolution, contemporary Chinese health
care is an enormous achievement.

A fundamental element in Chinese medicine is the rural health
care system. Eighty percent of China's people work in the
countryside, but in the early years of the People's Republic,
medical personnel were concentrated in urban areas. It was
evident that if there were to be an equitable system of health
care, then the peasants - the largest and most impoverished
section of the society - could not be neglected.

Workers from urban hospitals - doctors, nurses, lab technicians,

administrators - were formed into mobile teams to service large
rural sectors.   Small hospitals were established in central
villages and medical teams made regular visits, on foot or by
donkey, to surrounding villages.   An essential role in this
system has been the "barefoot doctors".   They are young workers
from the agricultural communes.   Once the harvest is taken in
they come to the central hospital to receive some basic medical
training over the winter.   They return to their villages in
spring, to help sow the crops and to begin their work as peasant
doctors.   They are the first line in the health care system,
responsible for tending to minor ailments, helping the villages
improve sanitation and living conditions, and alerting the
mobile medical team in case of emergency.

The integration of traditional medicine with Western scientific
methods has also come about because of China's lack of trained
personnel and technical resources.   At the time of the
Revolution, there were very few Western-style scientific doctors.
But there were hundreds of thousands of practitioners of
traditional medicine who, despite their lack of scientific
knowledge, were trusted by the people and had some experience in
dealing with medical problems.   Because experienced personnel
were needed, the traditional doctors were incorporated into the
new health care system.   They now work in hospitals side by side
with Western-style doctors.   The traditional skills in
acupuncture, herbal remedies and diagnosis are respected, and
they complement the scientific knowledge of the Western-style
doctors.

Genetic Engineering
One of the most frightening aspects of population studies is the
new field of genetic engineering.   In 1976, in a popular
television series called "Interface: Science and Society",
British Columbia's Provincial Educational Media Centre produced
a number of interviews between David Suzuki and leading
scientists from the field of genetics.   The following is some of
the information that was made available at that time.

A gene is the unit of inheritance that affects a distinct
characteristic of an organism.   In humans, there are genes that
affect the colour of your eyes, the straightness of your hair,
the length of your toes, the shape of your chin, the size of
your brain: all the physical characteristics that make you
distinguishable from other people derive from the particular
arrangements of moleules that we know as genes.

Inside every human body cell, the genes link together to form
23 pairs of chromosomes.   In every pair, there is one
chromosome contributed by the mother, and one by the father.
They appear under magnification as bits of thread scattered in
the cell.   No one is quite sure how many genes are carried by
the 23 chromosomal pairs; some geneticists estimate that there
might be more than a billion in every cell of every individual.

Each gene is a sequence of molecules.   Every message that the

genes carry - for straight hair, long legs, ten fingers, two
eyes - comes from a particular sequence of molecules, just as
the meaning of a sentence comes from a particular sequence of
words. What gives the sequence of molecules meaning is the
chemical DNA, a very long spiral molecule.

Five in every two hundred children are born with a serious
genetic defect. One child in a thousand has Down's syndrome
(or mongolism), which results in severely impaired intelligence,
heart ailments, and deformities of the face and hands. One in
ten thousand babies is born with phenylketonuria, an enzyme
deficiency which causes gradual mental retardation.

Parents accept these risks; after all, all the odds do favour
having a reasonably healthy, intelligent child. But even if a
child were to be born with a defect, most parents would accept
and love the child, regardless of its handicaps.

As the fertilized egg divides and grows, the DNA code copies
itself in every new cell, so that the genetic blueprint for
the entire organism is present in every body cell. Thus, if
DNA from a skin cell, or brain cell or stomach cell could be
activated, it would be able to produce another organism,
identical to the one which provided the DNA. This method of
reproduction is known as cloning, and it is quite common in
plants and some animals. Strawberry plants, for example, put
out runners that can take root and produce a whole new plant.
If a salamander loses a leg, the cells in the area of the
amputation produce the genes necessary for growing a new limb.

Cloning has been induced artifically in plants and in frogs.
Scientists working in Ottawa, for example, have been able to
clone elm trees. Working from single cells, they produced
mutant elm trees that were resistant to Dutch elm disease.
There is great economic potential in the ability to clone super-
ior strains of plants.

More relevant to human reproduction is the successful cloning of
frogs. The nucleus (containing the genetic information) was
removed from a frog egg. The nucleus of a cell from the
stomach of another frog was injected into this egg. The
presence of the nucleus - with the full number of chromosomes
- "switched on" the egg: it began dividing as if it had been
fertilized. It eventually grew into a frog with exactly the
same genotype as the frog whose stomach cell nucleus had been
used.

If this becomes possible in human beings, we will be able to
produce perfect genetic copies of ourselves. We could create
individuals whose genotypes were known in advance. Perhaps
great scientists or artists or statesmen could be cloned so
that there would be many Einsteins, Picassos and Gandhis. We
could not of course, duplicate the environment that produced
these individuals. We do not know the importance of environment
in developing character. But we could produce individuals with

the same basic genetic make-up as the humans we wanted to copy.

The possibility of copying human beings, for whatever purpose,
is disturbing. We like to believe in the uniqueness and
importance of the individual, and as long as we reproduce
sexually, individuals will always be genetically unique. But if
we clone our offspring, this sense of the individual, as a
unique and unrepeatable creation, will disappear.

The threats of genetic engineering are serious but as yet they
affect only a small number of people. The desperately urgent
population problems of the world are focussed on survival -
enough food and removal of the threat of death by disease.
And survival is most urgent among the world's poor.

Identify the issues

1.   When were death rates dropping fastest in developing
     countries?

2.   The argument for population control is that it makes
     possible a high quality of life for a few rather than
     a lower level of life for many. Where would you rather
     be, in a family with one other child or in a family with
     three or more brothers or sisters?

3.   In what kinds of climates are most of the world's
     peoples found? What problems of health might these
     climates pose?

"Nowhere are disparities in wealth more visible than in cities,
where airconditioned skycrapers, automobiles and glittering
store windows contrast dramatically with surrounding slums and
squatter settlements. In the design and management of human
settlements, these disparities also are reflected in housing,
access to public services, modes of transport and social
segregation. On a larger scale, there are also the inequalities
between cities of different sizes and between urban and rural
areas." From Habitat Preparatory Paper.

CHAPTER SIX

Poor and Rich

If the world's present population of over four billion persons became one town of 1,000, there would be only 60 North Americans. These 60 would receive half of the town's income, and they would have 15 times as many possessions per person as the remainder of the people.

The 60 would have an average life expectancy of 70 years. The other 940 would average less than 40 years. The lowest income group among the North Americans would be better off by far than the average of the rest. The 60 North Americans would extract the raw materials essential to their standard of living from the property of the other 940. While doing so, they would try to convince the other 940 to limit their population growth on the grounds that resources are limited.

Try to imagine the number of North Americans that would have to become soldiers. Think of the material and human resources that would have to be devoted to military efforts in order to keep the rest of the town at its present disadvantage.

The problem of the 940 is serious. But if we look at the situation of the very, very poor it becomes disastrous. There are 900 million absolute poor people in the world, this is to say very poor by world average standards, subsisting on incomes of less than $75 a year.

It is the scale of this problem today and the slow progress being made toward a solution that is causing the greatest concern.

The heaviest concentration of absolute poverty is in Asia. India, Pakistan, Bangladesh and Indonesia are particularly afflicted. In these countries, one out of every two individuals is in this category. In Africa most of the countries are plagued with both absolute and relative poverty. In Latin America conditions are slightly better than in these two other major areas of the world. When you look at a list of the world's poorest countries it seems that Africa is worst off. Of the countries with a per capita GNP of less than $100, a literacy rate of less than 20 percent, and the share of the GNP produced by manufacturing of less than 10 percent, most of the countries which may be described in this way are African. But it must be remembered that there are many more people in the Asian countries.

The overwhelming majority of the absolute poor are found in rural areas. This is because productivity on the millions of small subsistence farms is so very low. There has been practically no increase whatever in the output of these small family hold-ings over the past ten years. The problem is immense. The size of the average holding is small, and it is fragmented. More than 50 million of these families are farming less than one hectare, which is about 2½ acres.

Conditions in the rural settlements cannot be improved without quite new efforts from external sources. One of the most urgent needs is the improvement of the water supply - the provision of clean water to offset disease and to provide a healthier diet. Commonest diseases among rural poor are intimately related to polluted water.

Cholera, typhoid and parasites of various kinds are almost normal conditions in many, many villages of the developing world. In addition, standing water - in flooded rice "paddies," fish ponds, or irrigation channels - harbours the snail that is responsible for bilharzia, a debilitating disease. Some 200 million people are its victims. Another 20 million suffer from "river blindness," a disease that is traced to black fly infestation of running water. And tropical swampy areas have long been recognized as the home of the malaria mosquito, an insect that has now developed a resistance to DDT.

There are other problems confronting the poor in the country-side. There is the inadequate transportation system for access to jobs away from the land. There are housing problems, leading to intensive use of shelter, even multiple occupation of the places where they live. The most extreme form is the shift system of bed hiring in which several families occupy the same room.

In the urban scene the scarcity of jobs, indeed the tendency for capital-intensive developments to reduce job opportunities, is creating a sense of hopelessness among the urban poor.

Employment in the urban areas of the developing world is at two levels. One is the organized, modern, formal sector, character-ized by capital-intensive technology, relatively high wages, large-scale operations, and corporate and government organiza-tion.

The other is the unorganized, traditional, informal sector - labour-intensive, small-scale operations, using traditional methods, and providing modest earnings to the individual or family owner.

In the modern sector, wages are usually protected by labour legislation and trade union activity. In the informal sector, there is easier entry, but less job security and lower earnings.

Though jobs in the modern sector may be more desirable, they are often beyond the reach of the poor. They require literacy, experience, and a level of training the poor find difficult to acquire; and in a labour-surplus market, employers can afford to insist on exceptional qualifications.

The formal sector can eliminate jobs on an alarming scale. At the cost of $100,000, for example, a corporation may set up a plastic footwear plant, with only 40 employees, that can displace 5,000 traditional shoemakers and their suppliers.

In ways such as these the capital-intensive nature of the modern sector has kept openings for additional workers down, yet migration to the cities continues to swell the labour pool. In some developing countries, manufacturing techniques have already become so mechanized that an investment of $50,000 to $70,000 is often required to create a single new job.

It is not surprising then, that the informal sector is a critical component in urban employment. It provides, for example, nearly half of all the jobs in Lima, more than half in Bombay and Jakarta; and over two-thirds in Belo Horizonte.

And yet, the fact is that governments tend to view the informal sector with little enthusiasm. They consider it backward, inefficient, and a painful reminder of a less sophisticated past.

These discriminations against the poor are compounded by limited access to public services. There are heavy biases in the design, location, pricing, and delivery of such services.

Though most cities, for example, have access to them, they are largely reserved for the rich minority, even though the privileged have less incidence of illness than the poor. Nor is it surprising that the poor are so often ill, considering the squalor in which they must live. Frequently they have no public water supply or sewerage services whatever. And they often have to pay up to 20 times more for water supplies by street vendors than middle and upper-income families do for water piped by the city into their homes.

But if the poor are denied equitable access to water, sanitation, and health, they fare equally badly with education. Many of their children receive no formal education at all simply because they live beyond a feasible distance to the nearest school. Thus, though half the total population of the capital of one African country lives in the slum areas, all of the schools, with one exception, are located elsewhere in the city. The result is that the primary school enrollment is only 36 percent in the poor areas, but 90 percent throughout the rest of the capital.

Public transportation is another vital service the poor are often without. Their incomes are so low they can rarely afford it. And even if they could afford it, it often does not exist in the peripheral areas of the city where they generally live.

While the wealthy drive their cars, and the moderate-income
workers ride the bus, the poor walk to work - frequently as
much as two hours each way. Such distances are a penalty both
to their energy and to their earnings. And as the cities grow
larger, so their commuting grows longer. Studies indicate that
in a city of a million, the poor's average journey to work is
three miles; in a city of five million, seven miles.

Board of Chance
Jan Van Ettinger of the Ministry of Housing and Physical Planning
in the Netherlands has developed a model of the world's poor with
which he calculates the chances of children achieving their
potential. The general form of the model is shown in Fig. 6.1.
The actual development possible for a given child is represented
by the letter "Z". The potential quality of this same child is
represented by "X" and the nature of the environment within
which the child will live is indicated by the "Y" value in the
model. Someone born with a talent of 5.5 in a 4.5 environment
can only reach a level of 2.5.

Board of chance (with development levels Z)

Y \ X	0	1	2	3	4	5	6	7	8	9
10	0,5	1,4	2,4	3,3	4,3	5,2	6,2	7,1	8,1	9,0
9	0,4	1,3	2,1	3,0	3,8	4,7	5,5	6,4	7,2	8,1
8	0,4	1,1	1,9	2,6	3,4	4,1	4,9	5,6	6,4	7,1
7	0,3	1,0	1,6	2,3	2,9	3,6	4,2	4,9	5,5	6,2
6	0,3	0,8	1,4	1,9	2,5	3,0	3,6	4,1	4,7	5,2
5	0,2	0,7	1,1	1,6	2,0	2,5 (Z)	2,9	3,4	3,8	4,3
4	0,2	0,5	0,9	1,2	1,6	1,9	2,3	2,6	3,0	3,3
3	0,1	0,4	0,6	0,9	1,1	1,4	1,6	1,9	2,1	2,4
2	0,1	0,2	0,4	0,5	0,7	0,8	1,0	1,1	1,3	1,4
1	0,0	0,1	0,1	0,2	0,2	0,3	0,3	0,4	0,4	0,5

Y → quality of the environment

X → talent (potential quality of the individual)

Fig. 6.1 Board of Chance

Every hour, according to Ettinger, 15,000 children are born.
The mental and physical qualities that will characterize them
are matters of chance. The genetic allocation of talents is a
chance event. The environment within which they will grow is

also a chance event.

The distribution of genetic factors is similar to the distribution of any other random element - a large number in the category
of average and a much smaller number at the extremes of very high
and very low. Distribution of environmental quality is
difficult. There are large numbers at the bottom of the scale
and very few at the top, the place where environmental quality
is best.

As a result of these things the 15,000 children are distributed
as follows:

Talent

0	1	2	3	4	5	6	7	8	9	10
	41	459	1391	2456	3153	3153	2456	1391	459	41

Environment

0	1	2	3	4	5	6	7	8	9	10
	1222	2718	3138	2870	2242	1508	842	360	94	6

Using these figures along with Fig. 6.1 Ettinger estimates that
the 15,000 children born every hour on the average only achieve
one third of their potential quality. Furthermore, the majority
face life with little or no chance of reaching even that level
of quality.

North and South America
There is a sharp contrast within the Americas in per capita
income and level of literacy. Canada and the U.S. as the top
rich stand far above Honduras and Bolivia, the bottom poor.
See Fig. 6.2. Per capita income differences between these two
groups are $6,000 against $300, and literacy contrasts show
almost 100 percent against 40 percent. There are several other
countries of Latin America that are only slightly better off
than Honduras and Bolivia in terms of income and literacy.
Guatemala, El Salvador, Nicaragua, Ecuador and Paraguay each has
less than $600 per capital annual income and a literacy level
below 70 percent.

Africa
Julius Nyerere, one of the important leaders in post-colonial
Africa, expressed the feelings of many Africans when he
described the poor-rich divisions throughout the world. Here
are some of the things he had to say when he spoke to a U.S.
audience a few years ago.

Poverty is not the real problem of the modern world, for we have
the knowledge and the resources which will enable us to overcome
poverty. The real problem of the modern world, the thing which

creates misery, wars and hatred amongst men, is the division of
mankind into rich and poor.

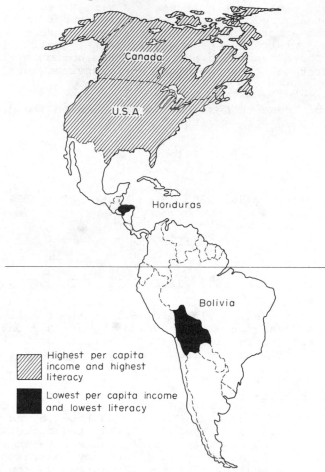

Fig. 6.2 Poor and Rich in the Americas

We can see this division at two levels. Within nation states
there are a few individuals who have great wealth and whose
wealth gives them great power. But the vast majority of the
people suffer from varying degrees of poverty and deprivation.
Even in a country like the United States this division can be
seen. In countries like India, Portugal or Brazil the contrast
between the wealth of a few privileged individuals and the dire
poverty of the masses is a crying scandal. And looking at the
world as a collection of nation states we see the same pattern
repeated: there are a few wealthy nations which dominate the
whole world, economically and therefore politically, and a mass
of smaller and poor nations whose destiny, it appears, is to be

dominated. The significance about this division between rich
and poor is not simply that one man has more food than he can
eat, more clothes than he can wear, and more houses than he can
live in, while others are hungry, unclad or homeless. The
significant thing about the division between rich and poor, and
rich and poor nations, is not simply that one has the resources
to provide comfort for all its citizens and the other cannot
provide basic services. The reality and the depth of the
problem arises because the man who is rich has power over the
lives of those who are poor, and the rich nation has power over
the policies of those who are not rich. And even more important
is that a social and economic system, nationally and internationally, supports these divisions, and constantly increases
them so that the rich get even richer and more powerful, while
the poor get relatively ever poorer and less able to control
their own future.

This continues despite all talk of human equality, of the fight
against poverty, and of development. Still rich individuals
within nations and rich nations within the world go on getting
richer, very much richer, much faster than the poor nations can
overcome their poverty. Sometimes this happens through the
deliberate decisions of the rich who use their wealth and their
power to that end. But often, perhaps more often, it happens
naturally as a result of the normal workings of social and
economic systems men have constructed for themselves.

Both nationally and internationally this division of mankind
into a tiny minority of rich and a great majority of poor is
rapidly becoming intolerable to the majority, as it should be.
The poor nations and the poor peoples of the world are already
in rebellion. If they do not succeed in securing a change which
leads towards greater justice then that rebellion will become
an explosion.

Nyerere's comments are important because he comes from a country
which, like most of Africa, was recently colonial territory.
See Fig. 6.3. Many Africans feel - rightly or wrongly - that it
is the influence of their former European colonial overlords
that keeps them in poverty.

In studies extending over the years 1971 to 1975, United Nations
committees have identified the least developed of the world's
developing nations. Most of these very poor nations are in
Africa and most of them were, until recently, colonial territories. See Fig. 6.4.

Islam
In the mounting tension between the poorer third world nations
and the richer industrialized nations of Europe and North
America, one large region of the world has been overlooked - the
culture area of Islam. Yet within this area are many of the
most impoverished nations on earth alongside some of the top ten
wealthiest countries.

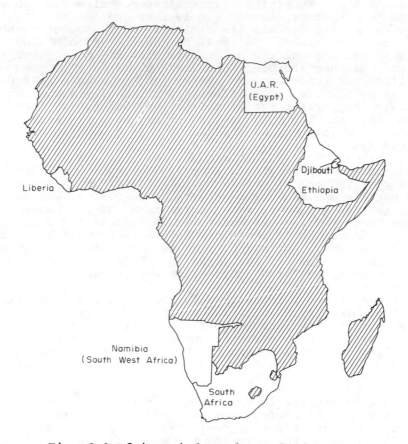

Parts of Africa that obtained independence
between January 1951 and July 1977

Fig. 6.3 African independence 1951 - 1977

The surprise is that the poor-rich debate does not focus on
these differences. Half of the least developed countries shown
on Fig. 6.4 are within the culture area of Islam. So are
Kuwait, United Arab Emirates, Saudi Arabia and Iran - countries
that rank among the wealthiest in the world because of their oil
resources.

It may be that Islam's religious ties are stronger than their
economic tensions. The following account traces some of the
history of Islam and shows how these ties were forged over a
long period of time.

Every spring jets from Tehran, Kuala Lumpur, Bombay, and
Casablanca converge on the city of Mecca in Saudi Arabia. Ships

from Yemen and Tanzania bring passengers to Mecca's port, Jidda. They continue on to Mecca, joining other pilgrims who may have walked, ridden camels, or driven cars. National differences are forgotten as are differences in wealth, social status, and education. All believers dress in the same ceremonial clothes to pray together as equals and to go through the rituals that remain unchanged after more than thirteen centuries. Shrouded in black cloth they walk seven times around a cube-shaped building. They read from the holy book of revelations, the Koran. Everyone is certain that his neighbour, like him, is a Muslim, that is a member of Islam, for entry into Mecca by non-Muslims is forbidden. A pilgrimage to Mecca is the ambition of every faithful Muslim.

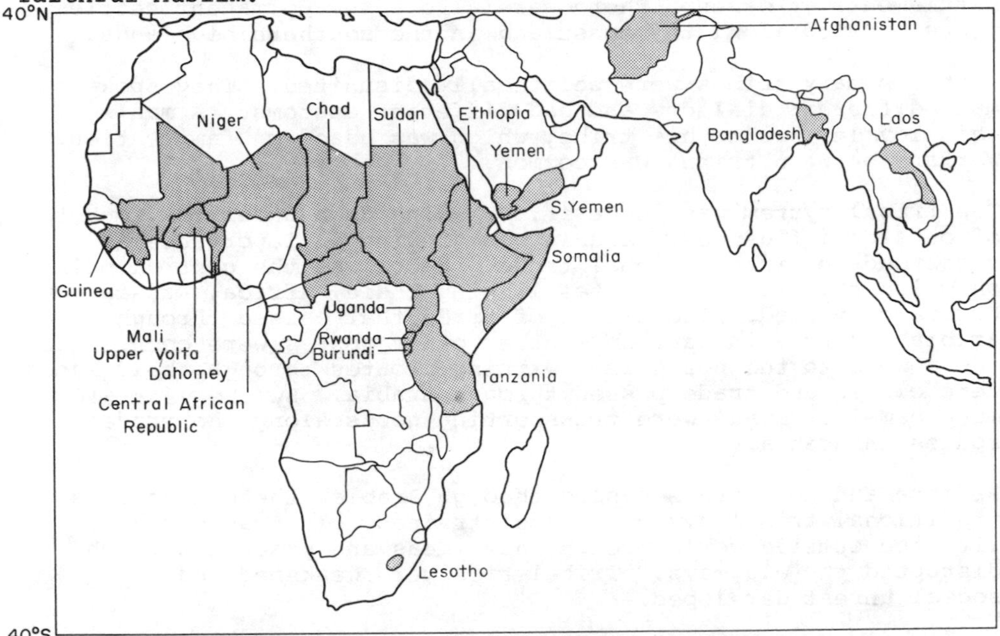

Fig. 6.4 20 of the least developed countries, 1971
(GNP less than $100; literacy less than 20%;
Proportion of GNP in manufacturing less than 10%)

The prophet Mohammed, who founded Islam, was born in Mecca. His religion spread from there across North Africa to the west, north to the Balkan countries and southern Russia, and east through Persia and India to the islands of Indonesia.

In 600 A.D. two great empires controlled most of the territory of Southwest Asia. The eastern rim of the Mediterranean was under the rule of the Byzantine Empire. The Byzantines carried on the Christian tradition of Rome and the cultural inheritance of Greece. Their capital was at Constantinople.

Bordering the eastern edge of the Byzantine lands was the Persian Empire. The Persian Empire was also a long-established civilization. It was known for its high development of fine arts.

Between these two great empires there was constant friction. The Persians made periodic raids into Byzantine lands and the Byzantines would, of course, retaliate. This continuous warring weakened both empires at a time when a new power came into being on their southern borders.

Previously neither empire had to worry about a threat from its neighbours to the south. The Arabian peninsula was peopled by many scattered tribes. The vast deserts of that area were dotted with camps of nomadic tribes and with agricultural settlements at oases. There were also a few permanent settlements located along the coast and in the southern highlands.

Arabia's many tribes were politically disunited. They spoke many different dialects and had different customs. A man's main loyalty was to his tribe, which was based on family ties. Warfare between tribes was common.

The tribal system was, however, breaking down under the impact of outside influences. Arabia was growing in importance as a crossroads of international trade. Mecca was the central point on which several trade routes linking India, Africa, Russia, and Europe converged. The amount of trade that passed through Arabia depended in part on whether other routes were open. When the powers to the north were warring, routes through their lands were closed and trade passed through Arabia. By the year 610 many camel caravans were transporting goods along the trade routes in Arabia.

As more and more trade passed through Arabia, the peninsula's traditional tribal system became strained. Increased contact with the outside world brought new ideas and practices which disrupted the old ways. Tribal ties were weakened and social unrest developed.

The time was ripe for the right man with the right idea to lead Arabia out of its turmoil and set it on a new and stable footing. That man was Mohammed and his idea was the religious system we call Islam. Under Mohammed's leadership the tribes of Arabia were at long last united.

Mohammed was born around 570 in Mecca, the richest city in Arabia. Orphaned at an early age, he was raised first by his grandfather and later by an uncle. As a young man he was exposed to a wide variety of ideas in his contacts with the business community of Mecca and in his travels with trade caravans. Eventually he became a prominent member of the merchant and administrative class in Mecca. He earned respect particularly for his ability to settle disputes arising between clans. This leadership and administrative experience aided him later in organizing his new state religion.

When Mohammed reached his forties he began to have visions. He
believed the angel Gabriel spoke to him. It became his practice
to retreat to a cave for evenings of contemplation. His dreams
and visions continued for seven years before he began telling
his family and friends about them. By this time he was old
enough to command respect in a society that valued age.

Mohammed believed he had been chosen to be a prophet in order
to transmit God's word to the Arab people. He drew on many of
the ideas and practices which were commonly accepted in his time,
but formed them into a new pattern. Thus, Mohammed's new
religion, Islam, blended easily with Arab culture and customs
and at the same time provided a basis for a new unity.

The central concept of Mohammed's teachings was that there is
only one God, and not many as the Arabian tribes had believed.
This idea, though new to Arabia, had long been believed in
other parts of the Near East by Christians and Jews and had been
carried to Arabia by both traders and Jewish immigrants.
Mohammed felt he had been chosen by the one God to carry His
doctrine to the Arab people.

One of the most important practices of Islam - the pilgrimage -
is rooted in Arabic tribal practice. Arab tribes had long made
pilgrimages to Mecca, a centre for believers in many gods.
Mohammed retained the pilgrimage idea and kept Mecca as a holy
city, though he only permitted the worship of one God there.

Another long-established Arab practice became an important
means of spreading Islam. In Mohammed's day, raiding trade
caravans and settlements was common. Mohammed included the
practices of warring and looting in his theology. War to spread
peace became a holy aim and any Muslim who died in battle for
his religion was assured of paradise. Success in war was
interpreted as a sign of God's favour.

The one doctrine that probably did the most to advance the
acceptance of Islam among diverse peoples and cultures was the
doctrine of the brotherhood of believers. Formerly, in Arab
lands, loyalties had been limited to blood relations. Islam
built upon this family-centred loyalty by extending brotherhood
to embrace all those who accepted the religion. Those who
accepted Islam came under its laws. This approach proved itself
a powerful force to unite people across national, economic and
racial lines.

Mohammed's new religion did not flourish at first. He and his
small band of followers, composed mainly of relatives and
friends, encountered much opposition from the older religious
leaders of Mecca. In 622 the little band left Mecca for Medina,
where Mohammed hoped to find more people who could be converted
to the new religion.

In Medina the number of Islam's faithful began to grow.
Mohammed led raiding parties against caravans in order to obtain

funds for Islam. He built a mosque in Medina to which increasing numbers of converts flocked. Finally, in 630, Mohammed's
armies were strong enough to return to Mecca as conquerors.

Mecca became the principal holy city for the governing religion.
Since no distinction was made between religious laws and
political and civil laws, Mecca also became the capital and
administrative centre of Mohammed's new Islamic state.
Mohammed was the leader of not only the religion but also the
state and its armies.

On Mohammed's death in 632 leadership of Islam fell to his son-
in-law, Abu-Bakr. He received the title of caliph, meaning
successor to the Prophet. He took over Mohammed's duties as
religious leader, chief-of-state, judge, law-giver, and
commander-in-chief of the army.

Abu-Bakr was not immediately recognized as the rightful leader
of Arabia. Many tribes which had been converted to Islam during
Mohammed's time rejected the new religious and political system
as soon as Mohammed was no longer alive to provide strong leadership. They wished to free themselves from Mecca's political
control and especially from contributing to Islam's treasury.

The caliph sent out his army to regain control. Within a year
central Arabia had been conquered. The army became an effective
organization for spreading the new religion as it moved around
Arabia suppressing revolts. By the end of 634 the Islamic
armies had conquered all of Arabia and had reached the borders
of the Byzantine and Persian empires to the north. The warring
tribes of Arabia, now united by religious zeal, began to think
of the possibilities for converts and riches that lay beyond
their borders.

The Arabs not only had the power to attempt conquest in Persian
and Byzantine lands. They had strong motives for moving out
from the peninsula at this time. For several years rainfall in
the peninsula had been much lower than usual. Both grazing and
irrigated lands were drying up and many people were forced to
look elsewhere for a livelihood. Many felt that they had nothing to lose in attempting to expand into other, richer lands.
United under the banners of Islam, the Arabs began to push their
way into the territories of both empires.

The first military objective was Syria, a rich province of the
Byzantine Empire. The Muslims sought control of the important
trade routes which led into Syria and the riches harboured in
Syria's cities. In 635 the rich trade centre of Damascus was
captured. A year later the Byzantine forces were routed and
the Mediterranean coast from Palestine as far as the Taurus
Mountains came under Muslim rule. By 650 the Muslims had
occupied Byzantine territories as far as the island of Cyprus.

But the small Muslim state did not limit its military attention
to Syria alone. While campaigns were waged on the Syrian front,

the armies marched on Ctesiphon, the Persian stronghold. In
637 it fell, and Islamic control in the northeast extended from
the Persian Gulf to the city of Mosul. Muslims marched eastward toward Sus and Isfahan.

The armies encountered little resistance in their march. Their
entry into Persia coincided with a general breakdown in the
Persian government. The Persians were unable to organize themselves against the invaders and finally, in the midst of the
chaos, the king was murdered by one of his own companions.

After the first surges into the Byzantine and Persian empires,
expansion stopped for a while as the Muslims organized and
consolidated their new and sizable empire. Damascus, more
central to the whole empire, became the administrative headquarters of the new state. Islam, in becoming a world power,
adopted the complicated administrative methods used by the
Byzantine Christians. The simple methods used to rule the
tribes of Arabia were no longer adequate.

During this period of consolidation a split developed in the
ranks of Islam. A struggle over leadership developed into a
civil war. A new caliph was finally chosen, but the issues
raised at that time are kept alive today by the different Muslim
sects that grew out of the conflict.

Islam began to expand again once its internal problems were
settled. Raids across the Amu Darya River in the year 675
introduced the Muslims to their Turkish neighbours in the northeast. By 700 Kabul in Afghanistan was invaded and the king was
made to pay tribute. By 700 too Islam had spread westward
across northern Africa as far as Morocco.

The farthest Arab conquests toward the northeast in Asia was
Kashgar. To the southeast they pushed as far as the Indus
River by the year 750.

By this time Islam was much too widespread to be controlled
effectively from any single centre of government. Communications were slow and peoples and customs varied greatly from place
to place. Thus, after 750, different parts of the Islamic
Empire began to break off into separate states. Eastern Persia
was the first to secede. The Persian governor acted independ-
ently in matters of state. However, the Persian people kept
the Muslim faith and ties were maintained with the caliph,
whose headqaurters had moved to the new city of Baghdad.

The period from 750 to 1400 was one of little Islamic expansion
to the north. For part of this long period, Islam was on the
defensive against European Christians and Mongols. The major
events of the period involved the movements of outsiders into
previously Islamic lands, where they then became Muslims themselves. Though in general Islam, the religion, maintained its
previous territorial extent, Islam as a political organization
became divided into several independent states ruled by

different groups of peoples.

In the centuries that followed, Islam as a religious movement
kept its grip on the lands it had conquered or otherwise had
won over to the Muslim faith. Between 1400 and 1600 it
expanded into the areas we now know as Bangladesh, Malaysia and
Indonesia.

Today the Muslim faith predominates in all of North Africa
as far south as central Nigeria, all of Southwest Asia, the
central Asian region of the Soviet Union, Pakistan, Bangladesh,
and a major part of Southeast Asia.

Women
The debate between poor and rich nations tends to overshadow
the equally serious contrasts within countries. These contrasts
are sharpest between women in the poorer segments of society
and men in the richer domains.

At the United Nations Women's Conference in Mexico City, 1975,
there was fresh evidence of the continuing inequality between
women and men. And wherever there is inequality in status or
opportunity there is inevitably inequality of income. One of
the most glaring cases of prejudice came from Saudi Arabia's
spokesman Mr. Jamil Baroody.

In his view women already have more equality than men. Women
are the mothers, wives, sisters and daughters of men. A man
works to support a woman until he dies and she inherits his
wealth. Women from all over the world enjoy unwritten
privileges. An international conference such as the one in
Mexico City is disruptive and upsets many time-honoured
institutions.

One report from the Mexico City Conference pointed out the
tendency to explain the sexual division of labour by referring
to differences in the physical strength of men and women.

Yet, according to the Yale University Cross-Cultural Survey,
some of the most demanding types of heavy work are given to
women in many cultures. Water-carrying, for instance, is
regarded as an exclusively feminine task in 119 cultures.
Burden-bearing is regarded as an exclusively feminine task in
59 cultures. There are 36 known cultures in which the building
of dwellings is left to women. Laundering, which before the
advent of washing machines was one of the most strenuous tasks,
until very recently was a typically feminine job everywhere in
Western civilization.

Another study summed up vividly the extent to which minor
technical developments improve the lives of women. In the
various places in East Africa where hand-pounding of cereals
has been replaced by small-capacity power-driven mills, an
average village family consumes about 3 kilograms of maize
daily and to pound this takes about an hour. East African

village women will take advantage of a commercial mill even
though they have to carry a 24 kilogram load for four miles and
take a bus for a further five miles. They do this in spite of
the costs of grinding and transportation, which amount to
two-thirds of the value of the cereal.

Collecting and carrying fire-wood is one of the heavy chores of
African women, the study pointed out. And this has become
increasingly tiring and time-consuming as deforestation has
forced women to walk longer and longer distances to find the
quantity they need.

A third report presented at the Women's Conference dealt with
the education of women. From earliest infancy, in most countries
of the world, boys are encouraged in their studies but girls
receive no help and may even, at times, be prevented from
studying. While they are at school, girls may be called home at
any time to look after sick brothers and sisters, to do the
shopping, or to help with the cooking. Girls attend clubs, join
sports associations and take part in excursions or travel much
less frequently than their brothers. If a girl goes to school
and does well neither her teachers nor her family will encourage
her to be ambitious. She may become a teacher, but only in
primary or secondary school. She will very seldom become a
research worker, particularly in the scientific field.

A large number of callings will be virtually barred to her,
either because the training required takes too long and is too
expensive, or because they are not thought to be suited to
feminine capacities.

The paper also looked at another important aspect of education
and social values; physical education and dress. For girls,
said the study, physical education is not always regarded sympa-
thetically by parents, and yet it is one of the foundations for
giving women real equality. It goes hand in hand with
simplification of women's dress.

Handicapped
Poverty is aggravated wherever the built environment in human
settlements does not take account of the needs of the physically
or mentally disabled. And a large number of poor people fall
into these categories.

In its report to the Vancouver Habitat Conference the Government of Sweden described some of its experiences in making
provision in the built environment for the nation's handicapped
population. The most surprising aspect of the Swedish report
was the large numbers involved.

Sweden has a population of 8,125,000. Of these 1,240,000 are
under 17 years of age and 1,225,000 over 65 years of age.

The physically disabled - 25,000 people are confined to wheel-
chairs, 230,000 are considered to have grave motor problems

and a further 250,000 have similar problems.

The hard of hearing - 7,000 people are totally deaf and
325,000 need a hearing aid. 650,000 Swedes consider themselves
to have problems with hearing.

Impaired vision - 12,000 are blind and a further 160,000 have
such poor vision that they have problems in going about their
daily business.

Epileptics - 60,000 people suffer from this difficulty.

Allergies - 1 million Swedes have to seek medical attention for
allergic conditions.

Mental illness - What is classed as mental illness and what is
classed as mentally sound varies according to cultural circumstances and values. A metal illness is commonly described in
psychiatric circles as changes in a person's perception and
behaviour. The line of demarcation between sick and healthy
patterns of perception and behaviour is vague. Often this line
is determined by the inability or ability of a person to satisfy
the performance requirements of a given environment.

In the course of a routine medical examination of 1,000 civil
servants in the Stockholm area in 1970, half of the men were
suffering from some mental or psycho-somatic disorder, while
20 percent were having nervous trouble.

About 40 percent of all cases of early retirement can be traced
to mental illness.

If we examine the lives of Swedish people from childhood through
the various stages of adult life up to old age, it becomes
clear that practically everyone is afflicted by handicaps.
People who have never at any time in their lives been handicapped
are a minority. Many will at some time in their lives break a
leg or an arm and experience difficulty in managing everyday
routines. Furthermore, all of us become in time old and more
and more confused and weak.

Until the mid-sixties, plans to modernize housing stock were
mainly concerned with building as many homes as possible and
with improving the quality of the individual dwellings as far as
budgets would permit. Families in which the wife remained at
home had been the basis and guiding principle of housing
planning. Later, the number of women going out to work grew,
and this was particularly noticeable during the economic booms
of the sixties when there was a large demand for labour.

Authorities began to study how community services in residential
areas could be improved and expanded. In addition to taking
some of the burden of the household chores off the shoulders of
the women, there was concern about supervision facilities for
children, the role of the school in the environment, help for

the old and disabled in their daily routines, and improvement of recreational facilities.

Brickebacken in Orebro, some 200 km west of Stockholm, is an example of a housing estate from the late sixties, designed on the basis of these ideas. The estate provides accommodation for 5,000 people in 1,300 flats in two-storey blocks and 400 flats in four six-storey blocks. Some 70 of the flats in the six-storey blocks are let to retired people, while a further ten have been specially adapted to meet the needs of the physically disabled. A special service is provided for these flats so that tenants can get help from staff during emergencies. A covered way links the six-storey blocks with the service centre.

Plans are in hand to extend these provisions for handicapped people. Instead of treating them in special institutions authorities are working on designs to provide equality of services and of facilities in all public environments.

Tackling Poverty

For abour 4 years the World Bank has focussed its efforts on the world's poor. Here are some of the things that are being done. The rural areas have been chosen to begin an assault on poverty because the overwhelming majority of the absolute poor are there. The poverty problem in the countryside revolves primarily around the low productivity of the millions of small subsistence farms. Despite the growth of the GNP in most developing countries, the increase in output of these small family holdings over the past decade has been so low as to be virtually imperceptible.

The scale of the problem is immense. More than 100 million families - some 700 million individuals - are involved. The size of the average holding is not only small, but often frag-mented. More than 50 million of these families are farming less than one hectare.

The objective is that by 1985 output will be growing at an average rate of 5 percent per year.

One of the most innovative of the rural development projects undertaken by the Bank has been a $10 million credit to assist the Tanzanian government to bolster the productivity and living standards of farm families in the Kigoma region where per capita incomes are among the lowest in the world. The project provided economic and social services to 250,000 individuals in 135 newly-established villages, substantially improving their crop production and doubling their incomes. It included a credit and marketing system; primary schools, health centres, and improved water supply; clearing the area of the tsetse fly; regional radio-telephone communications; and a program of adaptive agri-cultural research. The project could serve as a model for new settlements elsewhere.

Though the new rural development projects are innovative, they are designed to provide a substantial economic rate of return

at a low investment per individual served so that they can be
readily extended to additional areas as additional resources
become available.

But the closer we get to the core of the problem of poverty in
the countryside, the more difficult, complicated, and time-
consuming the task becomes.

One road block is the issue of appropriate technology. The
agricultural methods of the wealthy nations in the temperate
zone are frequently unsuited to the environment of many
developing countries, where poor farmers are often struggling to
subsist on semi-arid, or marginal land. There is a critical
need for new agricultural technologies tailored to these
conditions. The Bank helps to meet this need.

One technique in use is satellite remote sensing imagery in the
survey and evaluation of potential land and water resources.
This new tool is proving valuable in many aspects of project
planning, and several countries are using it - Indonesia, India,
Bangladesh, Nepal, and Kenya.

Another problem is the pricing and subsidy policies some governments impose on the rural sector. These policies are usually
imposed to provide cheap food for the cities. But if prices are
kept artificially low in relation to costs, farmers have no
incentive to expand production. This is especially true of
small farmers who simply have no margin for risk.

Just because a man is poor it does not mean that he is naive.
The truth is that millions of small farmers - even without
elaborate inputs - could increase their productivity if they
could be given one simple assurance: that at harvest time they
would be able to sell their additional produce at a rewarding
price.

The small farmer is almost always discriminated against by
public institutions that tend to favour the larger and more
prosperous producers. It is the larger farmer who enjoys easy
access to public credit, research, water allocations, and
scarce supplies of petroleum, pesticides, and fertilizers.

The assault on poverty in the rural areas was launched because
that is where most of the absolute poor currently are. But
they live in the cities of the developing world as well.
Roughly 200 million are there now. More are coming, and coming
soon.

The Bank has been giving increased attention to this issue. It
is immensely complex - even more so than the problem of poverty
in the countryside. But a much more comprehensive effort now
seems possible to assist governments to reduce urban poverty.

Poverty is a word that has largely lost its power to convey
reality. At least that is true among most of those who have

never known it in its most abject form.

But if we have not personally endured it - if most of the affluent world has never experienced it - there are 900 million individuals alive today, more than 40 percent of the total population of the developing countries who not only know it, but in their wretched circumstances are living examples of it.

Identify the Issues

1. What is the weekly income of the world's absolute poor?

2. What are the obligations of the rich countries in relation to poverty? What are the obligations of the poor countries?

3. What is meant by poverty? Does the word have the same meaning everywhere?

PHOTOGRAPHS, PAGES 122 - 145

These photographs have been selected to illustrate some of the conditions described in this book. As you look at them consider the following questions.

1. Locate on an atlas as many as you can of the places named. Which area has most pictures - the developed or the developing world? Why is this?

2. Which of the rural or urban scenes look like the place where you live? Which ones are different? Make a list of 3 similarities and/or 3 differences.

3. Select the one picture which, in your opinion, shows the worst conditions of human life and work. Suggest some reasons for the bad conditions.

(Photo credits: pages 122, 123(top), 123(bottom), 125(top), 125(bottom), 126(top), 127(top), 127(bottom), 128(top), 129, 130(top), 131, 132(bottom), 133, 134(top), 134(bottom), 135 (top), 137(bottom), 138, 139(bottom), 141(top), 142, 143, 144(top), 144(bottom) - United Nations; pages 124(top), 130 (bottom), 136(top), 136(bottom), Canadian Government; page 124(bottom) - Israeli Government; pages 126(bottom), 128 (bottom), 132(top) - South African Government; pages 135 (bottom), 141(bottom) - Iraqi Embassy; page 137 (top) - Thailand Government; pages 139(top), 140(top), 140(bottom) - Australian Government; page 145 - British Government.)

Vancouver, British Columbia, scene of Habitat Conference, 1976

R.Buckminster Fuller at Habitat News Conference, Vancouver,1976.

L to R; Enrique Penalosa, Secretary-General of Habitat; Maurice
Strong, former Secretary-General of Environment U.N. Conference,
Stockholm, 1972; Barbara Ward, President of International
Institute for Environment and Development. Photo taken at
Habitat News Conference, Vancouver, 1976.

Inuit catching Arctic Char at fish traps

Israeli kibbutz

Graffiti, New York

Urban renewal, New York

Pedestrian mall, Tokyo

Soweto Black Township, Johannesburg, South Africa

Village women using a common well, Upper Volta

Fishing with a cast net, Niger River, Mali

Ancient irrigation system, Madras State, India

Zulu huts, South Africa

Planting rice near Dacca, Bangladesh

Dacca street, Bangladesh

Large family, rural Indonesia

Group of children in Barbados

Transkei Black territory, South Africa

Colombian photographer preparing film for Habitat Conference.
Scene shows a squatter settlement in Bogota.

African quarter of Abidjan, Ivory Coast

Rural development project, Nigeria

Rural market town, India

Herdsman tending his goats in one of the drier areas of Senegal

Bagdad, Iraq, showing benefits of oil wealth

Bringing Canadian wheat from the farms
to the waterfront elevators

Shipping Canadian wheat down the Great Lakes

Rice boats on a Thailand river

Irrigated alfalfa field in Iran. Wealth from
oil makes modern agriculture possible

Milk distribution in Mauritius

Brisbane, Australia, scene of 1974 floods

Bauxite plant, Jamaica

Baby seal, Phillip Island, Victoria, Australia

Fairy penguins, Phillip Island, Victoria, Australia

Desalination plant, Kuwait

Oil refinery, Kirkuk, Iraq

Women chopping straw for later mixing with clay for bricks, Peru

Tao Payoh Housing Estate, Singapore

Mud-cement bricks, Upper Volta

Harvesting totora reeds, Lake Titicaca, Peru.
These reeds are used for building homes

Carrying coal from underground to the
tunnel entrance, Britain, 1840

"Human survival at the most basic level requires air, water,
food and shelter. In the planning and management of human
settlements, these biological needs are subject to degrees of
quantity, quality, access, even cost. Some specific problems:
future food needs of cities and development of food distribution
and marketing networks, remedies to problems of pollution, and
techniques and laws for environmental safeguards, standards for
water and air purity, and acceptable living densities and
interior space in individual dwellings. In each of these areas,
minimum standards can be specified and actual conditions
scientifically measured." From Habitat Preparatory Paper.

CHAPTER SEVEN

Life Support

If you travelled across parts of Asia, where more than half the
world lives, you would see two out of every three people hungry
or suffering from one of the sicknesses caused by diet
deficiencies. These are diseases that shrivel the muscles,
swell the stomachs of children, and damage the bones. They may
dull the mind and weaken the body. A large part of Africa and
Latin America also has a shortage of food. Today's challenge
is to produce not only more food for two thirds of the world,
but more of the right kinds.

Because people are hungry, they are not strong enough to grow
more food or produce goods to exchange for food. Because they
are poor and uneducated, they cannot get or use modern tools and
methods to raise more food.

Their problem is an old one. Mass starvation or famines are
part of the earliest history of man. China is said to have had
at least 1,800 famines since 108 B.C. More than 14 million died
in an 1876 - 1878 famine that reached from India to China.

England suffered at least seven famines every century from 1200
to 1600. Food shortages were so severe throughout Europe in the
middle 1800s that a whole decade is called "the hungry forties."
It was in that decade that Ireland lost nearly half its population, partly by emigration, but many from starvation.

Again and again famines have overtaken mankind and destroyed
millions. As recently as 1930 five millions died in a famine
in China.

It seems incredible, therefore, that, as recently as 1972, the
whole world felt assured that the ages of famine scourges had
finally come to an end. Henceforth mankind's problems were to
be those of surpluses, not shortages.

A year later, several years of drought reached a crisis along
the southern fringes of the Sahara and whole communities from
Mauritania to Ethiopia were wiped out by the famines that
followed the drought. Whence, then, came the extraordinary
optimism of 1972?

The answer is the Green Revolution, the widespread application
of science and technology to agriculture. Mexico was first to
show success in the development of new wheat varieties. Later
the same technique was successfully applied to Northwest India.

From 1970 to 1972 there had been spectacular growth rates in
food production both from fishing and from grain growing -
growth rates that exceeded those of population - and grain
stocks in the main exporting countries were high.

These were the roots of the short-lived optimism of 1972. By
1974 two sudden crop failures in several areas of the world,
plus the oil price crisis of 1973, totally changed the picture.
Stocks were rapidly reduced and the new, higher prices put the
Green Revolution beyond the reach of the poorer countries.

Optimism returned early in 1977 as wheat stocks were rebuilt.
Experts reported that for the first time in five years, the
world was entering its primary growing season without fear that
crop failures might generate a food crisis for any broad section
of the globe.

Reason for the new outlook was the biggest increase in global
wheat stocks ever experienced and a smaller buildup in other
grains, with projections indicating another increase for 1977.

Malnutrition
Quite apart from shortages of food, there are the many who are
not getting enough of the right kinds of food. Most of the
common deficiency diseases are the result of shortages of
protein in the diet. Proteins, which supply the amino acids
needed for the growth and replacement of body tissues, are
needed by everyone, and are especially important in young
children and pregnant women. The period of fastest growth for
humans is from five months before birth to ten months after. At
the end of the first year the brain has reached 2/3 of its
adult weight. Severe malnutrition, and particularly the shortage of protein in this early period, permanently reduces the
number of brain cells. The damage cannot be made up by proper
feeding later on.

Malnutrition occurs even when a person has a completely
adequate diet in terms of calories.

The unit commonly used to measure diets is a calorie. This is
the energy needed to heat one kilogram of water one degree
centigrade. A calorie of food is the amount that will produce
that much energy when "burned" in the body. Nutritionists say
the number of calories people need varies widely. Age, weight,
sex, activity, and climate make a difference. On the average,
good health requires 3,000 calories a day.

Cereals, potatoes, and sugar alone can provide these calories
and support life, but not health. In South Asia these foods
make up 60 percent of diet, but in North America less than 10
percent.

The contrast is clearer if you can imagine you are an ordinary
person in a South Asian village. Rice or some other cereal
would be the main dish at every meal - with only one serving.

You would eat two meals a day.

With the rice or cereal you would have about two tablespoons of
a green vegetable or half a small apple, but not both; you would
also have one tablespoon of nuts or beans, one of sugar, and one
of oil or fat. Once a week you would add enough beef or fish to
make a hamburger the size of a golf ball. Your ration of dairy
products would be equal to a glass of milk a day. You would
have no seconds and no between-meal snacks or soft drinks.

This would keep you alive, at least until you had a serious
illness because there would be sufficient calories. But your
resistance to disease would be low, your capacity for study or
work severely limited, and you would be shorter than you are by
several inches, all because of inadequate amounts of protein and
vitamins in your diet.

There are millions of children who are under-nourished at the
present time. Sudden disasters can quickly add to this number.
To produce enough food to correct this deficiency, as well as to
provide for the constantly increasing numbers who move into the
cities, will require a fundamental change in the productivity of
agricultural regions.

Women and Food
The problem of malnutrition is compounded by the subservient
position of women in many developing world societies, and therefore the smaller amount of food of the right kind that is
available to them. The world food crisis is a much more serious
matter when we consider that it is affecting future generations
through deficiencies in mothers.

The following accounts illustrate the special role of women in
the provision of food. These 3 are typical of many millions
throughout the world.

Pumla Njenga from Kenya was married at 15. She bore her first
child at 16 and has borne 9 children, 6 of whom still live.
Her husband went to the city to find work two years ago. He
rarely returns to the village and seldom sends any money home.

Pumla produces almost all the family food in the fields about
a mile from their village home. She wakes in the early light
before dawn and, without breakfast, straps her baby to her back
and walks that mile to the field, where she works for 10 hours,
stopping midway in hard physical labour to eat a bit of bread
or dried vegetable. The work is physically demanding, as is
the labour of all subsistence farmers, who work with a few very
simple tools. Some of the young men in her village have gone to
attend an agricultural training course to learn more efficient
methods. Pumla thought of going, but women were not asked to
apply.

Food comes to the Njenga home in its most raw and natural state.
For example, grains must be pounded by hand, consuming about 2

hours of Pumla's day. Before her little girls, ages 5 and 7,
were old enough to collect and carry firewood, Pumla also did
that. It took about 1 hour to get the wood for the cooking
fire. In the early evening after pounding the grain, Pumla goes
to fetch water, a journey of another mile each way, which takes
her roughly 1 hour. Some women in East Africa spend up to 6
hours a day carrying water.

Food is served in wooden bowls. Small children and men - in
this case, Pumla's father-in-law - are served first, the older
children next, and Pumla herself eats whatever is left after the
rest of the family has eaten. The meal is not a social occasion
nor a period for family conversation and sharing. Pumla works
hard to keep her family alive and is too tired for such things.

The family consumes little or no protein and few vitamins. They
are malnourished.

Maria Carlucci from Italy was married at 18. She bore her first
child at 19 and has borne 6 children, all of whom are living.
Her husband usually works at odd jobs, but recently there is
little work. He is deeply disturbed at not providing income and
has left the family. Maria now does domestic work fairly
regularly, but cannot receive public assistance as only male
heads of families are eligible.

Most of the Carlucci family food is purchased with a little
money Maria brings home from her domestic duties. Because the
income varies from day to day, the food is purchased daily.
Maria goes to several markets in and around the poor section of
Naples on her way home from work. Getting the food usually
takes her about 2 hours. Like other women in her culture and
class, she is responsible for preparing food for the younger
children plus the working men of the family. Older children are
given a small share of whatever money there is, and are expected
to shift for themselves. These youngsters live by their wits in
the streets.

Maria does all the cooking in the evening on two small gas burn-
ers. There is no oven in the home and sometimes one evening's
cooking must last several days.

Maria, like Pumla, serves the small children and the men first.
Her widowed father and unmarried brother live with the family.
There are plates and forks for everyone and spoons for the small
children. The meal is not a family occasion with the very
special exception of Sunday when the family spends the whole day
together preparing and eating the one main meal.

Maria's main concern is to provide enough food to fill the
stomachs of her family. Meals consist of pasta, little meat,
rarely vegetables, and hardly ever fruit. Three of Maria's
children suffer from rickets.

Sally Wilson from the United States was married at 21. She bore

her first child at 23. She has 3 children, all of whom are
living. Her husband is an engineer who formerly earned $22,000
a year, but is now unemployed.

Sally used to buy all the food once a week in one supermarket
and did some shopping only once a month. She now goes to the
market daily, going where there are sales, and where food stamps
are accepted. Obtaining food stamps consumes on an average 2
hours a week. Shopping sometimes takes up to 2 hours a day now
rather than 2 hours a week.

Sally uses fewer frozen and prepared foods now. She spends much
more time peeling vegetables and making casseroles and other
budget dishes.

Sally used to prepare breakfast and dinner for the entire family,
and the children were given money for hot lunches at school.
Now all the meals are jointly prepared by Sally and her husband,
including packing sandwiches for the children's lunch. Sally
has a part-time job as a typist so she doesn't have the time she
once had to spend cooking and preparing meals. She is glad that
her husband is willing to help with the cooking. If he doesn't
get a job soon, Sally will try to find full-time work.

Although the Wilsons eat less meat, they eat more fresh vegetables, and very few cookies and cakes.

World Grain Consumption
Of all the sources of man's food energy, grains are by far the
main supply. Rice provides 21 percent of total food energy,
wheat just under 20 percent and corn (or maize) 5 percent.
Other grains add up to 7 percent.

Figure 7.1 shows that annual per capita grain consumption
exceeds 600 pounds in the developed world but is often below 200
in developing countries. The large consumption in developed
countries is mostly indirect - fed to animals for production of
high protein meat.

One half of all the people in the world get 60 percent of their
energy from rice. Although it is lower than other important
grains in protein, it is high in calories, with 3,600 per kilogram.

There are two main groups of rice: upland or dry-land rice, and
paddy or irrigated rice. While dry-land rice is grown without
irrigation, it needs a great deal of soil moisture - at least 75
cm of rain in summer. With less rain, yields will be seriously
reduced and farmers will do better with other crops like wheat.

In the major rice-producing areas such as China, India, and
Southeast Asia, 90 percent of the rice is paddy. In these areas,
too, most agriculture is still noncommercial. That is, the
farmer grows crops almost entirely for his own family's need.
But even among commercial farms, paddy is more important than

dry-land rice.

To get the largest yield, seeds are planted in seed beds to
sprout. When the seedlings are about eight inches high, they
are transplanted by hand into a field with a thin mixture of mud
and water. The plants grow to maturity standing in water.
Close to harvest time the fields dry out and the crop is then
ready.

This method has been used for centuries in Asia, where it is
more widely understood and practiced than anywhere else.

In another method of paddy culture, the seed is sown directly in
the fields, usually before flooding. In some places, such as
Arkansas and California, seeds are sown from airplanes directly
on to flooded fields. After the plants have matured, the fields
are harvested just like the transplanted rice. This method
requires less hand labour than the transplanted rice.

Paddy culture needs a great deal of water. During the ninety
days that the plants are growing, 15 cm of water must be kept
on the fields. In humid areas, this equals 38 cm per acre
during the growing season. In arid areas, 90 cm are required.
Most of the water evaporates or seeps into the ground; it is not
used by the plant itself.

The water must be available at the proper time. Usually a
farmer must have access to a river, lake, or ground water so
that he can flood his fields after plowing and before setting
out the seedlings. He must be able to control the amount of
water, and this may call for costly irrigation equipment or a
great deal of labour.

In dry areas, the fields must be irrigated throughout the
growing season. In most of India and Southeast Asia heavy seasonal rains keep the fields flooded during the growing season.

Because of the need for a large volume of water and the cost of
irrigation, paddy culture, like dry-land rice, is seldom found
in areas where the summer rainfall is less than 75 cm.

More acres are planted to wheat than to any other grain. Like
rice, it is important in the diet of many countries. For a
cereal it is high in calories, the most common varieties producing about 3,300 per kilogram. It has a higher protein content
than any other cereal grain and is the grain most used for flour.
Many people prefer it baked as bread.

Wheat may be grown throughout the agricultural realm; it adapts
better than any other grain, except barley, to varying soils
and climates. It needs only a fairly short growing season,
about 100 days, so that its cultivation can extend to the coldest borders of the agricultural realm. Moreover, wheat may be
grown in areas with as little as 30 cm of rain a year.

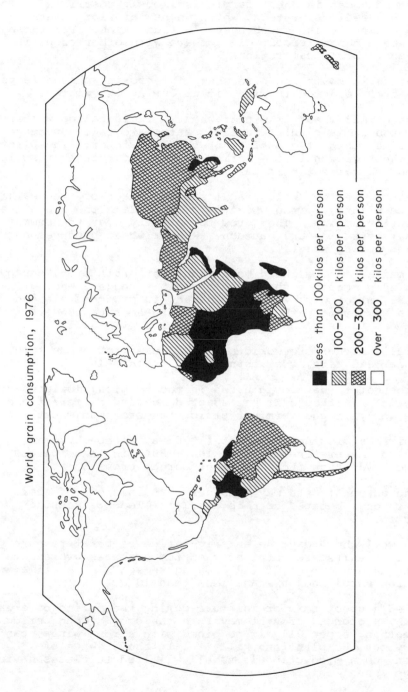

Fig. 7.1 World grain consumption, 1976

World grain consumption, 1976

Less than 100 kilos per person
100-200 kilos per person
200-300 kilos per person
Over 300 kilos per person

Only in humid areas is wheat farming seriously restricted. Too
much moisture reduces protein, which means inferior plants;
excessive moisture also encourages plant diseases. For these
reasons, wheat cannot profitably compete with other crops in
tropical and subtropical regions.

Sometimes, as in southern China where the growing season is year
round, wheat is planted in rice fields during the winter.

75 percent of all wheat is winter wheat. It is called winter
wheat because it is planted in early autumn to take advantage
of fall rains, then it goes dormant for the winter. The plants
continue their growth in the spring, taking advantage of spring
rains, and are harvested in early summer.

Where winters are very cold, and there is danger of the weather
killing the plants, spring wheat is grown. Here the seeds are
planted in the spring. They grow to maturity over the summer
and are harvested in early autumn. Winter wheat produces higher
yields than spring wheat.

Corn, or maize, is the third most important grain crop, occupying about 20 percent of the world's grain acreage. When ground
into a meal, mixed with water and baked, it produces a bread
that is an important part of diet in Latin America, and to a
lesser extent in Asia and eastern Europe.

Only a small part of the world's corn is used for human food.
Unlike wheat and rice, most corn is fed to animals.

Corn is thought to have originated in the tropical lowlands of
South America. Although it has adapted to very different areas,
its needs for rain and warmth restrict it more than wheat.

Corn requires a growing season of 130 days, although some
varieties can mature in less than 100. But, in these places,
yields are lower than those of other cereal crops.

Spring and autumn frosts may endanger corn in areas of short
growing seasons, because corn is easily killed by freezing
temperatures.

Corn does well where daytime and night time temperatures are
warm. Best results are obtained when temperatures average 23°C
during the major portion of the growing season. Night time
temperatures should not average less than 13°C.

Plants need a great deal of moisture during the period of greatest growth; prolonged drought may ruin the crop. Long periods
of dry weather, especially if combined with strong winds, can
easily dry out the plant and kill it. In the absence of
irrigation, corn production is usually limited to places having
an average annual rainfall over 75 cm.

In Mexico, for thousands of years, corn has been the traditional

grain. The tradition is so strong that Indians in the northwestern part of the country have selected varieties and developed farming methods that permit them to grow corn under near
desert conditions.

They plant a few seeds in little mounds 4 metres apart - very
unlike the closely planted rows found in North America. The
wide spacing gives the roots plenty of room to spread out and
capture the little moisture available.

Northwestern Mexico never knew wheat until long after the farmers worked out their system for growing corn. Wheat might have
yielded more food for less work. Yet even after wheat was
known, the farmers clung to their old ways.

Corn is an excellent grain for feeding animals. It has a high
carbohydrate and oil content, and it is therefore particularly
suitable for fattening. Corn produces 900 calories per kilogram. In addition, the plant can be harvested green, chopped
into small pieces, and allowed to ferment to form what is called
silage. As silage, corn is a tasty form of roughage, ideal for
feeding cattle.

In addition to its use as food for humans and feed for animals,
corn is also an important industrial crop in some parts of the
world. In the United States, it is the source of a number of
food products including starch, corn syrup, and corn oil.

Sea Harvests
The world's main fishing grounds are shown in Fig. 7.2. The
three biggest grounds are located at the junction of warm and
cold ocean currents where the mixing of waters of different
temperatures and salinity, in areas of shallow water, provide
favourable conditions for the growth of plankton - the principal
food of fish. The increase in total catch between 1955 and 1965
was an impressive 80 percent, in sharp constrast to the production increase in agricultural commodities for the same period,
and in sharp contrast to the increase in fish catch over the
preceding 20 years. Between 1935 and 1955 total world fish
catch rose by only 25 percent. The new increases are due to a
much-expanded use of trawlers by which the sea bottom is scoured
for fish, and to an intensified exploitation of fish off the
Pacific coast of South America. In 1965 and 1966, for the first
time, intensive trawling off the Northwest Pacific coast was
carried on by large Soviet fleets.

Between 1965 and 1975 there was a drop in the South American
catch because of the loss of anchovie stocks, but elsewhere the
trend toward increased exploitation continued.

Fish provides the much-needed protein element in man's diet - an
element mainly provided by meat in Canada and the United States,
but almost totally provided by fish in the countries of East
Asia. We have greatly increased the output of meat by improving
the strains of cattle, and by developing new forage crops.

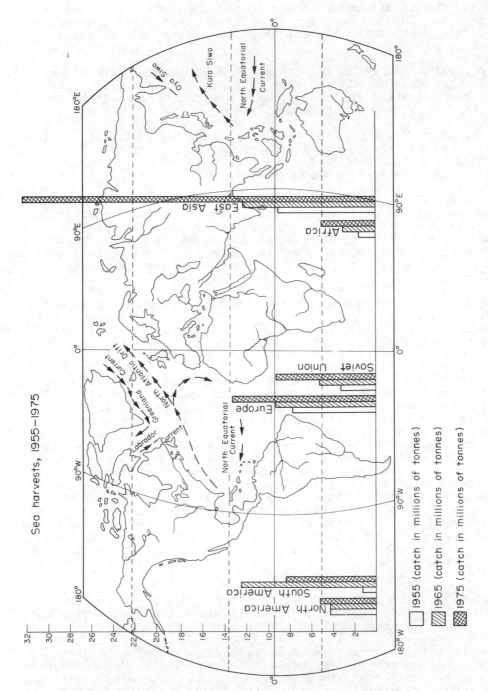

Sea harvests, 1955–1975

Fig. 7.2 Sea harvests, 1955 – 1975

Could not the same be done with fish? Should we not be able to improve the productivity of the sea and the fisherman by scientific methods? These are the questions now being asked in the light of the pressing need for food. To date, Japan seems to be the only country that takes this question seriously. For the most part her efforts at aquaculture have been concentrated in tidal coasts and in inland fresh waters, but these same efforts, with the aid of modern technical resources, could be extended into offshore areas of shallow water.

Japan's fish catch is twice that of any other country. For the most part this catch consists of a wide variety of fish from tunas to sardines caught in coastal waters, but a substantial portion of the total tonnage comes from aquaculture. One large town on the shores of Tokyo Bay is totally dependent on a clam industry. Seed stock is scattered at regular intervals on a hand-prepared sea-bottom, and the area is then protected from predators for the two or three years required for clam growth. More recently tractors have been employed to smooth and improve the tidal lands. In ponds, reservoirs, lakes, streams, and above all, in rice paddies there is a long-standing fish-rearing tradition. Young carp, about one inch in length, are placed in the fields shortly after transplanting in June, and six-inch-long fish are harvested when the fields dry out in September.

Other parts of the world are developing agriculture on smaller scales. In Israel 1 acre carp ponds each produce 2300 kilograms of protein-rich fish per year. Scots and Norwegians farm salmon, while Americans cultivate trout and catfish - in both instances for sport.

75,000,000 metric tonnes of fish are caught each year. That is expected to rise to 80,000,000 tonnes by 1980. Fish that are currently classed as "trash" could add 40 million more tonnes. But our lack of knowledge of fish is highlighted by the unexpected disappearance of the king of protein, the Peruvian anchovy. In the past this has provided 20 percent of all fish caught. We don't know if the anchovy has been overfished or if there has been a harmful shift in ocean currents as a result of climatic shifts.

The Japanese eat 45 kilograms of meat per year; North Americans 110. Only 3 of the 45 are in the form of beef. The rest is fish. Japanese people make good use of their sea harvests. It enables them to reduce their dependence on arable land for protein supplies. With their population pressure and shortage of oil and gas, they still manage to be number one in the export of petroleum based fertilizers (30 percent of the world's exports).

Asia's Small Farms

When industrialization began in Europe, the rate of migration to the cities was quite small, less than 1 percent. In the recent drift to the cities in the developing world, however, the growth has been more like 3 percent, so the increased demand for agricultural production is very much greater.

The small farmer with his few acres of land may not seem an
important person, but when we consider that there are 100
million of such farmers in the world it is a very different
story. In fact it is these small farmers who are the best users
of land. Their productivity per acre is much greater than that
found in the large farms. They are the ones with whom the hope
of increased food production must lie.

Millions of Asian families earn their livlihood and sustenance
from small plots of land on which they cultivate their staple
food, rice. As populations grow, however, greater pressure
is being put on these people and their land to produce sufficient
food just to feed themselves, with very little left over.

Multiple cropping is one way of intensifying production from the
same land and it has been practiced and refined by farmers in
many locations for centuries. It has only been recently,
however, that these intensive multiple cropping systems have
begun to receive serious attention from the scientific community
concerned with improving agricultural production.

Small Asian farms are, for the most part, characterized by a
diversity of crop, animal and off-farm activities, all of which
contribute to the cash flow of the farming system. It has been
normal practice for scientists developing agricultural production technology to pay attention only to the field areas where
major crops are grown. However, there is often an additional
homestead production area surrounding the house or farmyard
where the farm family lives. This area provides a wide assort-
ment of crops that contribute diversity and quality to the
family's diet. The importance of this area to the family
depends on both farm size and its cash flow, but for a low-
income subsistence farmer the homestead is as important as his
cultivated field area.

A great majority of the small farms in East and Southeast Asia
depend on rainfall, and only partially on irrigation to supply
the water needed to grow their rice crop. In most instances
only one crop is harvested, even where partial irrigation is
available. It is these areas that offer considerable potential
for increased production through intensive cropping. Two crops
of rice, or at least rice followed by an upland crop, are
possible if new procedures can be introduced.

Normally farmers wait until the monsoon rains have deposited
enough water on their fields so they can puddle the soil and
transplant young rice seedlings into the resulting water saturated mud. With new early-maturing rice varieties, however, it
is possible to plant rice seed directly into non-puddled soil
at the start of the rains in regions where the monsoon starts
gradually. Direct seeding eliminates the traditional long wait
until the monsoon is well established.

The new method permits growing two short season rice crops dur-
during the rainy period. The first one can be harvested soon
enough to allow time for a second to be transplanted in the
normal fashion.

Where the rains begin suddenly rather than gradually, direct
seeding is not possible and transplanted puddle rice must be
grown. In many areas, however, there is still enough moisture
available after the rice has been harvested to plant another
crop such as a vegetable.

The potential number of combinations of crops, crop varieties,
and physical characteristics is mind boggling, but it is the
task of the cropping systems research program to sort these
out and come up with more productive crop combinations than
those farmers are presently using.

Climatic Shifts
Over and above the dangers that affect food production year by
year - storms, floods, earthquakes and weather changes - there
are the long-term changes in weather that can profoundly alter
the food supply for half a continent. The drought that was
experienced in Europe in the summer of 1976 was matched by an
excessively wet summer in the western part of Canada.

Early in 1977 the U.S. experienced extremely low temperatures -
so low that there was a serious shortage of heating oil and gas.
See. Fig. 7.3. for the shift in the westerlies storm tracks
that caused the big freeze.

In England, the average growing season is now two weeks shorter
than it was in 1950. Mean temperatures peaked in 1945 with a
steady drop since. Although the world wide average drop of 1.5
degrees Celcius doesn't sound like much, it is effecting growing
seasons, fishing patterns and animal migrations.

Reid Bryson, University of Wisconsin climatologist, says that
an accumulation of dust in the atmosphere began the cooling
trend.

Wind blown dust from mechanized agricultural operations, dust
from overgrazed arid lands, smoke from slash and burn land
clearings in the tropics, and natural phenomenon such as
volcanic dust, salt water spray, and organic emissions all
contributed. Bryson points out that the dust has a more
pronounced cooling effect on the polar regions than on the
tropics.

Compounding the cooling trend was a greenhouse effect caused by
past heavy dependence on fossil fuels for power and heat. The
resulting carbon dioxide formed a layer of insulation letting
the sunlight in but not letting the heat out. The dust blanket
has now overcome that warmth.

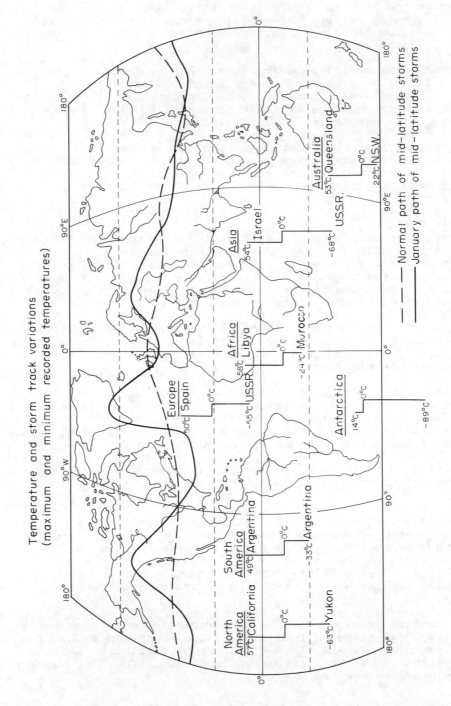

Fig. 7.3 Temperature and storm track variations

According to one report, the past 1600 years show many major shifts of climate with drops in temperature lasting 40 years followed by 70 years of slow increase back to "normal". Under these circumstances we could see the demise of Canada, China and the Northern USSR as major forces in world food production. Only the U.S. and Argentina, of the main growing areas, would escape the loss of their productive capacities.

From 1933 to 1960, there has been an enormous increase in world population. Major dams and irrigation systems were built during this period based on prevailing rainfall patterns. Under conditions of a cooling trend the green revolution in Mexico, Pakistan and India could fade away because the hybrid plants were developed within a particular weather pattern. The USSR, China, and Southern Asia would need more food imports.

Bryson believes that the period from 1890 to 1945 amounted merely to a brief respite from the "little ice age" that has held the world in its grip ever since the sixteenth century.

Before the little ice age, grapes were widely cultivated in England, and the French complained of English wine makers dumping their wares in European markets. As early as the tenth century, the Vikings had established prosperous colonies in Greenland, having named the island for its verdant pastures. By the early fifteenth century, however, these colonies were wiped out by cold and hunger and now four-fifths of Greenland lies buried under an ice cap.

From the evidence found in sea-floor sediments, peat bogs, and tree rings, the earth's long-term climatological history has been full of ups and downs. Even the little ice age is only a minor squiggle in swings from warm periods and true ice ages.

There is agreement among researchers that the earth is now heading very slowly into another major ice age such as the one that brought the glaciers deep into North America more than 10,000 years ago.

One of climatology's more surprising conclusions, derived from investigations of sea-floor sediments, is that for the past 700,000 years, global temperatures have been as high as they are now for only 5 percent of the time.

Experts used to think that intervals as warm as the present lasted 100,000 years or so. Instead, they appear to be short, infrequent episodes. Another surprising finding is that transitions have taken place with great rapidity, often within a century.

Nutrition, Wealth, and Health
Recognition of the instability of the climatic environment of agriculture adds urgency to the task of providing adequate nutrition, wealth, and health to the billions of mankind.

It is clear from Fig. 7.4 and Fig. 7.5 that only in the developed world are all three of these needs properly met.

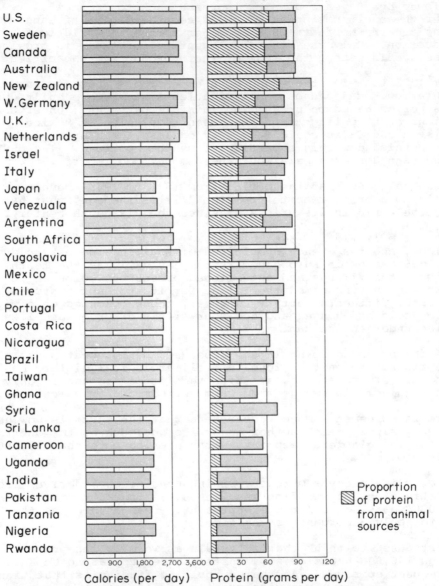

Fig. 7.4 Nutrition and wealth, 1976

The number of people suffering from malnutrition still stands at the staggering level of 500 million. There are one billion more who would benefit greatly from a more varied diet. The largest concentration is in Asia, Southeast Asia and Sub-Saharan

Africa. Clinical surveys and hospital records indicate that
malnutrition wherever it exists is severest among infants, pre-
school children and pregnant women; that it is most prevalent
in depressed rural areas and the slums of great cities; that the
problem is frequently accompanied by a lack of calories as well
as a lack of protein.

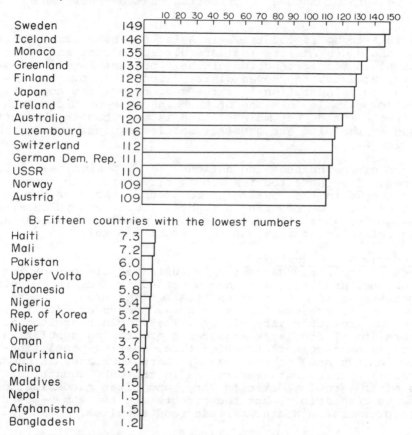

A. Fourteen countries with the highest number of beds per
   10,000 inhabitants

Sweden	149
Iceland	146
Monaco	135
Greenland	133
Finland	128
Japan	127
Ireland	126
Australia	120
Luxembourg	116
Switzerland	112
German Dem. Rep.	111
USSR	110
Norway	109
Austria	109

B. Fifteen countries with the lowest numbers

Haiti	7.3
Mali	7.2
Pakistan	6.0
Upper Volta	6.0
Indonesia	5.8
Nigeria	5.4
Rep. of Korea	5.2
Niger	4.5
Oman	3.7
Mauritania	3.6
China	3.4
Maldives	1.5
Nepal	1.5
Afghanistan	1.5
Bangladesh	1.2

Fig. 7.5 Number of hospital beds, selected countries

The world can be divided into five groups on the basis of
levels of nutrition. The first group consists of the industrialized nations, where food is plentiful but pockets of poverty
persist. Here governments are able to deal with problems of
malnutrition through food assistance to the poor, nutrition and
health programs and nutrition-education programs. The chief
members of the group are the U.S., Canada, the nations of
Western Europe, Japan, Australia, New Zealand, Hong Kong and
Singapore.

The second group consists of the nations with centrally planned
economies, where government control of food supplies and distribution protects the populations against malnutrition due to
hunger. In this category are China, Taiwan, North Korea, South
Korea and Vietnam.

In the third group are the nations of the Organization of
Petroleum Exporting Countries (OPEC), with enormous wealth but
with a pattern of income distribution that may not benefit the
poor.

Fourth is a group of countries in Asia, the Near East, Central
America and South America that are already almost self-
sufficient in food production at their present level of demand.
There is, however, an uneven distribution of income that is
reflected in malnutrition in large segments of the population.
Brazil, for example, has one of the highest economic growth
rates in the world, but malnutrition is very bad in the northeast and in the slum and squatter settlements surrounding the
large cities.

The fifth group includes the nations the UN designates as least
developed. They have too few economic resources to provide
for the people in the lowest income groups. Many of the countries are exposed to recurring droughts, floods or cyclones; some
are ravaged by war. All of these least developed nations are
poor in natural resources and investment capital.

North American Breadbasket
One area of the world has not only sustained its per capita
level of food production; it has exceeded it and, in so doing,
has focussed world attention on itself. The area is North
America and the reasons for an increased dependence on it by
the rest of the world vary widely. They include ecological
deterioration of food systems because of growing population
pressure, mismanagement of agriculture, soaring population-
induced demands and, in some cases, sharp increases in demand
as a result of new found wealth, as in the OPEC countries. The
causes of the growing deficits vary, and often a combination of
factors is responsible, but the effects are the same - ever
greater pressure on North American food supplies.

As a result, North America today finds itself with an almost
monopolistic control of the world's exportable grain supplies,
a situation for which there is no historical precedent. In a
world of food scarcity, where there may not be enough food to go
around, North America must decide who gets how much food and on
what terms. The governments of the United States and Canada
have not consciously sought the responsibility, any more than
the countries of the Middle East have planned their geographical
location astride the world's richest oil fields, but it is a
reality and it must be reckoned with.

Throughout much of the period since World War Two, the world has
had two major food reserves: stocks of grain held by the

principal exporting countries and cropland idled under farm
programs in the United States. During the sixties and early
seventies some 50 million acres out of a total U.S. cropland
base of 350 million acres was held out of production to support
prices. Stocks of grain held by the exporting countries were
readily available for use when needed. Cropland that had been
idled under farm programs in the U.S. could be brought back into
production within a year. Together, grain stockpiles and cropland reserves provided security for all mankind, a cushion
against food disasters.

Until a few years ago it seemed likely that surplus stocks and
idled cropland would be part of the landscape for a long time.
Then, suddenly, things began to change. The global demand for
food, a result of the relentless growth of population and rising
affluence, began to outstrip the productive capacity of the
world's farmers and fishermen. The world fish catch, which had
tripled between 1950 and 1970 and moved to a new high virtually
every year, stabilized. Most of the idled U.S. cropland was
returned to use, but still food reserves were not rebuilt.

Another factor contributing to instability was a decision made
by Soviet political leaders to offset crop shortfalls with
imports.

This policy, apparently made in early 1972, may not be an
irreversible one, but neither will it be abandoned easily.
Soviet herds and flocks have been building steadily throughout
the seventies as a result of this policy. So too have the
expectations and appetites of Soviet consumers.

There are then four major factors contributing to instability
in the world food economy today: the decline of grain reserves;
the disappearance of idled cropland in the United States; the
dangerous dependence of the entire world on the food surplus of
one geographic-climatic region; and the decision by the Soviet
government to offset shortfalls through imports rather than
through belt-tightening. All but one, the overwhelming dependence on North America, have emerged quite recently.

The obvious question is: why has one region emerged as a
supplier of food to the rest of the world? If one were to
select the single dominant factor reshaping world trade patterns
in recent decades, it would be the varying rates of population
growth. While North American population has grown slowly, most
of the rest of the world has been experiencing extremely rapid
growth.

The question now before the international community is whether
the food trends of the past several years will continue. One
thing seems certain. The rapid growth in dependence on North
America cannot continue for much longer without exceeding the
region's capacity to respond.

The Changing Pattern of World Grain Trade

Region	1960	1970	1976
	(Million Metric Tonnes)		
North America	+ 39	+ 56	+ 94
Latin America	0	+ 4	- 3
Western Europe	- 25	- 30	- 17
E.Europe & USSR	0	+ 1	- 25
Africa	- 2	- 5	- 10
Asia	- 17	- 37	- 47
Australia & N.Z.	+ 6	+ 12	+ 8

Plus sign indicates net exports; minus sign, net imports.

Canada

Ample evidence already exists of the strains being felt in
North American agriculture. Canada's story is typical of most
of the continent.

The farmland acreage in Canada is not nearly as large as is
popularly supposed. Just because the country is the world's
second largest country with one of the world's lowest population
densities, it is easy to assume there is no limit to the
agricultural resources and the food resources available. This
is far from being the case.

Only 7½ percent of Canada is agricultural land, that is a total
of 174 million acres. Out of this total only 108 million acres
are improved land and only about 69 million of these are under
crops. Even if all 108 million acres were under crop it would
be just sufficient to feed a population of 30 million people at
present levels - this is less than the population Canada will
have in the year 2000. It is difficult for Canadians to realize
that a small country like Britain is already growing sufficient
food to feed that number of people.

Most of the urban growth in Canada is taking place in three
of the nation's most fertile areas; south-central Ontario, the
St. Lawrence lowlands in Quebec, and the Lower Mainland in
British Columbia. Together, these three areas contain 24
million acres of the finest agricultural land in Canada. Much
of it is unique because of mild climate, good rainfall, and
excellent soil.

In the Niagara Peninsula of Ontario, the acreage devoted to
tender fruit trees and vineyards has been declining for years.
Recently, over a 5 year period about 520 acres per year were
taken out of production. Over 80 percent of the losses were to
urban uses.

The reasons for the loss of land to urban uses are not hard to

find.   An acre of the best farmland might sell for $700 if it
were to be used for growing crops.   But if the same acre were to
become part of a residential development, the price might be
$50,000.   In such an economic climate, only government inter-
vention can save the land.

In a survey in the Niagara fruit belt, local farmers were asked
about their land.   About one-third said they did not care about
future patterns of development in the area.   Some 40 percent
felt that saving the fruit belt would be a good thing, but that
the present economics of fruit growing and the high prices do
not justify such action.   It is hard to blame a farmer for
wanting to sell if the price is right; 90 percent of farmers
would let their land go if they got a good price.

Declining fertility of prairie farmland makes it essential that
none of the best land be urbanized.   Soil fertility decline is
not a well known problem because massive doses of fertilizers
continue to counter the decline, and even increase yield.   But
in reality all the best prairie farmland has already lost one
third of its native productivity.   In addition large acreages
are being ruined by bad cultivation practices that encourage
high salinity.

Agricultural land is therefore being lost by bad farming
practices as well as by urbanization.   So a double erosion of
available farmland is taking place.   A double counteraction is
therefore needed if productivity is to be maintained.

It is often claimed that the sale of agricultural land for
urban development provides farmers with a just reward for a
lifetime of underpaid labour.   While this may be true, it does
not alter the fact that some of the best wheat land is being
lost to urban development every year.   In a recent 7 year period
16,000 acres of Class 1 land were lost to the city of Edmonton.
That land could have produced 11,200 tonnes of wheat per year.
This should be compared with total Canadian wheat production
of 17 million tonnes which is over 1,500 times the potential
of the urban land lost in Edmonton.   By these measures the
impact of Canadian urbanization on global food production is not
very big.   But this cannot be said if the same process is
multiplied again and again around North America.

Every acre lost is one acre too many in a world where millions
are malnourished or starving.   The 11,200 tonnes of wheat lost
to Edmonton each year could provide dietary essentials for
16,000 starving people.

Solutions
Every country in the world has the capacity to feed itself.   The
problem of hunger is not a natural one of scarcity: it is one
of the social and political order we live in.   That is typical
of the comments made by many leading westerners.   It is an
extreme viewpoint.   It almost implies that countries should be
able to solve their food problems without any external aid.

The views of the Canadian International Development Agency are close to this optimistic outlook. In 1975 this was the Canadian view.

The opportunities for increased agricultural production through-out the developing world are great despite the bleatings of those who paint pictures of doom. In that area of the world bordering on and between the tropics of Capricorn and Cancer, there is a vast potential for agriculture and food production almost untapped. Much of this area is farmed or grazed under technologies that differ little from those discovered thousands of years ago. Yet the basic ingredients of a productive agri-culture - water, responsive soil, suitable year-round growing conditions, and abundant light - hold an immense promise for an abundance beyond anything yet attained by man.

The Indus-Ganges-Brahmaputra plain of northern India and Bangladesh could, if properly exploited, almost double present world grain output. Southern Sudan, an area of tens of thousands of square miles, receives each year more than 400 billion cubic metres of rain and runoff, of which only about 70 billion cubic metres passes into the Nile river. This water forms large swamps, drains into underground aquifers and pools, evaporates under the relentless sun of the dry season, and produces a coarse and heavy vegetation that is of limited use to man. Of the regions in the world that are still available for the development of agriculture, the southern Sudan is probably the largest area that can readily be developed. Not far behind are the vast grazing areas of the Sahel, parts of West, East, and Southern Africa, and Latin America.

The potential of those areas in the tropical and subtropical developing regions where there are large expanses of land still unexploited for agriculture is, however, probably surpassed by the potential of those other parts, now cultivated by traditional means, where modern farm technologies could greatly increase production. New crop varieties of the major grains and starchy roots offer significant advantages in yield and nutrient content over indigenous biological materials; modern methods of irrigation and rainwater harvesting have a potential water-use efficiency of close to 90 percent, a sharp contrast with tradit-ional irrigation efficiencies of between 10 and 20 percent. Multiple cropping and intercropping systems adapted to tropical climates and soils can increase land yields by 10 tonnes annually per hectare per crop. (Yield per unit of land per period of time is now replacing yield per unit of land as the critical output measure for tropical circumstances).

This is not all. New methods of using plant residues for inte-grated crop-livestock programs hold promise of higher returns to small farmers, of making efficient use of plant materials unfit for human consumption, and of yielding a major source of quality protein for human nutrition. New means of storing and processing food commodities will eliminate waste and open opportunities for rural industry and development.

Improved implements for farming permit greater efficiency and timing of agricultural operations, while easing some of the drudgery of peasant work. New pasture grasses and legumes, new methods of controlling animal diseases, new techniques of animal and range husbandry, new breeds of livestock open major avenues for increasing the yields of animal and grazing agricultures. These are only a few examples. Modern technology holds one of the keys to abundance, the potential of the tropical world holds another.

A more realistic view takes account of the fundamental constraints of climate, the difficulties of expanding production in cold deserts, hot deserts, and wet tropics.

Summers are so short and cool that few plants grow in the cold deserts of northern Canada or northern Siberia. There is only enough food in the cold climates to support a few scattered people, and most of them live by hunting and fishing rather than farming.

An extreme example of winter cold is found at Verkhoyansk in Siberia. Here the average temperature in January is -50° C.

In some cold climates the ground is frozen all year round to a depth of a thousand feet. These are the regions of permafrost where any water in the soil is ice. Even during the short summers, only a shallow top layer melts. This water, unable to soak down into the frozen earth below, remains in the surface layer of soil until it freezes once again.

No major crop can grow outdoors in such a short, cool summer, even where permafrost is absent. New varieties of crops would have to be developed.

If we did have a grain that could be harvested a few weeks after it is planted, it would need expensive soil care in cold climates. The soils are highly acid and since the elements most plants need for nutrition wash out of them, they would have to be heavily fertilized.

The cold climates, it has been said, are well suited to grazing, and small herds of reindeer are raised in some areas. The vegetation, however, is sparse and grows very slowly. A few animals soon eat everything within reach, so they have to be moved frequently from place to place. It is estimated that each reindeer needs about five square miles of land. Before larger herds can be fed, new varieties of grass would be necessary.

Life is almost as hard on men as on plants or animals. Not very many people would live in these regions if they could help it.

The hot deserts are quite a different story. All that they need is water. Irrigated patches of desert are among the most productive farm lands on earth. Some of them have supported dense populations for thousands of years. Long before Europeans

began to clear forests to make room for farms, irrigated
deserts in Africa and Asia had developed very advanced civil-
izations.

There is usually plenty of sun, which most food plants need,
and the soils are fertile. They are free from most insect
pests, which in wetter regions can ruin crops.

There are oases in the deserts, most of which tap underground
water. The fields watered by the Nile River make up one of the
oldest farming regions on earth. Some of the most productive
United States farm lands are in former desert areas of the
Southwest.

Irrigated fields and oases, however, make up only a tiny fraction of the vast dry wastelands. The rain that does fall often
comes in the form of violent storms. After ten years with
virtually no rain, some places in Egypt received 6 cm in the
eleventh year, most of it from a single shower. Ouargla in
Algeria had more than 20 cm of rain in one year after several
dry years.

Wide ranges of temperatures that kill plants are a feature of
such deserts as the Sahara. Days are sunny, hot, and very
windy. Nights are cold and still. It is not unknown for water
to freeze at night even after daytime temperatures of 32° C.
The hot winds carry sand or dust that cuts the skin.

Not very many forms of life exist. Plants are of two kinds,
neither of them useful either as human food or as animal fodder.

One variety has seeds that can stand being dried out, baked in
the hot sun, and frozen in the cold night for months or even
years until one of the rare rains comes. Then they sprout,
grow, flower, and bear seeds within a few weeks.

The second variety of desert plants stores water or else sends
down long roots to reach underground supplies.

Deserts, then will have to have water. In the developing
regions of the world, sources of water not already used can only
be tapped by building very costly irrigation works.

The wet tropical rain forests of South America, Africa, or Asia,
present a solid mass of vegetation extending as far as the eye
can see. There are more than a thousand species of plants in
a single acre.

Inside the forests are scattered tribes who may never have
farmed. They live by hunting, and by collecting wild fruits,
nuts, and vegetables.

In clearings and on the fringes of the forest, other groups of
villagers farm by an old method known as "slash and burn."
They cut down the trees in a patch of the forest, burn what they

can, and plant a crop between the charred logs.

After a year or two, the heavy rains of the wet tropics dissolve the minerals needed by food crops, and drain them out of the soil. The villagers cut another patch of forest and repeat the process. This method produces small quantities of food.

Whatever the future potential of technology applied to agriculture, it is clear that present efforts in that direction are meeting with significant success. In many countries, for instance, fortified grains have been developed in order to compensate for the lack of vitamins and minerals and amino acids in cereals. And in Colombia a kind of thin gruel has been developed which serves as a hot drink. It consists of a high protein mixture made up of a variety of chemicals. This gruel has been particularly valuable for feeding infants.

Identify the Issues

1. What was the green revolution? Where was it most successful?

2. There are food sources that could be tapped if cultural biases were removed; e.g. if cattle in India were not sacred, there would be a lot of beef available for everyone in that country. Should governments interfere with religious/cultural beliefs such as this one when so many do not have enough food?

3. What single, large, new source of food could most easily be developed and used?

"As cities grow, so do the problems of pollution. Air and water
contamination are an immediate threat to health. But there are
other environmental problems: traffic congestion, overcrowding
of parks and loss of open spaces, rising levels of garbage and
waste, fire and other public safety hazards, noise and noxious
smells, social alienation and rising crime. In most countries,
these problems are aggravated by underdevelopment and mass
poverty. Industries use high-pollutant energy sources, traffic
is worsened by the mingling of automobiles with carts, bicycles
and animals, and squatter settlements are criss-crossed with
open sewers. Low levels of municipal revenue make solutions
harder. A mile of modern subway construction for example, can
cost as much as 10,000 small homes." From Habitat Preparatory
Paper.

CHAPTER EIGHT

Hazards of the Environment

The environment of mankind is a complex of natural and man made
elements - land and water, climate and soils, buildings,
industries, streets, television and books.

Climate has always profoundly affected the distribution of
people throughout this total environment. In the higher
latitudes of the Canadian Arctic or Soviet Siberia it is too cold
for dense settlement. In the lower latitudes of the Sahara or
Arabia it is too hot and dry.

The main climates that favour dense settlement are the temperate
mid latitudes, a few tropical climates, and the monsoon lands of
east, south and southeast Asia. See Fig. 8.1. It is the high
concentrations of people in these few areas of the world,
especially in the urban concentrations that have focussed
attention on environmental hazards.

The gloom and doom prophets of the environment were operating at
a high point in 1970. Disaster seemed inevitable in all directions. Paul Ehrlich's scenario of that year took the viewpoint of an observer of 1980 looking back on the tragedy of the
earth that was.

The scenario went something like this. The end of the ocean
came late in the summer of 1979, and it came even more rapidly
than the biologists had expected. There had been signs for more
than a decade, commencing with the discovery in 1968 that DDT
slows down photosynthesis in marine plant life. There had been
the final gasp of the whaling industry in 1973, and the end of
the Peruvian anchovy fishery in 1975. Indeed, a score of other
fisheries had disappeared quietly from over exploitation and
various eco-catastrophes by 1977.

And so on. It was a far cry from the optimism of the late 1940s
when the U.S. was busy urging all North Americans to buy two
cars, to raise their standards of living to new heights, to take
advantage of the vast amount of resources that were waiting to
be consumed.

In 1972 came the United Nations Stockholm Conference. That was
the beginning of a much more realistic approach to the problems
of the environment. At that conference it was evident that many
nations did not see the environmental crisis the way we do. For
them the dominant consideration was a higher standard of living
no matter what cost to the environment - a flashback to the
thinking of so many in the industrial revolution in Britain 200

173

years ago.

The beginnings of the present phase of environmental concerns go
back to the mid-1960s. They were triggered by space travel and
the view it brought of the earth as a finite and rather small
body in space.

"Spaceship earth" came into common use to imply that the earth
was a very fragile and closely knit system. Damage to the
water supply in one part of this system, to take one example,
could effect the whole planet. So could damage to other things -
natural resources, air, soil. The analogy of a spacecraft facing the constant risk of a dangerous accident came to a head in
the concern over nuclear arsenals, and the possibility of
accidental use of these weapons of destruction.

Today the world "environment" implies much more than the
physical resources of the earth. It defines the total environment within which people live and work. The worker who is on
night shift and has to sleep in the daytime under conditions of
high noise level suffers from a very bad environment.

Many people in developing countries travel long distances to
work in poor facilities. The journeys are often a source of
physical and nervous fatigue.

Even in the countryside the working environment is changed with
the rapid expansion of mechanization in agriculture. The
occupational accident rate is as high in some countries in that
kind of work as it is for miners or construction workers. Furthermore the widespread use of fertilizers, weedkillers, and
pesticides pose enormous problems for the long-term health of
the environment and the food it produces for humans.

What it all boils down to is that it is no longer possible
either in urban or rural settings to make a sharp distinction
between occupational disease and generally poor health, between
health problems or environmental problems resulting from work
and those that come from the general environment in which the
work is carried on.

Australia

Australia experiences three major storm types: the tornado, the
'southerly buster', and the tropical cyclone. The tornado is
the most localised in effect: its path is seldom more than a
fraction of a kilometre wide or more than a few kilometres long.
It can demolish everything in its path.

At Brighton, Victoria, on 2 February 1918, one of these storms
reached a speed of 300 km/h. Tornadoes are rare in the southern
states, but they occur more frequently in Queensland and other
northern parts of the continent. A tornado devastated the
Queensland town of Killarney in November 1968.

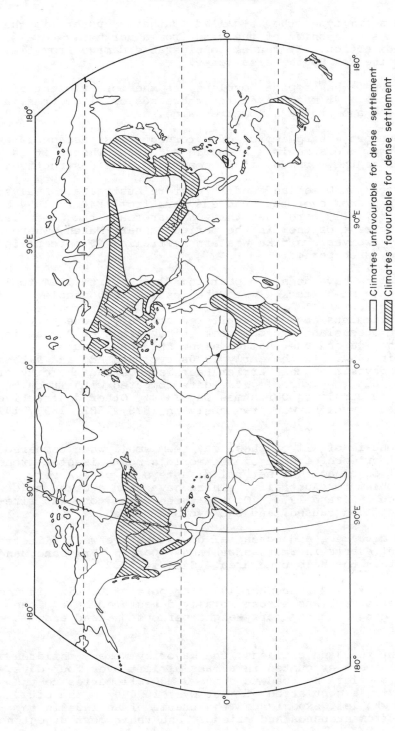

Fig. 8.1 Climate and settlement

☐ Climates unfavourable for dense settlement

▨ Climates favourable for dense settlement

The second storm type, the so-called southerly buster, is the
result of a sudden shift of the wind from a northerly to a
southerly direction. It causes considerable damage from time to
time along the New South Wales coast.

The third type, the tropical cyclone, is the most violent of all
in its effects. It may travel for thousands of kilometres, and
often affects a belt 500 kilometres wide.

Unlike the short, sharp impact of a tornado, its passage takes
several hours, and sometimes a couple of days. Though it is not
as powerful as the tornado, it is generally more destructive.

Cyclones occur in Queenland and in Western Australia. Analysis
of cyclonic storms over the hundred-years from 1844 to 1954 has
shown that slightly more than three a year reach the Queensland
coast, 60 percent of them in the period January-March, whereas
three every two years strike Western Australia, 80 percent in
the January-March period.

Heavy sufferers have been the pearling fleets: from 1844 to 1954
300 ships have been wrecked with the loss of 1000 people.

Coastal settlements have also suffered severely. One very
destructive Queensland cyclone took thirty lives at Mackay in
1918; another caused vast damage along the coast south of
Bundaberg in 1954. In the early 1970s cyclones Ada and Althea
struck and devastated the Barrier Reef islands and the city of
Townsville, but they were lightweights compared with Tracy,
which came to Darwin on Christmas Day 1974. Other destructive
cyclones had struck Darwin previously in 1878, 1882, 1897, 1917,
and 1937.

Though the scale of all of these may seem small when compared
with the experience of some of the world's most disaster-prone
regions, it is clear that natural disasters do pose a very
serious problem for Australia. There have been a dozen major
ones between 1964 and 1974. Of the three worst, one was fire-
caused, one flood-caused, and one cyclone-caused.

Australian disasters and potential disasters are well illustrated in recent events in 3 urban centres - Darwin, Brisbane, and
Westernport in the Melbourne area. See Fig. 8.2.

On the night of 24-25 December 1974 the port of Darwin, in the
Northern Territory, was almost totally devastated by cyclone
Tracy, bringing death to forty-eight persons on land and
nineteen at sea.

Twenty-eight thousand citizens, the majority women, children and
older people were evacuated in a mass airlift over four days.
Another 11,000 left by road to drive 3,200 kilometres to the
south, leaving a population of just over 10,000 in the city.
The people who left experienced the trauma of an indefinite
separation from husbands and friends, and their most urgent need

was comfort and assurance that families would be reunited as
soon as possible.

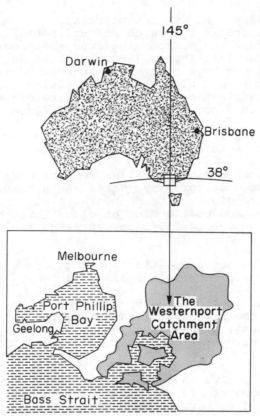

Fig. 8.2 Environmental problems in three Australian areas

Those left behind had to try to re-establish themselves, but
their needs were complex and could be resolved only in a day-to-
day piecemeal manner.

Although Darwin is tropical, the cyclone brought freezing rain
and winds and these things, coupled with the aftermath of fear,
reduced the body temperature to an almost unknown low. Almost
all goods and chattels were saturated, and whatever was dry was
used as body covering. People improvised as best they could,
with the desperate need to be warm and dry uppermost in the
minds of all.

Since there was no sanitation, special care had to be exercised
in hygiene. All perishables were collected from homes and
buried or burnt. Human waste was similarly buried. Survival
from day to day was the prime urgency.

Less than a year earlier a different kind of disaster hit
Brisbane in northeast Australia.

The Brisbane Valley contains two major rivers, the Bremer and
Brisbane, and two cities, Ipswich and Brisbane. In the 19th
century both rivers and surrounding land suffered several
record floods, the last in the 1890s. In the 20th century
several minor floods have occurred. In common with other cities
urban sprawl spread out along the flood plains over the past 60
years. This, despite the advice of hydrologists that residents
of both cities could not be protected from floods.

In January 1974 the right climatic conditions for severe flooding were about to enfold Brisbane and Ipswich.

In January 1974 the North Australian monsoon moved further
south than it had done for many years. As a result, heavy rains,
and widespread flooding occurred in almost all areas of the
State. Few areas had no flooding at all. Throughout January
the Weather Bureau issued 262 flood warnings for most rivers in
the State.

Fortunately because of population spacing, few areas held the
same potential for personal loss as did Brisbane and Ipswich.

Most Brisbane and Ipswich people were sound asleep and oblivious
to the start of the six days of rain and high water which began
at 3 a.m. on Friday, January 25. Brisbane woke up to a most
depressing day, with the rain lashing down and continuing un-
abated until 3 p.m.

Then it eased slightly. But the effects were soon to be felt.
Major flooding occurred in all the Brisbane creeks, with levels
very near those of an earlier storm in February and April, 1972,
when extensive damage was done.

At 8 p.m. the rain increased in intensity again, and between 9
p.m. and midnight some areas registered falls of 180 mm.

Intense rain continued on Saturday. By Saturday afternoon
flooding in the creeks had subsided. But the Brisbane River
height had increased, and its backwater then started to lift
the level in the creeks.

About the same time, cyclone Wanda crossed the coast at Double
Island Point. In its wake came an intense flow of very moist
air which produced extremely heavy rain along the ranges
immediately west of the coastline.

This continued for the next two days. The heaviest rain fell in
the D'Aguilar Range, and in one period of 24 hours Mt. Mee had
324 mm.

Cyclone Wanda practically blew itself out in the following 24
hours. But the monsoonal trough it brought south with it stay-

ed, and generally very heavy rainfalls were recorded over the next 48 hours, with 485 mm at Enoggera Reservoir. Then the rains eased.

The first part of the Brisbane Valley to respond to the monsoonal rainfalls was the Stanley River, where major flood levels rose quickly.

Meanwhile, exceptionally heavy rain had been falling in the middle and lower reaches of the Brisbane River, including the Bremer River.

Unprecedented flooding in Ipswich and the Bremer River area at this stage was due entirely to the Bremer and local area run-off.

The most devastating feature of the Ipswich flooding was the velocity of the water, which was much greater than in the 1893 flood.

In the Brisbane city area, the first minor flooding on the river occurred at high tide about midday on Friday and again at midnight.

The tides were higher than normal and, as well as including some storm surge, the river contained a big contribution from the flooded metropolitan creeks.

River levels continued to rise in Brisbane, and at 2.15 a.m. on Tuesday, January 29, reached their highest point.

Flooding eased gradually in Brisbane, and by 6 a.m. on Thursday, January 31, had dropped to a safe level. And then, for many, started the heartbreaking job of counting the losses and the cost - 16 dead, thousands homeless, and more than $75 million property loss.

Westernport is a story of potential disaster. Intense utilization of the area poses a threat to both wildlife and recreational sites. A major study is now underway to anticipate and prevent the kinds of developments that would destroy this particular environment.

The catchment area covers some 3000 km^2 around the shores of Westernport Bay, a deep-water harbour about 56 km from the heart of Melbourne.

About 40,000 people live in the region on farms and in several towns. About 12 percent of the land is in its natural state.

Development has so far had only a mild effect on the enclosed waters of the Bay and the related open waters nearby. The total area of these waters is about 1600 km^2.

The Bay and the adjacent open waters constitute the phase of the system most seriously threatened by urban, industrial,

rural and recreational activity. For this reason the study is
concerned with dangers posed to the waters, the shores and the
bed of Westernport Bay.

Westernport Bay and its beaches, swamps, mangroves, mud flats
and rocks support a prolific and varied population of wildlife,
some of it rare. Among the birds, 200 varieties have been
reported, including penguins, pelicans, mutton birds, swans,
ibis, duck, spoonbills, oyster catchers and white-faced herons.
Near the entrance to the Bay, seals thrive in one of Australia's
largest colonies. Elsewhere, the region supports koalas and
at least two species close to extinction - the potoroo, or rat
kangaroo, and the New Holland mouse.

In the waters and the bed of the Bay, marine life is richly
diversified. The fishing is good; so, too, are the opportunities for swimming and water sports. In brief, Westernport Bay
has all the elements needed for the recreation of Melbourne's
urban-weary masses.

In itself, that exposes the environment to stresses; but the
main threat comes from the growth pressures generated by the
city itself. Now populated by around 2.5 million people, the
city by the year 2000 is expected to have a population of four
to five million. Unchecked, this growth would inevitably
swallow much of the Westernport region, absorbing it into a
Melbourne megalopolis.

Such rural land as remained would be subjected to more intensive
farming practices. As for urban and industrial developments,
the attractions of Westernport would prove irresistable: deep,
sheltered waters for ships; natural gas energy from the Bass
Strait fields for industry; adjacent markets; a flat hinterland
easy to connect to existing rail, road, power, water and
community services.

Westernport poses the problem of how to utilize a resource,
using the word "utilize" in the broad sense which includes
conservation.

For the authorities, "utilizing" Westernport involves them in
arbitrating between the competing claims of various sectors of
society.

One of the focal problems is the susceptibility to pollution
particularly in the northern reaches where the most extensive
mudflats are found and the tidal flushing is least adequate.
Phillip Island, located across the mouth, restricts the
entrances to the Bay to 200 yards in the eastern opening and
five miles in the western opening. As a result, the exchange of
water in the Bay is slow, with the dominant tidal movements
passing through the western opening. Of the tidal waters
entering the western opening, thirty percent merely move in and
out of the entrance channel.

Westernport has been recognised as a fine port with deep,
sheltered anchorage since it was discovered and named by George
Bass in January, 1798, but it was adjoining Port Phillip Bay
which became Victoria's major commercial and industrial port.
Now with a dramatic increase in deep draught shipping, particularly for industrial cargoes, the importance of Westernport
has increased because the entrance to Port Phillip Bay is too
shallow for these new vessels. No other harbour on the Victorian coast, and few in Australia, can match Westernport's deep
sheltered waters. Almost completely landlocked, its depth at
the entrance exceeds 30 metres, dropping to a minimum at low
water of 14 metres in the Northern Arm and 15 metres in the
Western Arm.

Other factors add to its value as an industrial port. In the
vicinity of Hastings, the deep water channel is flanked on both
sides by large tracts of flat land suitable for heavy industrial development. It is close to the Melbourne-Dandenong-
Berwick axis, where the thrust of Melbourne's growth is greatest.
Similarly it is close to the Melbourne-Gippsland axis with its
rich resources. The large labour and consumer market of
Melbourne is nearby, and it is central to the entire market of
Southeast Australia.   The area is also well served by land
transportation.

The first moves in the development of industrial potential began
with the choice, in 1963, of Crib Point as the site for an oil
refinery.

Now almost any form of development within the drainage catchment
of the bay, whether for residential, recreational or industrial
purposes, will require control to prevent pollution.

To the task of finding answers, government and industry have so
far allocated more than $2 million.

This is a beginning. The study won't completely solve all
problems, but should at least avert any possibility of an
ecological disaster by neglect or default.

Earthquakes
It was inevitable that an altogether new concern for the human
environment would emerge in the 1960s. The rapid growth in the
world's population had begun in earnest in the 1950s, and with
the increase in numbers of people, particularly those in urban
areas, there had to come an increasing confrontation with
nature. The most obvious examples are the people killed by
earthquake. If there are more people on the surface of the
earth then it's natural that with the same frequency of earthquakes more lives will be endangered.

We need not only to protect the environment from man's destructive efforts but also to protect mankind from the devastation
wrought by nature.

In one recent year, more than 110,000 people died and 215
million others were affected as a result of natural disasters in
different parts of the world. Most of this toll occurred in
disaster-prone developing countries. It has been established
that between the years 1947 and 1970 more than one million lives
were lost through various kinds of natural disasters. The
region most severely affected was Asia.

Not only is the loss of life enormous. There is also a very
severe dislocation of economic life accompanying these natural
disasters. In five countries of Central America, for example,
between the years 1960 and 1975 disaster damage averaged 2.3
percent of the gross national product in these countries taken
together. In addition to this direct economic destruction there
were many indirect effects - greater incidence of certain
diseases, some flooding and some dislocation of people from
their homes and from their social lives. In the major
Nicaraguan earthquake in 1972, the total reconstruction costs
were close to $1 billion (U.S.) - that is to say 50 percent of
the gross national product for that year.

The devastating earthquake that hit China in 1976 took half a
million lives.

Fig. 8.3 and the following list of 20th century hurricanes show
something of the extent of these natural disasters.

1900 A hurricane and storm surge killed about 6,000 persons
     in the Galveston, Tex., area.

1928 About 1,800 persons died in a hurricane and floods in the
     Lake Okeechobee area of Florida. The storm also killed
     1,100 persons in Puerto Rico and the West Indies.

1932 The storm surge following a hurricane drowned 2,500 persons
     in Santa Cruz del Sur, Cuba.

1935 The barometer fell to 66.93 cm during a hurricane that
     struck Tampa, Fla. This was the lowest reading ever
     recorded in the Western Hemisphere. More than 400 persons
     were killed in the storm. Winds reached from 240 to 320
     km/hour in the Florida Keys.

1938 A hurricane killed about 600 persons in southern New
     England and on Long Island, N.Y.

1954 Hurricane Hazel killed 1,000 people in Haiti and 80 in
     Toronto.

1955 Hurricane Diane caused about $1-3/4 billion in damage from
     North Carolina to New England. The storm killed 184 per-
     sons.

1957 Hurricane Audrey struck Louisiana, Mississippi, and Texas,
     killing 390 persons.

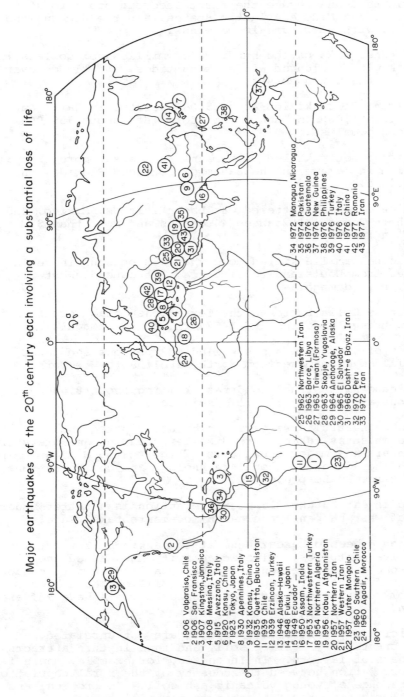

Major earthquakes of the 20th century each involving a substantial loss of life

Fig. 8.3 Major earthquakes of the 20th Century

1   1906 Valparaiso, Chile
2   1906 San Fransisco
3   1907 Kingston, Jamaica
4   1908 Messina, Italy
5   1915 Avezzano, Italy
6   1920 Kansu, China
7   1923 Tokyo, Japan
8   1930 Apennines, Italy
9   1932 Kansu, China
10 1935 Quetta, Baluchistan
11 1939 Chile
12 1939 Erzincan, Turkey
13 1946 Alaska-Hawaii
14 1948 Fukui, Japan
15 1949 Ecuador
16 1950 Assam, India
17 1953 Northwestern Turkey
18 1954 Northern Algeria
19 1956 Kabul, Afghanistan
20 1957 Northern Iran
21 1957 Western Iran
22 1957 Outer Mongolia
23 1960 Southern Chile
24 1960 Agadir, Morocco
25 1962 Northwestern Iran
26 1963 Barce, Libya
27 1963 Taiwan (Formosa)
28 1963 Skopje, Yugoslavia
29 1964 Anchorage, Alaska
30 1965 El Salvador
31 1968 Dasht-e Bayaz, Iran
32 1970 Peru
33 1972 Iran
34 1972 Managua, Nicaragua
35 1974 Pakistan
36 1976 Guatemala
37 1976 New Guinea
38 1976 Philippines
39 1976 Turkey
40 1976 Italy
41 1976 China
42 1977 Romania
43 1977 Iran

1960 Hurricane Donna became the first recorded storm to strike
     Florida, the Middle Atlantic States, and the New England
     States, with hurricane-force winds.

1961 Hurricane Carla caused hundreds of millions of dollars in
     damage with prolonged winds, high tides, and floods over
     most of the Texas coast.

1963 Hurricane Flora killed about 5,000 persons in Haiti and
     more than 1,000 in Cuba. The storm left about 750,000
     persons homeless.

1965 Hurricane Betsy killed 76 persons and caused more than $1
     billion in damage in the Bahamas, southern Florida, and
     Louisiana.

1967 Hurricane Beulah battered Caribbean islands, Mexico, and
     southern Texas. It caused 44 deaths and more than $1
     billion in damage.

1969 Hurricane Camille killed more than 250 persons in seven
     states from Louisiana to Virginia. It caused about $1½
     billion in damage.

1970 Hurricane Celia battered the Texas coast near Corpus Chris-
     ti, causing 11 deaths and $467 million in damage.

1972 Floods of Hurricane Agnes killed 122 persons and caused
     $2 billion in damage from North Carolina to New York.

1974 Hurricane Fifi struck Honduras, killing about 8,000
     persons and causing $1 billion in damage.

Many of these natural disasters can be anticipated and
preventive measures taken. Pre-disaster planning and disaster
prevention are now major endeavours of the United Nations. In
fact, with the advent of global technology and communications,
most disasters can be prevented.

First step in earthquake disaster prevention is a better understanding of what happens when earth movements take place.

Volcanoes have been of great benefit to mankind. Yet, during
the last five centuries, volcanic activity has caused the
death of some 200,000 persons, and has resulted in a tremendous
amount of suffering and property loss. Millions have been
driven from their homes, and even greater numbers have suffered
starvation.

The beneficial and destructive aspects are not unrelated.
Volcanoes create very fertile soil, and this in turn attracts
large numbers of farmers. In Indonesia, for example, there is
a close correlation between the density of the rural population
and the presence of young volcanic-ash soil. In tropical and
subtropical regions, rapid leaching removes plant nutrients

from the soil. But volcanic ash is rich in plant nutrients,
largely contained in glass which is readily broken down by
weathering, releasing the nutrients for plant use. Thus ash
renews the fertility of the soil.

The richest soils tend to be closest to the volcanoes, attracting the agricultural population into the areas which are most
subject to volcanic destruction. Again turning to Indonesia
for example, the region close to the base of Merapi, in central
Java, is highly fertile, and more than a million people live in
villages in the adjacent river valleys and on the flanks of the
mountains. Yet Merapi is one of the most active and dangerous
volcanoes in the world, and every few decades eruptions take
several thousand lives.

Ash thrown into the air by explosion is deposited as a blanket
of fragments that usually decrease in average size with increasing distance from the vent. The coarsest fragments commonly
pile up directly around the vent to form a pumice cone. The
finer material is carried by the wind, often scattered in different directions, to distances of hundreds of kilometres and the
resulting ash deposit may be extending many times farther down
wind than up wind.

Rain falling through clouds of ash in the air may form mud balls
as much as a centimetre in diameter, and heavy falls may result
in layers of these over areas of a few square kilometres.

The finer ash is seldom hot enough when it reaches the ground to
start fires. Commonly, however, the weight of deposited ash
causes roofs to cave in. Thus, during the 1971 eruption of
Fuego, in Guatemala, a thickness of 30 cm of ash 8 km west of
the volcano caused about one fifth of the roofs in the town of
Yepocapa to collapse.

When it is dry, the ash may be light enough for the roof to
support it, but rain may rapidly increase its weight and result
in sudden collapse of the roof. There have been very numerous
examples of collapse of roofs under loads of ash since the
destruction of Pompeii in 79 A.D., and not uncommonly people
have been killed as a result. An obvious remedy is to shovel
the ash off the roof before the load gets too great.

Working outdoors during a heavy ash fall may be difficult,
however, due to breathing of the ash-laden air and to the intense darkness that often prevails. The sharp ash particles
are extremely irritating to the respiratory passages, and in-
halation of excessive amounts of ash may result in death.
Ordinary industrial dust masks are very effective, although the
filters may have to be cleaned frequently; an ordinary cloth
tied across the face, especially when it is dampened, provides
reasonably good protection. Goggles may be desirable to prevent
irritation of the eyes.

Heavy ash falls may disrupt water supplies by clogging streams

and wells, or filters in water systems, and water may become
acid from leaching of the ash. During the Katmai eruption the
people of Kodiak had to be supplied with water from ships in the
harbour; and during the eruption of Irazu, Costa Rica, in 1963,
ash suspended in river water clogged the filters in the water
works of the city of San Jose. Suspended ash can be removed
from piped water by a temporary filter, or even a cloth bag tied
over the faucet. As soon as the possibility of a dangerously
heavy ash fall becomes apparent, sufficient water to serve
essential needs for several days should be stored indoors. Ash
washed from the streets of San Jose during the Irazu eruption
blocked the storm drains, causing flooding during subsequent
rains.

Ash flows can issue from vents at the summit of big composite
cones, or from fissures not directly associated with any large
cone. A good example was the one that formed Crater Lake, in
Oregon, about 6,000 years ago.

The great speed and often great volume of ash flows make it impossible to control them in any way. Lessening their destruc-
tiveness in the future depends on recognition of conditions in
the volcano, and prediction of the eruption long enough to
permit evacuation of the endangered area.

Earthquake prediction took a new twist in 1977 as a result of
the work of a Japanese scientist, Tsunesi Rikitaki.

He recently finished compiling 157 case histories of strange
behavior of animals before big quakes in Japan, China and
Europe during the last 300 years.

The yak, a Tibetan ox, is only one of several animals that may
be able to anticipate quakes.

Cats, mice, caged birds and even tigers in zoos have histories
of acting up before the ground begins to tremble.

In China, local governments keep several types of animals under
observation as an earthquake-forecasting measure. Detection of
strange animal behavior is credited with saving lives in the
1976 quake in China's Fukien Province.

Unusual movements of fish also have been a tip-off of an
approaching quake. Just before the quake that devastated Tokyo
and Yokahama in 1923, catfish were seen leaping from rivers like
trout, something they normally don't do.

There have been several cases in which mice and birds disappeared from a locality just before a major earthquake. Cats desert-
ed a number of villages in northern Italy two or three hours
before a severe quake hit there in 1975.

In other cases, caged birds begin flying violently and beating
against the bars of their cages.

Waste Management: A Case Study of Values/Analysis
Urbanized and industrialized areas produce large and increasing
amounts of waste materials for which acceptable disposal methods
have to be found. Industrial heartlands like Tokyo, Ruhr
Region, Southern Ukraine, and Northeastern United States pose
the greatest problems.

The following series of readings from the High School Geography
Project deal with the disposal of gaseous, liquid and solid
wastes in the New York Waste Management Region. See Fig. 8.4.
5 readings are provided for each of these three categories.

Fig. 8.4 New York Waste Management Region

Three small group discussions based on these readings will lead
naturally into a consideration and analysis of environmental
values. To ensure that this process of valuing is carried out,
the groups should tackle their discussions as follows:

1. Each group decides what are the two worst problems in the
    category under discussion - gaseous, liquid, or solid.

2. Best remedy for the two worst problems are then proposed
    by each group.

3. Finally one representative is taken from each group, to
    form a new group within which the conflicts created by the
    different solutions are faced, and new overall best remedies
    proposed.

Gaseous Readings

1. AIR AND HEALTH.

    When a city's air becomes so foul that it blackens stone
    buildings, withers plants, blisters paint, sends cleaning
    bills soaring, and makes people's eyes smart, it is time to
    ask how much of a health hazard it is.

    The evidence is strong that heavy smog in cities such as
    New York and Los Angeles can give patients suffering from
    respiratory ailments a turn for the worse. The evidence is
    not so strong that dirty air can cause the disease in the
    first place.

    Smog has been blamed for some major disasters. One of the
    earliest, recorded in 1948, was in the small industrial city
    of Donora, Pennsylvania. Half of its 12,000 people were
    sick during a period of protracted smog and 20 died. In New
    York City 168 deaths were attributed to a long drawn-out
    smog in 1966. The greatest loss of life ever reported as
    the result of air pollution was in London in 1952. Nearly
    4,000 people were said to have been killed by a heavy smog
    that lasted for days. But in all three of these cities
    those who died were already sick, though many who became ill
    at the time thought their illness was caused by smog.

    A Symposium on Air Pollution and Respiratory Diseases held
    in Buffalo, New York, heard a report on a state medical
    study. The researchers had found that many more workers
    were absent from their jobs because of respiratory diseases
    on days when the amount of sulphur dioxide and dust in the
    air was high than when only small quantities were present.
    However, the amount of carbon monoxide in the air seemed to
    make no difference so far as respiratory diseases were
    concerned.

    Professor Rene Dubos of Rockefeller University believes that
    the harmful effects of pollution are likely to increase as
    people are exposed to it over longer and longer periods of
    time. He wrote that people are exposed to massive doses of
    pollutants from the time of birth. It is possible that we
    will suffer the effects of pollution much more than previous
    generations have. He believes that people are engaged in a
    kind of chemical warfare of pollution against themselves,
    and especially against their children.

2.   THE SMOG SEASON.

The heaviest concentration of air pollution - the smog that
causes eye irritation and coughing in people, haze in the
air, and damage to paint and plants - results from a combination of four factors: fumes from man-made machines, sunlight that converts the fumes into damaging gases, lack of
wind to blow them away, and a temperature inversion that
keeps them from rising into the atmosphere.

In cities such as New York and Los Angeles where smog is
severe, it would be a boon if one could predict exactly the
hour or even days when all four will happen at once. Then
measures to prevent or control the pollution might be taken.
What is known can be summarized as follows:

Fumes are the only one of the four that can be forecast
fairly accurately. They are twice the amount in New York
and its neighbouring cities on working days as on weekends
and holidays. On working days the peak of pollution is
reached during the morning and evening rush hours, 7 to 10
A.M. and 4 to 7 P.M. These six hours are 25 percent of the
day but produce at least 37.8 percent of the car exhaust
fumes that account for most of the hydrocarbons in the air.

Sunlight is not as constant in New York as in Los Angeles -
one reason why the West Coast city is often said to have
the more distressing smogs. However, the sun does shine in
New York 59 percent of all the minutes between sunrise and
sunset. The month by month percentages of sunshine in New
York are as follows:

January	48	July	48
February	46	August	49
March	53	September	71
April	55	October	63
May	56	November	48
June	68	December	45

Winds above 7 miles an hour will prevent smog from accumulating to the point of discomfort. In New York City windless
conditions (less than 7 miles an hour) prevail:

> June through October: more than one third
>   of the time.

> December through March: less than one fourth
>   of the time.

> November, April, and May: between one third
>   and one fourth.

Temperature inversion is the name used for a condition in
the atmosphere where a cool or cold layer of air close to
the ground is overlain by a warmer layer. When a cool layer
of air exists next to the ground, the warmer air above acts
as a ceiling. The surface air cannot rise. Fumes and dust

accumulate in this surface layer. Pollution from the morning is still there when the evening rush hour begins. The
worst smogs in history have occurred when a temperature
inversion lasted for several days.

3. A BURNING PROBLEM.

The haze that hangs over the city may be simply moisture but
it is far more likely to be a man-made mixture of dust,
fumes, and gases. It is created by burning - the burning
of fuel in motor vehicles, factories, and power plants, and
the burning of refuse by incineration.

In some places it is the accumulation from hundreds of
thousands of separate engines and furnaces. In others it
may emanate almost entirely from a single source. In the
New York region the haze usually has a great many contrib-
utors.

It also has a great many ingredients. The principal ones
are grains of dust of various kinds, sulphur dioxide, carbon
monoxide, oxides of nitrogen, hydrocarbons, sulphuric acid
mist, organic aerosols, fluorides, and hydrogen sulphide.

The sources for 480,000 tonnes of dust in the region are as
follows:

	Dust Generated	Dust Discharged into Atmosphere
Heating of homes, offices, factories	25,000 tonnes	25,000 tonnes
Apartment house incinerators	15,000 tonnes	15,000 tonnes
Municipal incinerators	110,000 tonnes	55,000 tonnes
Open burning	120,000 tonnes	120,000 tonnes
Motor vehicles	30,000 tonnes	30,000 tonnes
Power plants using coal	105,000 tonnes	25,000 tonnes
Power plants using oil or gas	5,000 tonnes	5,000 tonnes
Other industrial processes	70,000 tonnes	10,000 tonnes
Total	480,000 tonnes	285,000 tonnes

Hydrocarbons in the air come entirely from two sources:
internal combustion engines and oil refining. Cars, trucks,
and buses produce 1,215 million tonnes of the region's annual
total of 1,470 million tonnes of hydrocarbons.

More than half the sulphur dioxide in the region's air comes
from the oil that heats houses, factories, and commercial
buildings. Coal and oil burned to create energy provide

most of the rest.

All coal and oil contain some sulphur, At high temperatures
it escapes as sulphur dioxide with a little sulphuric acid
mist. The sources of 1,940 million tonnes of sulphur
dioxide gas in the region's atmosphere were as follows:

Heating	1,150,000	tonnes
Power plants (coal)	485,000	tonnes
Power plants (oil)	165,000	tonnes
Oil refineries	115,000	tonnes
Motor vehicles	20,000	tonnes
Incineration	5,000	tonnes

4.   SELF-CLEANING AIR.

The amount of dust and other impurities that the atmosphere
can absorb without apparent visible effects is almost unlimited. As yet all the new air polluting machines available could not cloud the enormous mass of air that surrounds
the earth if only the dust and fumes could be evenly spread.

The layer of atmosphere that performs the self-cleaning
operation averages 11 km in thickness. It is called the
troposphere.

The main factor that enables the air we breathe to preserve
its quality is wind. Wind at a velocity of five miles an
hour will carry most impurities of the earth. Dust from
major volcanic explosions has been spread all over the world
because it has been lifted high enough to catch the prevailing air currents in the upper air.

Wind can also prevent one special pollutant - hydrocarbons
from automobile exhausts - from reacting with other gases
in the presence of sunlight to form more unpleasant gases.

In addition to the spreading out of pollution by winds, air
is cleansed by precipitation. As rain falls through the air
it carries down dust particles. It also dissolves gases and
carries them to the ground.

5.   INSIDE THE FACTORY CHIMNEY.

The principal industrial polluters are power plants and
petroleum refineries. All other industrial processes put
together produce only 3½ percent of the dust in the air.

However, factories other than power plants and petroleum
refineries do burn oil to heat their premises and so are
responsible for a certain percentage of the sulphur dioxide
in winter.

The possibilities of drastically reducing the gases from the
chimneys of heating plants, power plants, and oil refineries
are very good. Low pollution fuels are being used more and

more. Equipment to prevent gaseous wastes from escaping
from chimneys is increasingly common.

Most of the dust that gets into the air comes from incineration. Improved equipment is already being required to
reduce dust from apartment and municipal incinerators. This
is accomplished by devices which clean the smoke. If the
operation is large enough, it is feasible to install a trap
of some kind right in the chimney. Some of these traps
remove the dust by charging the smoke particles electrically
so they will stick to surfaces with the opposite charge.

Expectations are that the region will have less sulphur
pollutants in the year 2000 than in 1970. Assumptions are
that more heating will be done with gas or by electricity,
that almost no power will be generated by coal, and that the
sulphur dioxide released by oil will be cut 50 percent.

Liquid Readings

1. DOWN THE DRAIN.

The New York City Region pours 6 billion litres of liquid
wastes into sewers every day. The daily sewage contains
1,700 tonnes of organic matter that pollutes water.

Sanitary engineers measure the organic solids in liquid
wastes by the amount of oxygen required to decompose or
break them down and render them harmless. This is called
the Biochemical Oxygen Demand, abbreviated as BOD.

Water (H_2O) is 88 percent oxygen by weight, but wastes cannot extract it. This is the oxygen "breathed" by all plants
and animals that live in water. If the oxygen is taken off
to decompose wastes, none is left for fish. Nor will the
water be tasteful as drinking water for people. That is
why water is aerated in large fountains at waterworks and
reservoirs. The process puts as much oxygen into the water
as it will hold.

The Biochemical Oxygen Demand (BOD) of the New York Region's
liquid wastes amount to 700,000 tonnes.

In areas of sparse population and ample, fast-flowing
streams, BOD is easily satisfied because there is enough
oxygen to take care of wastes and still not deprive the fish.
But where large quantities of liquid wastes are produced,
it becomes necessary to treat them before they are discharged into river or lake or ocean if the water is not to be
contaminated.

Sewer treatment plants are simple operations, but they do
several different things. First, screens remove the coarser
nonorganic solids - tin cans, bottles, and the like. Then
settling tanks allow more of the heavier material to settle

out. Biological and chemical processes that result in the
decay of complex organic matter into simpler compounds are
encouraged. Some of the solid organic matter changes into
gases. Much of the rest becomes soluble compounds. In
these processes all of the disease-producing germs are destroyed.

The liquids flowing out of an efficient sewage treatment
plant are not recognizable as sewage and are generally
inoffensive as to odor or taste. Solids may have been
reduced by 90 percent and BOD by 80 percent. The liquids
actually may be quite rich in soluble compounds which favour
plant growth.

Improved treatment is likely to be the principal method of
keeping BOD within limits that can be met by the water
systems of the densely populated parts of the region.
Liquid wastes will increase because of increased affluence
and therefore increased consumption. This increase could
more than offset any reduction of BOD from improved industrial processes and recirculation of water.

2.   WATERS OF DEATH.

The bays and coves all along the coast line of New York
Region used to be famous for shellfish. The oyster and clam
beds, once highly productive and valued at millions of
dollars, lie abandoned. The oysters and clams are still
there and in many places thriving. But the sewage of
neighbouring cities and towns has polluted them so badly
that it is not safe to eat them.

Forty years ago the shad fishermen of the Hudson River were
a prosperous community, scattered for the most part in
towns along the west bank. Now they have ceased to exist.
The fish can no longer make it through the pollution of the
water between New York and New Jersey to their spawning
grounds upstream.

Thus, even in some of the thinly settled parts of the New
York Region, poor waste management has destroyed the fish
and wildlife areas. Trout have disappeared from polluted
streams in Sullivan County, by far the least densely populated county in the region.

Only a few miles west of the former shad fisheries lies a
marsh that once was a happy hunting ground for sportsmen
from New York, Newark, and a dozen smaller cities nearby.
Known as the Hackensack Meadows - the Hackensack River runs
through it - the marsh is dead and desolate today. The
wastes dumped there by one of the busiest industrial
sections of the country have poisoned both land and water.

3.   LIQUID WASTE CONTROLS

Steps to control the liquid wastes of a community are
usually considered only after the habitat has begun to de-
teriorate. As long as the water continues to be drinkable,
safe for swimming, and without any offensive odour, controls
are not even discussed.

In some of the more sparsely populated areas of the New York
Region this condition still prevails. The two counties of
the region with the fewest people produce only one fiftieth
as much waste as the two most populated counties. Within
a single county, conditions may be very different from place
to place. The southern half of Passaic County, New Jersey,
has twelve times the population of the northern half and
produces forty times as much liquid waste.

As population and liquid wastes increase, the first reaction
of communities is to enlarge their sewage systems. But when
it gets to the point of seriously polluting the bodies of
water into which the sewers empty, communities begin to
treat liquid wastes to reduce the BOD before the water is
discharged.

Yet New York City is still allowing millions of litres of
raw sewage every day to flow into the waters that surround
it.

Neither industries nor municipalities go to the expense of
treating their liquid wastes unless pushed somehow by the
pressure of public opinion. With costs increasing, more
stringent government controls may have to be adopted. These
controls are designed to reduce the amount of liquid wastes
discharged into rivers, lakes, and other waters.

Most controls probably would have to be imposed regionally
to be effective. A municipality may be reluctant to set
fees for local industries or regulate their liquid waste
discharges if neighbouring municipalities do not do so for
fear that some factories might be moved away and new ones
would not be attracted. Similarly regional action on
sewage treatment plants may be needed. Local governments
often refuse to treat their sewage properly unless forced to
do so by a higher authority such as a state agency.

4.   INDUSTRIAL WASTE

Among all the polluters of water in modern society, factories are commonly regarded as the worst offenders. Certainly they are the most obvious, but they do not always do
most of the damage. In the New York Region, industry
produces only 17 percent of the harmful liquid wastes.

The thirty-one counties of the New York Region are far from
equal producers of liquid wastes by industry. Six counties
produce only negligible quantities of the region's total:

four produce more than half, and five produce more than two thirds.

One factor to be considered in solving industrial liquid waste problems, especially for factories that consume a great deal of water, is the amount of water recirculated during the manufacturing process. Paper mills, for example, use enormous quantities of water, and the water has to be clean and fresh. For every tonne of pulp they produce, they have to flush away another tonne of waste which is dissolved or suspended in the water. Only very fast-flowing streams can handle the waste of a paper mill without being contaminated to the point where fish cannot live in them. If a factory recirculates its water, the water is treated and the BOD is reduced. In the paper industry as a whole, 32.1 percent of the water used is recirculated. In other industries needing large quantities of water, recirculation is as high as 77.4 percent and as low as 1.6 percent. Theoretically, for industry as a whole, 98 percent of the water intake can be recirculated.

Big industrial consumers of water nearly all discharge their liquid waste directly into the local waters, whether or not they treat it first to reduce the BOD. A survey of a dozen large industrial consumers of water in the New York Region showed that in only five cases was as much as 10 percent of the waste discharged channelled into public sewers.

5.   INDESTRUCTIBLE SUDS.

One day some years ago a mass of foam 12 metres high rose like an iceberg out of the Rock River in Illinois. It was below a dam over which the river, carrying the eventual run-off from thousands of washing machines and dishwashers, plunged in what was usually a handsome waterfall. But this day the churning water at the bottom produced one of the most spectacular displays of suds ever seen.

The incident occurred at the peak of a nation-wide argument over what synthetic detergents, replacing old-fashioned soap, were doing to the country's water supplies. Their popularity began after World War Two and soon they were being used more than soap. Within 20 years 80 percent of home washing was being done with detergents.

The chemical that helped make detergents better cleansers turned out to be a great sudser when it got into river water. This chemical, alkyl benzene sulfonate, is not "degradable"; that is, it will not disintegrate in water as do the chemicals in soap. So the alkyl benzene sulfonate kept building up in streams, and the faster it flowed or the more it was churned up the greater the foam it produced.

In many parts of the New York Region, and many other parts of the country where people got their water from streams or wells, so much of this chemical accumulated that a glass of water from the kitchen tap had a collar of foam on it.

Throughout the whole debate on detergents no one in authority urged a return to soap for most washing purposes. The
more powerful cleaning properties of detergents had won the
market. That they created a serious waste disposal problem
was not considered a good enough reason to give them up.
Instead, the waste problem was solved. A new substance,
linear alyklate sulfonate was marketed. It was just as good
a cleaning agent as the problem detergent, but it had the
added asset that it could be broken down by the action of
bacteria in rivers.

Solid Readings

1. THE POLITICAL GAME.

Everybody creates wastes; everybody has some responsibility
for getting rid of them. In this country "everybody" often
means the government; this is the politics of junk. For
government makes the rules, and wherever more than a few
people live or work near each other, government has a share
in the disposal.

In the New York Region there are literally thousands of
governmental units. At present, the responsibility for
managing the region's solid wastes is scattered among public
bodies that range from the federal government in Washington,
D.C., to the village council of the smallest settlement.

These agencies may and often do have conflicting views on
what is sound waste management. A town wants to use a given
piece of land for a dump, even though it will soon become an
eyesore. The county thinks the same piece of land would be
a great place for a park. The state sees it as land to be
condemned for a new highway. The federal government proposes to put it under water as part of a flood control project.

Which one of these wins is the essence of the process sometimes called "the political game." More players enter the
game as it becomes clear that political bodies with no
immediate responsibility for disposing of solid wastes have
an interest - agencies that deal with water supply, sewage
systems, industrial development, air pollution, zoning, and
urban renewal.

The political complexities are well illustrated in what The
New York Times once called "probably the world's biggest
garbage dump." This is the Hackensack Meadows in New
Jersey, 18,000 acres (about the size of Manhattan Island)
said to be worth a billion dollars in their unimproved
state. One side of the marsh is less than five kilometres
from New York's West Side; the other is even closer to
Newark. Millions of tonnes of New York City refuse, as much
as a million tonnes a year, have been dumped there. A great

deal of refuse has made a foundation for the few highways
that cross the Meadows.

For a hundred years plans of public and private groups to
develop all or part of the Meadows have failed because the
governments concerned could never agree on who should share
what. These governments were as follows:

The United States, mainly the Army Corps of Engineers

The state of New Jersey

Two counties - Bergen and Hudson

Fourteen cities or towns - Jersey City, Kearny, Secaucus,
North Bergen, Ridgefield, Little Ferry, Moonachie,
Teterboro, Carlstadt, East Rutherford, Lyndhurst,
Fairview, and North Arlington.

2.   REDUCING WASTE.

The trend in North America is toward consuming goods quickly,
then throwing them away. Not only are many items deliberately made for shorter life than was the case in the past, but
they are more elaborately packed. Furthermore, the wrapp-
ings are becoming more and more difficult to destroy.

The biggest single item in waste is paper. This now constitutes one half of the solid wastes in the United States and
the proportion is rising. If more than half of it could be
salvaged for reuse in paper mills the New York region's
annual rubbish heap in the year 2000 would be 20 million
tonnes smaller.

Factories and food processors could devise new manufacturing
methods or find different raw materials that would reduce
the weight or volume of their present refuse. The possibilities have hardly been explored as yet. But if containers -
bottles, cans, plastics, and paper cartons - could be made
of a reusable material, the waste reduction could be as much
as 10 percent. The ideal container is the ice cream cone.

Consumers and industry ought to be persuaded to return to
practices that produced less waste. Reusable diapers for
babies - the old-fashioned kind that got washed - and reusable crates for refrigerators are examples.

Wastes can sometimes be turned into a useful, profitable by-
product of the manufacturing process. One of the earliest
examples was cottonseed. Before Eli Whitney invented the
cotton gin in 1793, cottonseed was left to rot on the farm.
But after his invention, cottonseed piled up at the gins
where cotton was being processed. Cottonseed then became
a nuisance until it was discovered that it could be turned
into valuable products: oil, cattle feed, and fertilizer.

3. USE FOR JUNK.

New York has staged two World's Fairs on its trash. In 1939
and 1964 millions of people came to see exhibits and entertainment from virtually every country - all arranged on a
one-time marsh called Flushing Meadows, made into solid land
from the city's debris. In between the two fairs, the United Nations held its early Assembly meetings there, and since
1964 it has been a park.

A great deal of land in the New York Region has been created
in this way. Governor's Island in New York Bay is twice its
original size. Most of the new half, the largest of all
Coast Guard bases, is composed of landfill carried by truck
and barge from the excavation of the city's subway in the
early 1900s. The 587 hectare Great Kills Park on Staten
Island, one of the metropolis's biggest playgounds, consists
of millions of tonnes of city wastes deposited there 30
years ago.

At least two thirds of the region's refuse goes into making
new land - filling in low or swampy areas. Given the expected growth of both population and per capita waste, it is
estimated that in the year 2000 the region may triple its
production of solid wastes annually, if it can find places
to fill, and if this reamins the preferred disposal method.

4. BURN IT.

Of the more than 17 million tonnes of solid wastes produced
in the New York Region, one third was burned. The hope was
to get rid of it - or at least leave so little ash, smoke,
soot, or other residue that it would not be troublesome.

Incineration has become the region's favourite method of
disposal for any wastes that can be burned. Three fifths of
all the wastes burned in the region are consumed in New York
City incinerators, where a little less than half the
region's solid wastes originate.

But whether this is the best method is questioned by some
authorities. Certainly without controls over where refuse
is burned and what sort of incinerator is used, this method
of waste disposal could become troublesome. New York City,
for example, had to adopt stringent rules to prevent refuse
burning from putting unnecessary, dangerous, or objectionable
wastes into the city's air.

The early incinerators operated at temperatures that were
too low. Furnaces that generate 1000°C are needed if most
of the impurities that formerly escaped are to be consumed.
Devices are now used to catch impurities and wash them out.

The proportion of wastes which are disposed of by burning
is expected to drop, reducing air pollution. Several large
incinerators more than thirty years old have been shut down

and many small apartment houses closed their incinerators
and had the garbage collected by the city.

5.   CAR DUMPS.

Every year in New York City 25,000 automobiles are abandoned
on the streets. Some are simply left where they gave up,
others deliberately placed elsewhere. The owners remove the
license plates and anything portable that seems to be worth
carrying. This goes on in spite of the city's publicized
offer to remove free of charge any vehicle that a resident
wants to discard.

To dispose of this rubbish, New York City contracts with
wreckers to tow the derelicts away for scrap. At one time
it was thought that the city might make a profit on what the
wreckers were willing to pay. For even after the owner had
taken what he wanted from a car, parts could be salvaged.
But the private contractors grew increasingly reluctant to
pick up the junk. Before the wrecker comes, vandals remove
everything of the least value. An experienced gang can
strip an automobile clean in thirty seconds.

If we placed less emphasis on style changes, cars would not
go "out of fashion" and people would make them last longer.
Standardization of parts has been important in mass production. More standardization would increase the amount that
could be salvaged from a worn-out car. It might also make
less expensive the major repairs which would keep an old car
on the road.

Sometimes the wreckers or owners of "graveyards" try to
reduce the bulk by setting fire to the heaps of derelicts.
The result is a large addition to air pollution in the
vicinity but not much saving of space.

Identify the Issues

1.   What is the connection between increased population and
     increased danger from natural hazards?

2.   Discussions about environmental values often place people in
     one of two camps - those who feel that scientific and
     technological developments will solve our problems, and
     others who think that we must slow down development to pre-
     vent total destruction of our habitat. Which of these two
     do you favour?

3.   What changes should be made to cut down both the air
     pollution from automobiles, and the sizes of junk yards
     where derelict cars are dumped?

"In the planning, construction and management of human settlements we must find ways to use energy resources more efficiently
and give preference to those which are plentiful and renewable.
Innovative ideas and techniques are needed in conservation of
nonrenewable fuels, alternative sources (solar, wind, tidal
and geothermal), the role of nuclear power, and in correlations
between energy requirements and settlement design." From
Habitat Preparatory Paper.

CHAPTER NINE

Energy Crisis

The Arab Oil Embargo of 1973, in which oil prices skyrocketed, was the immediate cause of the world energy crisis. The oil price change marked a turning point in the history of non-renewable energy consumption. It caused a crisis in an international monetary system that was already in great danger of collapse.

For a time it was assumed that all would be well, but within a year it became clear to all that the international banking system was not coping with the $60 billion held by OPEC countries even though they had spent half of this amount on imports of goods and services. Even if new ways and means were found to recycle OPEC money, these ways could not absorb the $1 trillion that OPEC countries would have accumulated by 1980.

Arab action precipitated a crisis that would have hit us sooner or later without any change in present patterns of consumption. World oil extraction has been doubling every decade of this century. See Fig. 9.1. That is to say, between 1967 and 1977 we consumed more oil than in all the years before 1967. And this would have been repeated for 1977-1987 were it not for the 1973 boycott. How long could this rate of consumption last?

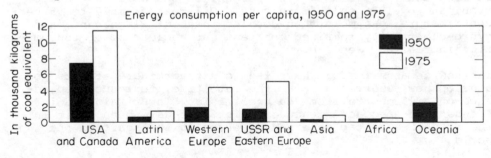

Fig. 9.1. Energy consumption per capita 1950 and 1975

There are many reasons for the escalation in rates of consumption. Sheer population numbers is one. Improved standard of living is another.

Mankind's first settlements were in the tropics. The invention of clothing, fire and shelter enabled gradual poleward expansion of settlement. With the discovery of coal, gas and petroleum as sources of heat it has been possible to establish large

settlements in very cold areas. In fact it has permitted the
settlement of the whole globe. Nearly 1 billion people now live
under climatic conditions that would have been quite unsuitable
for intensive settlement apart from coal, gas, and petroleum.

At the same time energy has been employed for cooling needs.
With an increase in the general standard of living there has
been a demand for more comfortable living conditions. These
have included refrigeration for the preservation of food, and
air conditioning, first in areas of work and in hospitals, and
then more generally in any place where people congregated.
Energy for these purposes is now required to meet the needs of
about 1½ billion people.

Oil and Gas
In 1950 the major energy consuming regions accounted for similar
shares of world production. By 1975 however, there were major
imbalances between what regions produced and what they consumed.

In 1975 Southwest Asia produced 36 percent of the world's supply
of oil, but consumed only two percent. The United States,
formerly a supplier of petroleum, is now unable to meet its own
needs, yet U.S. per capita oil consumption is about eight times
that of the rest of the world. Japan, the world's leading
energy importing nation, imports 99 percent of its oil supply.
The interrelationships and interdependence, then, between
producing and consuming nations is economically and politically
crucial. See Fig. 9.2.

The kinds of resources used for energy have changed dramatically.
In 1950 coal supplied over 61 percent of the world's consumption, and by 1975 only 32 percent. Oil rose from 27 to 45 percent: natural gas more than doubled to about 21 percent, and
hydro-electricity remained constant but nuclear power consumption increased. See Fig. 9.3.

The new demands for oil have led to extraordinary efforts to
develop new reserves and, at the same time, to reduce dependence on oil imports from Southwest Asia. In Britain and in
Scandanavia spectacular new oil platforms have been built in
the North Sea to tap undersea reserves in that part of the
world.

By 1977, a new one billion dollar platform - the world's biggest
- had been installed near the coast of Norway, on top of the
Statfjord oil field.

It stands 270 metres above the sea floor and is capable of
storing more than 200,000 tonnes of oil in its base.

The concrete platform was built in a sheltered fjord about midway between Stavanger and Bergen and then towed into place,
about 190 km offshore.

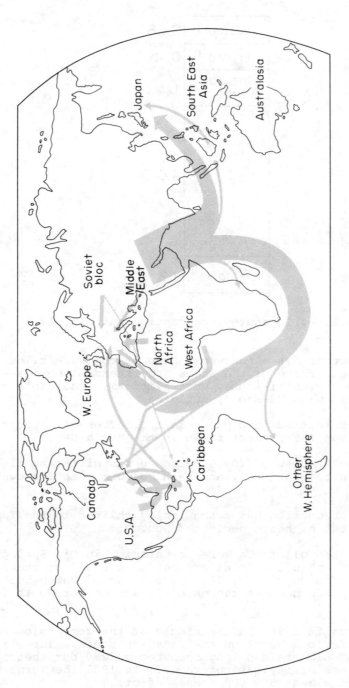

Fig. 9.2. Main world oil movements, 1975

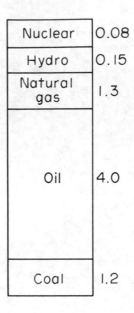

Fig. 9.3. World energy consumption pattern, 1975

The giant structure has a honeycomb base of concrete silos used for oil storage. Three of the silos are extended above sea level to support a multi-storey work platform. The whole struc-ture is as tall as an 83-storey building.

Statfjord A was settled into place in 150 metres of water to draw off oil from the richest field in the North Sea.

There is a regular crew of 200, living on six different floor levels, two men to a bedroom, and each bedroom with its own bathroom.

In Canada oil production has dramatically shifted to the Tar Sands, a rich but hitherto neglected source.

The first Canadian oil finds were in Ontario, in Oil Springs in Western Ontario in 1851. Total production for all of the 19th century never rose above 200,000 tonnes a year. Throughout this period the U.S. was seen as the main oil source for North America.

Then, in Alberta in 1936, in the middle of the depression years, the Turner Valley oil burst on the Canadian scene. The oil and gas reserves of Alberta had long been recognized but their extent and accessibility was not known. In 1937 the Turner Valley produced almost 500,000 tonnes of oil.

Alberta has never looked back. New discoveries quickly followed

Turner Valley. Production grew rapidly every year, and the
years of the Second World War added a special push to the
industry. By 1950 output had reached 4¼ million tonnes, by 1960
22 million, then up to 54 million by the year 1970. Today output is at the 85 million mark - supplying more than 80 percent
of all Canada's needs. Not all of these needs are being met
from Alberta, however, because of the way the pipelines are laid
out. Canadians export some Albertan oil to the U.S., then
import a similar amount from Venezuela and other places into
eastern Canada.

In addition to these large quantities of oil, Alberta produces
equally large quantities of gas. And in the background are the
new and hitherto almost untouched wealth of the Athabasca Tar
Sands.

These Sands contain as much as 50 billion tonnes of oil, more
than in all of the Arab countries of Southwest Asia. Why then
do we not use it to solve the western world's oil crisis? The
problem is cost. This oil does not lie in pools like other
fields. It is mixed with a sandy material which has to be spray-
ed with hot water jets before it can be taken to the surface.
There is an enormous amount of waste material involved in this
process, and this waste has to be taken away and dumped some-
where. The process is more like mining copper than oil.

While the price of oil was low it never paid to mine these tar
sands. Now that prices have risen so high it seems at last that
the Athabasca Sands are economically worthwhile. Enormous
amounts of money have been put into it in recent years by
governments, and by private industry. Yet a fear remains. What
if the prices of imported oil drop? Will it be worthwhile to
continue mining the sands? What will happen to the huge investments already made?

Canada is very much like the United States in energy consumption
per capita. See Fig. 9.4. And, since 1961, the rate of consumption has been increasing at an average rate of 7.3 percent
per year. The U.S. figure for the same period was 5.7 percent,
Sweden 8.8 percent, and Japan 17.7 percent.

Canada's consumption rate is higher than the U.S. because the
country is closer to the North Pole. Approximately 45 percent
of all energy consumed is related to settlement. Slightly more
than half goes into transportation, and a little less than half
is used in households and on farms. Of households use, 70 percent is for space heating. This means that about 15 percent of
all energy consumed in Canada is used to heat homes, one result
of living in a cold climate. The difference in housing stock,
period of construction, insulation quality and climatic differences explain the variations in energy use between Canadian
cities. Saskatoon, for example, devotes twice as much energy
per capita to its housing sector does as St. John's, Newfound-
land.

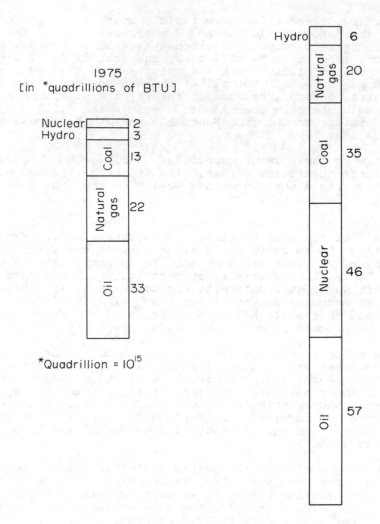

Fig. 9.4. U.S. and Canada
consumption patterns 1975 and 2000

The following additional statistics on world oil production,
transportation, and consumption for 1975 point up the present
state of dependence on others of so many large industrialized
countries. See also Fig. 9.5.

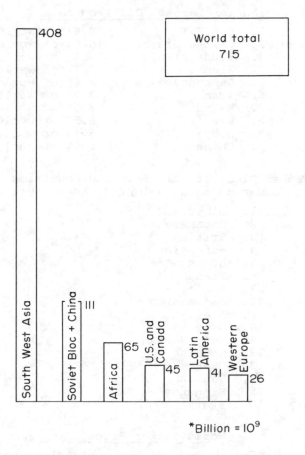

*Billion = 10^9

Fig. 9.5. World oil reserves, 1975

<u>The Ten Largest Oil Consumers</u>

1. U.S.A.
2. Japan
3. West Germany
4. Britain
5. France
6. Canada
7. Brazil
8. Sweden
9. Australia
10. Iran

The Ten Largest Oil Producers

1.   U.S.S.R.   18.5% of world production
2.   United States   15.0% of world production
3.   Saudi Arabia   14.1% of world production
4.   Iran   9.9% of world production
5.   Venezuela   4.0% of world production
6.   Iraq   3.7% of world production
7.   Nigeria   3.5% of world production
8.   Kuwait   3.5% of world production
9.   Libya   3.4% of world production
10. China   3.0% of world production

Tanker Fleet of Main Shipping Countries
(in order of total weight; 1 is biggest)

1.   Liberian
2.   Japanese
3.   British
4.   Norwegian
5.   Greek
6.   French
7.   U.S.A.
8.   Panamanian
9.   Italian
10. Swedish
11. West German
12. Spanish
13. USSR
14. Danish
15. Singapore
16. Brazilian

World Tanker Sizes

Size	Total Number
Under 100,000 tonnes	2600
100,000 - 250,000	600
250,000 - 500,000	300

Alternative Energy Sources

Buckminster Fuller, an advocate of conservation, is quite optimistic about the future. To him it is very clear that, using
proven energy resources, proven technologies using those resources, proven rates at which that technology can be employed, we
can, by 1985, have all of humanity enjoying the same energy that
is now enjoyed exclusively by North Americans. Evidence of
alternative energy sources, with the possible exception of
nuclear power, makes it difficult to accept this assertion.

Alternative energy resources are being studied and developed.
Some are environmentally controversial such as nuclear power.
Others, like coal, wind, and geothermal power are presently too

limited in scope. Solar energy, perhaps the most promising
major alternative, is too expensive. It will take years before
most of these alternative energy resources are ready for large-
scale operation.

In one country, Canada, for every man, woman, and child there
are 8,000 tons of coal available. It is a huge resource, bigger
in energy equivalent than all of the country's oil and gas
reserves. It is big enough to provide for Canada's energy needs
for a thousand years at the present rate of consumption. Why
is this coal resource not being used?

There are several reasons. For one thing coal has just been re-
discovered after 25 years of neglect. In one decade alone,
between 1951 and 1961, coal production in Canada fell from 19
million tonnes to 10 million tonnes. In the same period oil
production increased more than 400 percent while gas production
increased more than 800 percent. The problems of changing
equipment so that they burn coal instead of oil or gas are
costly and big.

A second group of problems relates to the technology of the
industry. The old ways of burning coal caused too much ash and
smoke for today's pollution-conscious consumers. To cope with
these pollutants a new processing method is being developed.
Coal is crushed, then expanded in a special type of burner so
that it behaves more like a liquid than a solid. As a result
the flame burns at a lower temperature and this cuts back on
pollution.

There is also under development a new type of coal gas, almost
identical to natural gas. Experts in the field claim that this
new type of gas can be produced from coal as cheaply as natural
gas can be mined and piped to market.

A third technological problem focuses on ways of mining. The
old ways are no longer suitable for handling the large quantities of coal now needed. This is especially true when the work
is carried on in mountain areas, and most of North America's
best coal lies in mountain areas. To date the Kaiser Company's
operations in British Columbia is the only modern approach to
large volume coal mining in a mountain area. Because of all
these factors, coal as a major energy resource must be classif-
ied as a future, not a present alternative.

In 1970, several years before the oil crisis, the National
Research Council of Canada was busy experimenting with windpower. Using the wind tunnels of the National Aeronautical Lab
two men worked on a device that is more properly called a wind
turbine than a windmill. It is totally different from conventional windmills.

To begin with it rotates at very high speed around a vertical
axis. This means that it is independent of wind direction, and
this greatly reduces the amount of mechanical devices that are

normally employed to shift a windmill to face the wind.   This
also cuts down on the weight.

Even earlier than 1970 Northern Canada had been experimenting
with wind power.   In villages such as Repulse Bay and Arctic Red
River, installations producing as much as 100 kilowatts have
been in regular use, using the high winds of the Arctic.   This
has also been true in other countries.   Several hundred thousand
wind pumps have been in use for some time in Australia, Southern
Africa and areas of the Mediterranean.   Wherever the small scale
technology is appropriate, windpower is a viable source of
energy.

As recently as 1950 there were 50,000 small windmill powered
electrical generators in use in the mid-West of the United
States alone.   Thirty years earlier the number ran into several
millions, but as oil and other sources of energy became available windmill power was dropped. Since the oil crisis the United
States has spent at least $1 million on windpower research.

There is one major handicap to extensive use of windpower.   Even
in the windiest locations the wind does not always blow.   Windmills therefore need some means of power storage, and traditionally this has been done with batteries.   Existing types of
batteries however, are not suitable for this kind of work, and a
good deal of reserach has yet to be done on suitable storage
systems.

There are other alternative sources - many of them.   Some have
been under consideration for a long time, like the water power
from tidal movements; some are quite fanciful, like the harnessing of energy at the point where rivers meet the sea.   The meeting of fresh and salt water releases large quantities of energy.
John Isaacs of the Scripps Institute of Oceanography has estimated that there is as much energy of this kind at the mouth of
the Columbia River as in all the existing dams on the river.

Geothermal energy, using the earth's natural heat, offers a
low cost, natural source potentially available to 146 nations of
the world.   Recently in the state of Idaho a geothermal well was
tapped about one mile from the state capital in Boise.   With an
initial budget of $3 million ten buildings are being heated from
this well.   This could easily be extended, say the authorities,
to provide space heating for 38 similar large buildings.   That
would be the equivalent of 4,000 homes.

The Imperial Valley of southeastern California contains enough
underground power to produce electricity for the needs of 10
million people.

About half of that amount could be tapped now with existing
technology and be competitive with fossil fuels and nuclear
power.

Sometime before the year 2000 the energy needs of 20 million people could be served from this geothermal source.

In a poor, rural community, 70 miles west of San Salvador,
capital of El Salvador, a modern plant is turning steam, siphon-
ed from beneath the country's lethal volcano belt, into electricity.

This geothermal energy could enable El Salvador to be one of the
first countries in the world to switch completely from oil to
renewable energy sources for all its power needs.

El Salvador is the eighth country in the world to own a geothermal plant, and the first in Central America.

The plant is powered by drilling down into steam reservoirs
around the volcanos to a depth of 1000 metres, using the same
technology as oil.

The steam pushes up at high pressure and is used to drive simple
electric turbines.

Unlike oil, volcanic power is cheap to tap, economical to produce, unlikely to run out and less polluting.

Solar energy is an obvious source of inexhaustible, pollution-
free energy. The potential is great. In a single day, the
earth intercepts a volume of thermal energy from the sun equal
to 100,000 times the world's total installed electric power
capacity. The areas, however, with the highest income of sun
energy are the deserts of sub-tropical latitudes, and these are
notoriously sparsely populated. Elsewhere solar radiation is
intermittent and disrupted by cloudiness. In polar regions
there is the additional problem of seasonal changes of dark and
light periods. In addition to the intermittent nature of the
energy source in the areas of high population density there is
the problem of conversion. Heating domestic water supplies
through roof tanks or greenhouses is not suitable for large
scale power production. One use, universally employed, is space-
craft and space stations.

More than a million Japanese housholds now use the sun for heating water. Dozens of new homes and public buildings use solar
energy not only to provide hot water but to heat the entire
structure, as well as to cool it.

And test structures are looking for even more efficient uses for
this natural energy that otherwise falls uselessly on tiled
roofs.

The one immediately available, large energy resource is nuclear.
It is probable that public opinion throughout the world will
choose this option in spite of concerns over radiation and waste
disposal.

Nuclear Power

Some authorities have stated bluntly that other systems are still at the science fiction stage when compared with nuclear power. For every nuclear power station, they say, 50,000 wind generators are needed. The largest operating windmill in the world only generates 200 kilowatts of power.

Nuclear power makes sense in developing countries. Poor countries have little cash reserves to cope with massive increases in oil prices. In Africa and Latin America the total amount of coal reserves is less than 3 percent of the world's total, so they cannot turn to coal as a substitute. Even firewood - traditional fuel for one third of mankind - is no longer available in sufficient quantities to provide a minimum energy supply.

Worldwide agreement that nuclear power is a necessity and an irreplaceable source of future energy supply is being claimed by Sigvard Eklund, director general of the International Atomic Energy Agency.

This consensus is based on an awareness that the present world consumption of about six billion tonnes of oil equivalent will more than double by the year 2000.

This will happen even if the maximum efforts at conserving energy are applied by industrial countries.

In the short term nuclear power offers an oil and gas substitute for electricity generation in many countries lacking hydro-carbons and coal.

In the longer term it holds out to the world a technologically mature solution to its increasing energy needs and places a safety net under the future development of mankind, since the potential of alternative energy sources is still at a laboratory stage.

Eklund predicts that the nuclear power share, which is today less than 10 percent of electricity and less than 3 percent of primary energy will grow to 35 percent of electrical energy and 15 percent of primary energy by the year 2000.

The Canadian Nuclear Association recently presented to the federal government 3 major reasons justifying nuclear energy production.

1. It is clean and safe and causes the least disturbance to the environment compared with other developed sources of electrical power.

2. It has been demonstrated to be cheaper. One nuclear power station has already saved Canada over $500 million worth of U.S. coal. Total energy cost of this power station was 25 percent below coal powered stations.

3. It reduces transportation requirements when generating
    centres are distant from fuel sources since, to generate
    the same amount of electricity with bituminous coal requires
    20,000 times the weight of the equivalent fuel.

Similar support for this alterative has been coming in from
other sources. In 1977 a committee of the World Health Organization came out in favour of nuclear energy.

The debate is far from being resolved. There is a persistent
and eloquent minority who insist that the dangers far outweigh
the advantages.

CANDU Reactor
Canadian research funds have been lavishly spent on nuclear
generators.

The country has 300,000 tonnes of uranium, sufficient to supply
its nuclear power needs, including projected expansions, for
many years to come. See Fig. 9.6.

The Canadian reactor system (CANDU) has proved to be very
acceptable throughout the world.

Nuclear power stations, in common with coal, oil, and natural
gas-fired stations, generate heat which is used to produce steam
which drives the blades of a turbine generator.

In a nuclear power station, the heat is produced by the splitting of a particular isotope of a uranium atom, U-235. This
process, called nuclear fission, is initiated when the nucleus
of a U-235 atom interacts with a neutron. The U-235 nucleus
immediately splits, producing lighter chemical elements known as
fission products, as well as giving out a large amount of heat
and more neutrons. Some of these ejected neutrons will interact
with the nuclei of other U-235 atoms, thus repeating the process.
The principle of nuclear power generation is to set up a controlled chain reaction whereby the fission process continues,
producing an uninterrupted flow of heat.

The Canadian reactor is called CANDU - for CANada, Deuterium,
and Uranium. Deuterium is a form of hydrogen, having one proton
and one neutron in its nucleus instead of just one proton as in
ordinary hydrogen, and in combination with oxygen it forms heavy
water.

Heavy water moleucles are very rare in nature, and the methods
used to concentrate heavy water from ordinary water make it
extremely expensive - about $250 per litre. Heavy water is used
in the CANDU, and some other systems, as a moderator to slow
down the speed of neutrons emitted by the fission process. When
travelling at slower speeds, these neutrons are more likely to
continue the fission reaction because at high speeds they may
pass through a U-235 atom without striking the nucleus and
making it split.

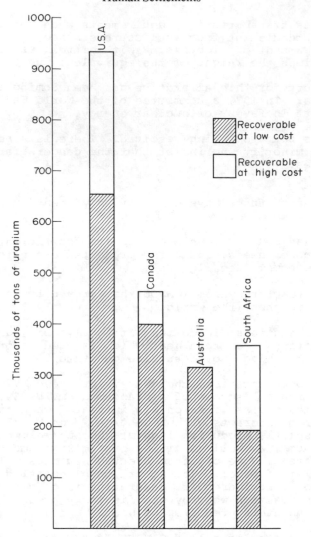

Fig. 9.6. World uranium reserves, 1975

The U in CANDU stands for uranium and indicates that natural
uranium is used as the fuel. It can only be used in systems
employing heavy water or graphite as moderators, since these
absorb relatively few of the neutrons emitted during the fission
reaction.

The core of a CANDU reactor is a tank called a calandria. It
contains the fuel and heavy water necessary for the fission process to take place. Heavy water surrounds a large number of
pressure tubes, which contain "bundles" with fuel pellets of
natural uranium inside. The coolant, also heavy water, but

separated from the heavy water moderator, is pumped through the
pressure tubes where it picks up heat from the fission reaction
taking place inside the fuel bundles. The coolant is then pumped on through boilers where the heat is used to make steam from
light water. This is the steam which drives the turbine.

The main objection to nuclear power is the fear of radioactive
materials being discharged into the environment by accident.
This possibility has led to public concern about the construction of nuclear power stations. In fact, the risk of such an
accident appears to be extremely low as the following table
shows.

Average Risk of Fatality by Various Causes

Accident Type	Total Number of accidents	Individual Chance per Year
Motor Vehicle	55,791	1 in 4,000
Falls	17,827	1 in 10,000
Fires & Hot Substances	7,451	1 in 25,000
Drowning	6,181	1 in 30,000
Firearms	2,309	1 in 100,000
Air Travel	1,778	1 in 100,000
Falling Objects	1,271	1 in 160,000
Electrocution	1,148	1 in 160,000
Lightning	160	1 in 2,000,000
Tornadoes	91	1 in 2,500,000
Hurricanes	93	1 in 2,500,000
All Accidents	111,992	1 in 1,600
Nuclear Reactor Accidents (100 plants)	-	1 in 500,000,000,000

Nuclear power stations release none of the usual chemical
pollutants but they do release small amounts of radioactivity.
Although the emissions from a coal-fired plant can cause more
deaths, those from a nuclear plant are probably more feared. It
is easier to monitor radioactivity and much more is known about
its effects on health than is the case for other pollutants.

The earth has contained radioactivity from its start. Mankind
has always experienced radiation as part of the natural environment.

The radioactive waste products in the discharged fuel bundles
from a reactor need to be stored in safety so that the radiation
does not escape. At one CANDU power station there are 40 waste
fuel bundles a day, each weighing 20 kilos. These discharged
fuel bundles are stored in pools of water on the reactor site
for five years. Following this initial period, the bundles are
transferred to storage sites in larger pools or in concrete
canisters. Eventually, it will be necessary to store wastes

indefinitely, possibly by deep burial in glass packages in some
geologically stable area.

An extensive research program is now underway on the permanent
storage of radioactive wastes in geologic formations.

In Canada both salt beds and impermeable granite are being
investigated as long-term storage sites, since there is geologic
evidence that they are suitable structures which have remained
undisturbed and dry for periods that are long, compared with the
radioactive lives of the wastes.

The recent discovery in Babon of two large underground deposits
of uranium in which large-scale fission had occurred naturally
a billion years ago lends support to the geologic storage
approach. Very little movement of the hazardous wastes had
taken place, despite the absence of any precautions.

It is possible that a new, safer form of nuclear power will be
available by the year 2000. It is known as fusion, not fission.
Once this source is operative the quantities of radiation
present in nuclear energy generators will be vastly reduced.

Existing nuclear power stations, like the CANDU reactor, work
through fission. Energy is released when the central nucleus of
an atom is split by bombardment with smaller atomic particles
called neutrons.

Fusion, on the other hand, forces together two nuclei - and
liberates a vastly greater amount of energy. This can be
accomplished by high heat, high pressures or both.

Although much energy is needed to get the operation started,
there comes a time when more energy comes out than goes in. And
since the main fuels are variations of hydrogen, and only small
amounts are needed for the amount of energy released, future
energy supplies are almost unlimited.

Thermonuclear fusion has important domestic implications since
a fusion reactor would produce infinitely more energy than it
would use. Current energy producers, such as oil or standard
nuclear power plans, consume huge amounts of energy, such as
electricity.

Energy for a Livable Planet
At Vancouver's Habitat Conference, Maurice F. Strong, then
Chairman of Canada's new national energy corporation, Petro-
Canada, and former Secretary-General of the United Nations
Environment Conference in Stockholm, 1972, summed up many of the
world's energy problems. Some of his ideas are summarized here.

Whatever patterns of settlement develop by the year 2000, human
settlement and the range of human activities occurring within
them will be dependent upon vast supplies of energy. The technology which makes a massive human population possible and the

technology which sustains wide ranges of settlement patterns, is a technology which produces and uses huge amounts of energy. People live under extremes of climate and enjoy a wide range of activities because they make use of energy in such vast and various ways.

I am concerned with present problems of energy supply and I am even more concerned with the future demand for energy. In considering the energy needs of the future, I once more affirm that we cannot afford to plan on the basis of past and current trends. If we assume that a decent standard of life for the world's people inevitably requires increasing per capita consumption of energy, we are most likely to be planning for an energy-starved world or an ecological disaster - or perhaps both.

It is obvious that urban problems are bound up with the use of energy. The energy needs of vast cities are most evident in the delivery systems that are required as the population multiplies. Urban populations require great quantities of water, food and fuel. Apart from the quantity of energy in the fuel itself, the delivery of these life-sustaining commodities requires a continuous use of energy. Even the physical components of the delivery systems - the steel for pipes, the cement for roads, the copper for wire - are produced through energy-intensive processes. The collecting and processing of a city's waste requires another energy-intensive system - though we sometimes choose a short-sighted saving of energy and, wantonly pollute rivers and lakes instead. Of course the building of the city itself, particularly the larger buildings, requires much energy. Better urban planning and more efficient processes can save energy, but monster cities must still be gluttonous users of energy.

If we are to make better use of energy in human settlements we must definitely break with past and current trends. Our experience in the recent past has made up wasteful, rather than wise, in the use of energy. Although energy use has recently increased most rapidly in the less wealthy areas of the world, in Africa and Asia, total consumption in these regions is still only a fraction of what it is in North America. In 1975, people in the United States wasted more fossil fuel than was used by two-thirds of the world's population.

The modern pattern has assumed that any extravagant style of life is entitled to the energy needed to support it. The jet plane makes it possible for executives and middle echelon managers to attend hundreds of meetings a year scattered across continents, or even across oceans, without serious question as to their utility. In northern climates, living and commercial areas have been completely enclosed and heated to shirt-sleeve temperatures in the midst of snow and blizzards. Indeed, in a country such as Canada, we have not troubled to implement a distinctive architecture for settlements which are sub-arctic, although our more thoughtful architects have produced appropriate designs. We have preferred increasing use of energy to creative

design or higher initial building costs. This prodigal use of
energy is a luxury of wealthy nations, and it is contrary to the
pattern of planning and development needed to cope with the expected world urban growth.

We must break from this pattern of rapid expansion in the use of
energy and we must stress the conservation and re-allocation of
energy. The figures for world energy use show that the major
breakthrough can be made in the rich countries. A 5 percent per
capita reduction in European energy consumption would save as
much energy as a 54 percent reduction in Africa. Though important energy savings can most readily be made in rich countries,
it is still vital for the poorest countries to stress conservation and efficiency of use.

From an economic point of view, poorer countries cannot afford
to import expensive energy, such as that derived from fossil
fuels. Also, the energy saved in one part of the world cannot
always be re-allocated elsewhere. Reducing consumption of hydro-
electric energy in Scandanavia does not make the saved energy
available in another region. Every country, therefore, is vital-
ly concerned with the more efficient use of energy. Even the
most modest savings possible in less wealthy nations will be
important for their development and their ability to meet the
growing needs of their population.

There is another aspect of the economics of saving energy. The
costs of new energy are likely to keep increasing, and we can
be certain that the discovery and development costs of new oil
will keep rising. I draw special attention to oil because, for
many purposes, particularly in transportation, we do not have
convenient or feasible substitutes. To the extent that various
energy sources are best suited to different kinds of use, a wise
energy policy will stress the allocation of energy according to
use. We may plan, for example, to reduce the use of fossil
fuels in space heating.

The ways of conserving energy and of utilizing alternate energy
sources are often quite obvious, but they are critically important if we are to have the necessary energy for the more crowded world of the year 2000. Some examples, first from large
settlements and industrialized economies, and later from rural
economies, will indicate the range of possibilities.

Industrial societies have often been extremely wasteful because
their planning has assumed an almost endless supply of low-cost
energy. The capital cost of buildings has been reduced, for
example, by minimizing insulation, accepting simplified window
design, and not using heat-exchangers in heating systems. Higher fuel costs have now changed the economics of such planning.

As one example of energy saved in industrial processes, when
heat from cement kilns is recaptured to preheat the limestone
feedstock, the total energy requirements for the production of
cement are reduced by about one-half. The short-sighted energy

policies which developed during times of abundance are nowhere
better illustrated than in a contention of the United States
Justice Department, in the 1930s, that paper companies should
not be allowed to sell the electricity they could produce by
using their process steam to generate power. Today, if all
industrial steam were also used to generate electricity, the
entire electrical needs of most secondary industries could be
met and there would be some surplus.

There are also some very encouraging examples. The State of
Connecticut has embarked on a ten-year program which will use
84 percent of the State's solid waste to produce 10 percent of
its electricity. Sweden now utilizes about one-third of the
waste heat from power plants for commercial purposes.

The possibilities for conservation of energy are enormous, from
the design of automobiles to turning off unneeded lights. Any
effective conservation effort will require good planning, more
effective government regulations, and individual commitment.
Changes in mortgage regulations could provide the incentive for
the better design and insulation of buildings. Transportation
systems using mini-buses and public-use automobiles can provide
alternatives between the energy-wasteful reliance upon private
cars and mass transit.

Again, governments can provide incentives with tax credits and
licensing regulations as well as by planning city streets for
use by public vehicles rather than private ones. If we can get
away from the idea that parking the car downtown is some kind
of basic right, methods of transporting people will change. All
these remedies have been possible for a decade. When will the
commitment of citizens be sufficient to spur governments into
action?

It is urgent to replace some uses of fossil fuels. The most
obvious alternate source is the sun. Using present technologies,
solar energy seems best suited to individual applications -
space and water heating for buildings - rather than to large-
scale solar installations for the generation of power. The
principal limitations on the use of solar energy are that it is
energy of low intensity and it is intermittent. Thus, it is not
practical to design a solar heating system to carry the full
heating load of a typical building as, doing so, would mean
building a large system which operated much of the time at only
a fraction of its capacity.

Energy storage is also difficult, requiring large installations
if solar energy is to be stored up for use at night or on the
coldest days. The possibilities vary with the climatic conditions. A solar house in Albuquerque, New Mexico, was designed to
use solar energy to meet from 70 percent of the load for space
and water heating. In Denver, where winter temperatures may be
below -30°C, solar energy met 26 percent of the heating needs of
a house. Solar energy systems may also be used for industrial
space heating.

Solar energy may be used in less wealthy countries, but the high
capital costs of man-made solar collection systems, makes it
more practical to use photosynthesis in plants as the fundamental means of capturing solar energy. There has recently been
much work in the development of faster growing species of trees,
in reforestation, and in the controlled cutting of trees for
fuel. While this work is also important in the struggle against
soil erosion, the cultivation of green plants as energy sources
will become more important with every passing year.

A time-honoured method of using the energy stored in green
plants is by feeding the plants to animals and then harnessing
the animals for work. Animals are not efficient energy convert-
ers however, and there are more direct methods of getting out
the energy captured by green plants. Biogas digesters are an
application of intermediate technology which is low-cost and
suitable for small-scale applications. Methane produced from
the process of biogasification can be burned as fuel as well as
used in engines to pump water or to generate electricity.

Studies carried out in the Gangetic Plain in India showed that
the most efficient use of methane from biogasification was as
a source of power for irrigation. Under the system tested in
these studies, the efficientcy of using biogas for irrigation
was measured by the increase in crop yields as more water was
available. Fuel for cooking was then obtained from water
hyacinths which in warm climates can produce large amounts of
dry matter for fuel.

Because this last example shows that options exist within energy
systems which we may think of as very simple, it should remind
us that all the uses of energy should be seen in the context of
systems. Our energy problems cannot be solved by the pushing of
pet projects, whether those projects are fusion reactors or
solar cookers. Any alternate energy source must be examined in
relation to other sources and also in relation to the range of
problems in a particular region of the world. Biogasification,
for example, should not be judged just as a source of energy for
people in less wealthy rural regions. It can also be vital to
stopping the advance of deforestation. In many countries, the
forest areas are dwindling at an alarming rate because wood
continues to be an inexpensive and available fuel. Biobasific-
ation also relates to another problem of our crowded world.
Waste disposal can be effectively achieved, dangers from infection can be reduced, nitrogen-rich sludge is available to
enrich the soil and, above all that, men can have clean, usable
energy if human and animal wastes are processed in biogas
digesters.

Biogasification may also be used in large-scale applications in
wealthier countries. A $4 million methane plant is being built
in Colorado to utilize animal waste from feedlots. The Energy
Policy Project of the Ford Foundation suggests that as much as
5.5 percent of United States energy needs could be recovered
from crop residues, feedlot waste, and urban refuse.

The possibilities of energy substitution are numerous, and I
could point to the present-day version of the wind-electric
plants which were common on farms across the North American
plains at the time when I was growing up in rural Manitoba.

Enough has been said to illustrate the critical point; energy
is vital to the quality of life in all forms of human settlements, and in all of those settlements there are possibilities
for more efficient use of energy and for utilization of alternate forms of energy. The great question remains - how can
energy best be utilized in order to maintain a basic standard of
life?

Identify the Issues

1. Which countries are most dependent on imported oil?
    Are these countries highly industrialized?

2. Power blackouts are inevitable if non-renewable energy
    resources are not conserved or suitable alternatives
    are not found in time. What should be cut first in
    the event of a blackout?

3. Investigate one source of alternative energy. Find out
    how much of your community's needs it could supply if
    it were now fully developed, provided its costs were
    not more than double present energy costs.

"The construction of shelter - not only housing but all buildings - must be recognized as an instrument of social, economic
and territorial planning. Governments must use this instrument
to achieve specific goals: attacking the housing problem by the
development of low-cost technology, using realistic building
codes, facilitating land tenure rights for low-income families,
providing innovative forms of credit for home building, stimulating economic activity through development of building material
industries and other construction suppliers, strengthening the
capacity of construction contracting firms and agencies, and
expanding employment." From Habitat Preparatory Paper.

CHAPTER TEN

Shelter for the Urban Millions

The improvement or provision of urban shelter is one of the basic starting-points in tackling the crisis in human settlements, and the control of land values is inseparably linked with shelter needs and the services that are part of these needs. Urban land is a scarce resource, so that without adequate control it quickly rises in value to the point where its purchase is beyond the reach of the average resident.

If the demand for land increases because of social conditions which have created a huge metropolitan centre, should not the land value increase be given to the people who created the additional value - the whole community?

In many instances this additional value, often called plus value, falls into the hands of private land owners who just happen to own the land at the right time. One of the strong views expressed at the Habitat Conference was that all such gains should be removed from private hands and given to the community.

Demand for urban housing is not just a demand for a certain amount of physical space. Location is critical because it determines whether or not people are going to be able to live close to their work, close to their friends, their cultural interests, education, and recreation. Location in fact affects a whole lifestyle. These important considerations point out the need for public control, if not public possession, of all aspects of land use.

Britain has developed an interesting approach to the problem of rising urban land values. It is called the "Community Land Act 1975" but it was preceded by 30 years of experience with a variety of less restrictive forms of land use control. It was therefore possible to add in the additional controls of the 1975 Act without disrupting the country's economy.

The British scheme relates only to land which is to be developed or redeveloped. It is not concerned with land that is to remain in its existing use, like agriculture or forestry. When new developments are about to take place the community purchases the land at its current use value, regardless of any future uses which may be made of the land.

Land banks are acquired in this way so that long-term planning becomes possible. Any public developments on such land - schools or government buildings - will cost less because the

land was acquired at an earlier time. This will keep taxation
levels low.

The essence of this British scheme is that the community takes
on the function of supplying land for private developments. It
secures the future needs of the community authority by purchas-
ing whatever land is needed and retaining the development value
for the benefit of the community as a whole.

In most countries the most frequently used land regulation is
price control. Cuba has established a ceiling on the maximum
allowable unit price of land. France and Spain have frozen land
prices in high priority development areas. Australia, Denmark
and Japan have a system of registration and evaluation of land
prices which involves periodic official pronouncements of prices
for specified areas.

The Netherlands is probably the most successful western country
in keeping land prices under control. By active participation
in the marketplace over many years, individual municipalities
have built up substantial land holdings. One result is that
this most densely populated country of Europe has had the lowest
rate of increase in land prices. The proportion of land costs
in the total costs of urban construction has remained stable for
the past 50 years.

Public sentiment over land values has been so strong that, in
1977, it forced the government of the Netherlands to resign
after almost four years in power, and only two months before
scheduled parliamentary elections.

Labour party Prime Minister Joop den Uyl submitted the resign-
ation of the five-party coalition to Queen Juliana. He told
Parliament he had been unable to resolve a cabinet conflict
over measures to regulate land sales.

The dispute on the land issue created a rift between leftwingers
in the cabinet, led by den Uyl's labourites, and the moderate
Christian Democrat bloc.

The leftwingers and a majority of the cabinet basically wanted
land prices regulated by the land's value to current users. The
Christian Democrats, however, demanded consideration for potential development value, including compensation for any drop in
valuation caused in scheduling a site for redevelopment. The
leftists said that this would open the way to increased land
speculation.

Urban land is very small in extent everywhere, even in the most
urbanized countries. See Fig. 10.1. But it is for this very
reason that the price controls imposed by many countries are so
essential.

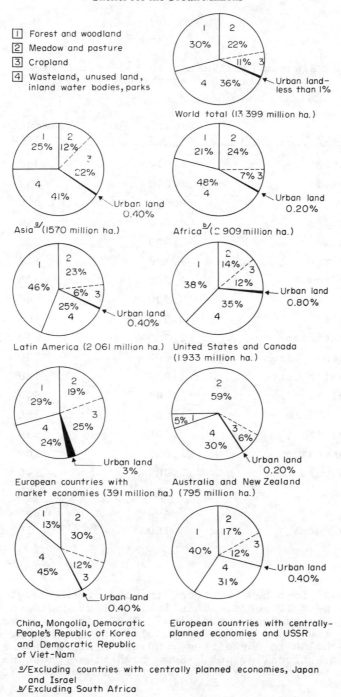

1 Forest and woodland
2 Meadow and pasture
3 Cropland
4 Wasteland, unused land,
  inland water bodies, parks

World total (13 399 million ha.)

Asia[a]/(1570 million ha.)

Africa[b]/(2 909 million ha.)

Latin America (2 061 million ha.)

United States and Canada
(1933 million ha.)

European countries with
market economies (391 million ha.)

Australia and New Zealand
(795 million ha.)

China, Mongolia, Democratic
People's Republic of Korea
and Democratic Republic
of Viet-Nam

European countries with centrally-
planned economies and USSR

a/Excluding countries with centrally planned economies, Japan
  and Israel
b/Excluding South Africa

Fig. 10.1. Major land uses, Selected Areas

Highest Land Values in Selected Cities
(Dollars per square metre, 1970)

City	Commercial Values	Residential Values
Zurich	14,000	350
Tokyo	11,000	850
New York	9,000	1,000
London	8,000	160
Paris	7,000	1,200
Beirut	4,800	120
Munich	4,500	600
Madrid	3,500	700
Milan	3,000	600
Amsterdam	2,700	170
Buenos Aires	2,600	200
Mexico City	1,800	180
Tel Aviv	1,700	500
Stockholm	1,000	150
Helsinki	1,000	170
Copenhagen	1,000	100
Taipei	1,000	140
Lima	300	50
La Paz	200	40
Calcutta	160	16

Shelter

Housing conditions have worsened in most of the developing world within the past 10 years. This is in direct contrast to the trends in the developed countries. There are three main reasons for this - the rapid growth of population, the migration of rural households to the cities, and the decline in the rate of increase in national output. Some countries' gross national product in real terms is lower now than it was in 1970.

Housing Requirements by 1980
(in millions)

Regions	Year	Population	Average Household Size	Dwelling Units Needed
World	1970	3,610	4.5	877
	1980	4,373	4.3	1,100
More developed regions	1970	1,084	3.4	342
	1980	1,181	3.2	395
Less developed regions	1970	2,526	5.2	535
	1980	3,192	5.0	705
Africa	1970	353	5.0	53
	1980	460	5.0	70
North America	1970	226	3.3	75
	1980	249	3.2	85
Latin America	1970	283	5.1	58
	1980	371	5.0	75
Asia	1970	2,027	5.1	462
	1980	2,514	4.8	604
Europe	1970	459	3.2	151
	1980	487	3.0	170
Oceanic	1970	19	3.8	5
	1980	24	3.7	6
USSR	1970	243	3.7	73
	1980	268	3.3	90

In the developed world there has been an additional cost item in the housing budget since 1973 due to the sudden big increase in the cost of energy. The role of building materials and methods of insulation has taken on a new priority.

Stone, concrete, and ordinary bricks have high heat conductivity and low heat capacity. Metal, often used for roof construction, is particularly poor in this respect. It will, for example, heat up to an extraordinary degree under the influence of direct isolation. Air spaces between the outer structural material and the interior panelling provide an effective heat transfer barrier. This type of construction provides for conservation of heating fuel and reduction of cooling needs.

In sunny climates, and especially where summers are hot, most

roofs are heat collectors and attic spaces, if present, can have
temperatures up to 50°C. Without adequate insulation, this
unwanted heat diffuses into the living spaces below, causing
discomfort. Artificial cooling may be needed.

If walls and roofs are white on the outside they reflect much of
the incoming energy and the building material does not heat up.
This suggests that these outer surfaces in sunny, warm climates
should be light. In cold climates dark surfaces are advantageous. The problems arise in climates where winters are cold and
summers warm but on balance it appears better to plan for
summer protection when the sun is high above the horizon and its
radiation intense.

In general, because of the large numbers of poor, homeless
people, if the housing conditions of the lowest income groups
are improved there will be an overall improvement in living
conditions. At the present time, however, housing policies
throughout the world merely increase the social inequalities.
Programs that are designed to promote the construction of housing through low-interest loans or tax exemptions generally
favour the economically strong groups. See Fig. 10.2. The poor
are too poor to be able to benefit. The provision of subsidized
public housing sometimes has a similar effect. The result - a
demand everywhere for new, less-costly approaches to housing.

In Mexico, it has been possible to construct dwelling units at
an average cost of $500. In one project, labour was manual,
including the production of bricks and the construction of the
"natural kiln" in which the bricks were fired.

As countries seek solutions to the slum and squatter problem
through housing, it is becoming clear that the housing units are
not the most important ingredients of a housing policy. The
site and the services to make life comfortable on such a site
seem to be the key.

The World Bank has embarked on "sites and services" schemes in
Senegal, China, Indonesia, and other place. More realistic
urban plans, based on more understanding and knowledge of the
nature of squatting and slum-dwellings are now being prepared
in many countries.

Thus, instead of always dreaming of high-rise dwellings with
elevators, planners now often provide the land on which the
squatter or slum dweller builds his own shanty, using whatever
materials he can lay his hands on.

Zambia Self-help Housing
Following independence in 1964, Zambia's urban population doubled, to reach 1.13 million by 1969. That figure represented 30
percent of the total population. The squatter population increased by 150 percent within the same five year period.

Squatter settlements represent a good illustration of self-

reliant development. Their populations have been able to create
shelter, however poor, five times faster than the public housing
authorities. Nearly all their dwellings are built by self-help
at weekends or in the evenings.

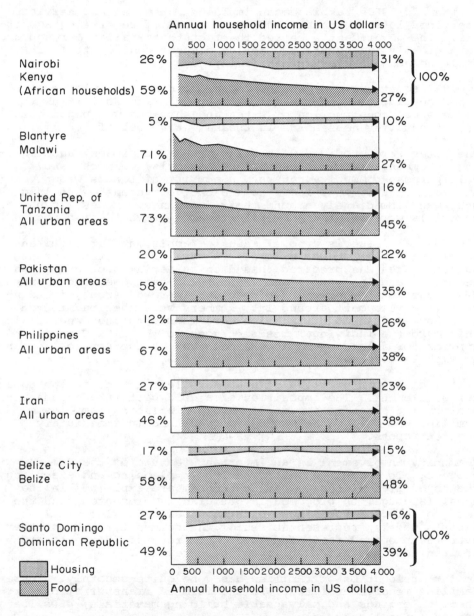

Fig. 10.2. Proportions of income spent
on housing and food

The housing, which is owner-occupied, is being continually improved. Within a few years, grass roofs are replaced by
corrugated iron, and sun-dried brick walls by concrete blocks.
At the same time, more rooms are added.

In the mid-1960s Zambia began implementing sites and services
(serviced lots on vacant land) as a means of resettling squatters. The government accepted the fact that available resources
were grossly inadequate to provide conventional contractor-
built houses for every urban family.

By 1972 squatters made up about one third of Zambia's total
urban population. In the following year, with World Bank
assistance, construction of sites and services was begun for
29,000 squatter households in Lusaka, at a cost of $40 million.

The sites were provided with water, roads, drainage, and lighting. Community facilities included schools, clinics, and
multipurpose community centres. Security of tenure was given in
the form of a 30-year lease to use the government-owned land
under and immediately around their dwellings. Modest loans for
materials were offered to residents to improve their homes.

The 30-year lease is a novel idea in Zambia, and it required
special legislation as follows. First a plan of the upgraded
squatter area was prepared, based on an aerial photograph, showing roads and land uses, and identifying each dwelling by number.
Next, the settlement was declared an "Improved Area", freezing
further development around it. Numbers were then painted on
each home and an identification card issued to the owner. With
this card the individual resident goes to the City Council and
applies for a lease much in the same way as one applies for an
automobile license.

Existing layouts and uses of space are left intact in the squatter settlement. The imposition of a grid pattern of roads and
minimum lot sizes is avoided to avoid displacing families.
Families who have to be moved are resettled in immediately
adjacent spots.

Community involvement is an important feature of the Zambian
project. To encourage participation in planning and execution,
the objectives of the upgrading program are explained in the
local language. A proposed layout plan is presented, and the
need to relocate some households is discussed. Technical
experts and key representatives of the community walk together
over the proposed roads and water main routes. Comments are
invited and, where feasible, changes are made.

So far, relocation of families has gone quite smoothly. These
families receive assistance in the form of transportation for
their belongings and salvageable building materials, plus loans
for additional materials.

The upgrading of the first squatter complex, involving 40,400

is now completed. Work has begun on the second complex for a
population of 50,000. This will be followed by work on the
remaining two smaller settlements.

Sweden Sites and Services Housing
In 1926 the City of Stockholm launched an entirely new system
of "Do-it-yourself" home construction, to reach the "less well-
to-do" and to improve their housing conditions.

The first proposal was for homes with one room plus kitchen and
with outer dimensions of 5 x 7 m. It was not intended to equip
them with pipes for water supply or drainage. Taps would be
provided nearby and households could fetch water. Land for
these houses would be leased by the city to the future land-
owners. The city would be responsible for the construction of
simple roads and would lend money for home construction.

This Swedish variant in "do-it-yourself" construction became
known as "The Magic House". But there was nothing magical about
those houses. They were simply a combination of municipally
owned land, administration, lending of funds, and belief in the
energy and ability of ordinary people.

In the spring of 1927 work was started on the first 200 houses.
The lucky families from the waiting list of 600 were selected
on the basis of a number of criteria. The most important of
these was family income. This income might not exceed the
average clerk's wage, while at the same time it might not be as
low as the average factory worker's wage. Thus it was necessary
for the wife of a factory worker to bring home a certain amount
of money if the family was to be judged capable of affording
the cost of the home.

Almost three quarters of those finally selected were manual
workers, most of them factory employees or building labourers.
Some had jobs as foremen or supervisors. Three quarters of the
builders lacked previous professional knowledge of house construction and were complete amateurs.

The city made two areas available for the scheme. These were
parcelled out into plots, roads were built and the land was
later leased to the prospective houseowners for a term of sixty
years.

The city assumed responsibility for laying cables and pipes for
water supply and sewage in the areas. All this was ready by
the time the home-builders started work. The city also provided
drawings of the types of houses to be built and purchased all
needed building materials in advance.

The total cost of a house was calculated to be 3.5 times the
average annual wage of a factory worker. The city loaned 90
percent of this sum to the home-builders. The money was made
available in the form of building materials and services. The
remaining 10 percent of the construction cost was to be covered

by the prospective owner through his own labour. Thus, the
home-builders did not need to have any capital of their own.

One big problem was how to cope with people who had never done
any building before. How could one be sure that these do-it-
yourself builders, who could only do their building in the
evenings and at week-ends, be able to complete the work in the
time allocated, so that the city could move on and open up new
areas?

Obviously, a certain amount of inspection was necessary on the
building sites, plus some educational effort. The problem was
solved by the city stationing building instructors on the sites.
It was soon found that one instructor could supervize the construction of 50 houses. He walked around from house to house
giving advice and instructions and correcting faults. Before
each new operation in the building process, the homebuilders
attended a meeting at which a run-through of the next stage of
construction was made. In time, the instructions were compiled
in the form of a manual with graphic illustrations and captions.

Work began with the digging of foundations and casting of
foundation walls. Wives and relatives usually helped the man
of the family. No special skill was required either for this or
for the laying of foundation walls of hollow concrete blocks.
In the middle of June the large structural components arrived
from the factory. Erection of these took a day with the help of
a couple of skilled building operatives who were included in the
component manufacturer's contract. Encouraged by the fact that
he had now produced something closely ressembling a finished
house, the builder and his family could launch themselves into
the job of putting in windows and erecting partition walls.
Electrical installations and plumbing were left to specialists
hired by the city authorities and paid via deductions from the
builders' loans.

In the early Fall most of the builders and their families could
nove into the houses and put the finishing touches to their
handiwork from a more comfortable position. By the time winter
arrived, the houses were finished and had been inspected. Only
a couple of the 200 builders got left behind - for reasons which
had nothing to do with the building. One of the big surprises
was that the workmanship was of a higher quality than that
normally found. The amateur builders had been careful and more
competent than professional workers.

In sharp contrast to these trends are the ideas of Buckminister
Fuller. To him technology is well able to handle all the demands for housing, and is able to handle it now. To him it is
highly feasible, with the knowledge that we now have, and with
the resources we have already mined, to have all of humanity
by 1985 enjoying a higher standard of living than ever before,
without anybody profiting at the expense of others. New home
designs and the maximum use of technology at the biggest scales
are the answers proposed by him.

Ideas like those of Buckminster Fuller dominated the urban planning scene for most of the post World War Two period. They
still dominate shelter and housing planning in some countries.
Singapore is one example of this massive high-rise approach.

Singapore Public Housing
Singapore is a small island nation sandwiched between Malaysia
and Indonesia. Its population is a little over two million, and
its total area about the same as that of a large metropolitan
urban centre. See Fig. 10.3.

Singapore

Fig. 10.3. Location of Singapore

Public housing in Singapore began in 1960 with the formation of
the Housing and Development Board. There was an urgent need to
provide families in the lower and middle income groups with
decent and safe housing at rents they could afford.

Today the efforts of the Housing Board are seen in the new
satellite towns and new Housing Board estates that have sprung
up - 200,000 new accommodations housing more than half of the
total population.

Imagine that you had come ashore with Raffles in 1819. You
would have found a Singapore of mangrove swamps and shrubs,
supporting a population of 150 people.

By 1900 the population had reached 250,000. By 1959, when the
present government took office, it stood at 1.5 million.

This rapid population growth created a housing crisis. Early
immigrants came in search of fortunes. They came without their
families. They came with no intention to stay. They planned to
save some money and to return home.

For them housing meant temporary shelters, just a bed for the
night and a roof over their heads. These early types of
'housing' soon grew into slums and were concentrated in China-
town. In time, these houses became honeycombed with cubicles,
with one family in each cubicle. It was common to find 100
people jammed into a single house.

Living conditions deteriorated. The lighting was poor, and
sanitation appalling. Ten families would share a single tap,
a single toilet, one kitchen. The street became the dining room,
a meeting place, the children's playground.

When things grew worse, families moved out to the city outskirts.
They erected shelters for themselves on any land they could find
- haphazard shelters of wood and attap, corrugated iron, old
scrap materials. These grew into squatter settlements. Eventually they formed a ring of squalor and misery around the
central city area. These slum and squatter settlements, apart
from being eyesores, were breeding grounds for disease, and they
were fire hazards.

This was the housing crisis that faced the government when it
came to power in 1959, and led to the massive program of high-
rise apartment buildings that have made the country a world
model of public housing.

In 1964, the Government launched a "Home Ownership for the
People" scheme to enable lower and middle income groups to own
some of the flats. Under this scheme the purchaser needed only
to make a down-payment of 20 percent of the selling price. The
balance was to be repaid monthly over 20 years, at an annual
interest rate of 6¼ percent.

During the first five-year building program the emphasis was
to build the maximum number of flats in the quickest time, at
the lowest cost. Only three types were built:

$$1\text{-Room Flat - floor area of 21 m}^2$$
$$2\text{-Room Flat - floor area of 39 m}^2$$
$$3\text{-Room Flat - floor area of 51 m}^2$$

All flats were built as self-contained units with individual
kitchens, bathrooms, water closets, piped water supply, electricity, gas and water-borne sewerage.

Now 10 percent of the housing units being built are of the

5-room type with a floor area of 121 m^2 per unit; 20 percent
4-room type with a floor area of 93 m^2 per unit; and 40 percent
3-room improved type. See Fig. 10.4.

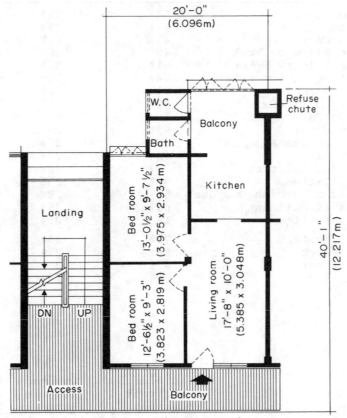

Typical 3-room (improved flat)

Fig. 10.4. 3-room improved flat

These 3 room flats have a floor area of 60 m^2. They are the
most popular and therefore the most numerous. They cost, in
present value, $3,750 (US dollars) plus land. They are sold to
tenants by the Government at a subsidized rate of $3,000.

The layout of housing estates is based on the "neighbourhood"
principle. The only people who need to commute outside the
neighbourhood are the bread-winners. Each neighbourhood has
between 2,000 and 5,000 families.

Tenants in the big high rises were asked two questions: what is
your degree of satisfaction with present living conditions, and
what is the extent of change you have experienced since relocation? The following two tables summarize the answers.

Item	Satis-factory	Accep-table	Unsatis-factory
Bus Service	57%	21%	22%
Taxi Service	63%	29%	8%
Nearness to City	49%	41%	10%
Nearness to Place of Work	40%	39%	21%
Nearness to Primary School	61%	24%	15%
Nearness to Secondary School	44%	35%	21%
Nearness to Market	81%	17%	2%
Availability of Goods	65%	28%	7%
Prices of Goods	16%	65%	19%
Nearness to Clinic	69%	24%	7%
Nearness to Police Station	37%	27%	36%
Public Security	65%	27%	8%
Playground for Children	33%	40%	27%
Parking Facilities	43%	28%	29%
Facilities for Rubbish Disposal	59%	28%	13%
Cleanliness of Building	41%	39%	20%
Efficiency of Lifts	14%	25%	61%
Opinion of Estate	72%	26%	2%
Opinion of Block	68%	27%	5%
Opinion of Floor	62%	25%	13%
Opinion of Flat	68%	24%	8%

Item	No Sig-nificant Change	Changed for the Better	Changed for the Worse
Employment	87%	8%	5%
Travelling Time to Work	47%	28%	25%
Household Income	42%	45%	13%
Public Security	38%	56%	6%
Health of Household Members	29%	67%	4%
Marketing Facilities	38%	51%	11%
Primary School	65%	28%	7%
Secondary School	71%	18%	11%
Travelling Time to Primary School	38%	38%	24%
Travelling Time to Secondary School	46%	26%	28%
Friendliness of Neighbours	63%	28%	9%
Type of People	65%	27%	8%
Amount of Noise	28%	41%	31%
Cleanliness of Neighbourhood	15%	75%	10%

In the overall picture it is clear that life has changed for the better, as seen by the tenants themselves: when asked to take everything into account, 26 percent said that life has become much better; 44 percent reported somewhat better; 18 percent mentioned that conditions have remained the same as before; 11 percent thought that life has become somewhat worse, and 1 percent indicated that things have changed very much for the worse.

In the colonial days of Singapore the minimum qualifications for obtaining a flat was five persons. In 1962 this number was reduced to three for those applying for one-room units. When the housing situation was drastically improved by the mid-1960s the minimum requirements dropped to two persons for any type of public housing unit. The effects of this new policy are twofold. On the one hand, it encourages the splitting of households and increases demand for public housing. On the other hand, the reduction of household size means a decrease in density in the housing unit and in the estate, thus lessening the population pressure on amenities and communal facilities. There is also a hidden contribution to family planning. People no longer need to have many children in order to qualify for public housing.

Identify the Issues

1. What is meant by "plus value" and why is it important in the process of tackling low cost housing?

2. What special problems would you expect to experience if you lived in a Singapore high-rise housing estate?

3. Find out what has happened to housing costs in relation to income in your community over the past 5 years. What proportion of income went to housing 5 years ago? Today?

"Based on national policies and strategies for human settlement
improvement and growth, a new and broadly based approach to
planning must seek a balance of social, territorial,
demographic, economic and ecological needs: intergrating human
settlement planning with economic development programmes,
narrowing differences in income, opportunity and living standards by special attention to isolated rural villages, urban
slums and squatter settlements, and other depresssed or marginal
areas, countering overconcentration in a few metropolitan areas
through decentralization of economic activity, development of
rural marketing and service centres, village amalgamation
programmes, and construction of new towns." From Habitat
Preparatory Paper.

CHAPTER ELEVEN

Planning for Tomorrow

The prevailing system of planning both in the United States and in the Soviet Union has been shaped by a technology of giantism, complexity and expense. It is past time, say many of the world's planners, to put a stop to this system, and devise a technology that moves in the opposite direction - towards smallness, simplicity, cheapness.

To strive for smallness means to try to bring organization and units of production back to a human scale. This is not a field in which precise definitions are possible, nor are they needed. When things get too large for human comfort, when the worth of the individual - a traditional christian value - is being eroded, it is time to scale down.

There are many reasons for favouring smallness. Small units of production use small resources - a very important point when concentrated, large resources are becoming scarce or inaccessible. Small units are ecologically sounder than big ones: the pollution or damage they may cause has a better chance of fitting into nature's tolerance margins. Small units can be used for decentralized production, leading to a more even population distribution, and better use of space.

In a sense both of these approaches are essential - the global U.S. or Soviet approach and the village style methods of many developing countries. The increasing complexity of human settlements demands a comprehensiveness in planning that links neighbourhood with provincial and national plans, something that has not been done before. At the same time the cry for human scale of planning is too insistent to be ignored.

In the past, urbanization problems were tackled on a piecemeal basis. Employment opportunities or social problems were often sufficient cause for a shift in policy. Sometimes programs concentrated entirely on remedial action, involving only the disadvantaged sections of the community.

Now urban and rural developments must be planned together since urban growth has the greatest effect on the valuable agricultural land bordering cities. It is this change of scale in planning policies that most clearly separates the new style of planning from traditional practice and, at the same time, poses the dilemma of a human scale of operation in an increasingly big and complex society.

National planning in the U.S. and Soviet Union is geared to

widespread growth in consumption of electricity, mechanization
and automation of both industry and agriculture, and generally
to a sharp rise in industrial productivity. Can the world's
resources serve this kind of huge growth rate in an increasingly
technological society?

Because people tend to work on the basis of past and current
trends, the developed world, communist and capitalist alike,
looks ahead to a society that is more and more technologically
oriented, consuming ever-increasing per capita quantities of
non-renewable resources. Mankind can live anywhere in artificial
environments, it is said, in dome cities in the Arctic or in
space stations orbiting the earth. The implications of this
kind of thinking and planning, when applied to all mankind and
to our total habitat, are rarely considered.

What about developing countries with their burgeoning populations and lopsided distributions? It is here that small is
beautiful as well as economically viable. Planning at the human
scale of the small community is often the only kind possible.

The most dramatic and poignant form of community participation
is seen in the organization of new squatter settlements by landless tenants.

Britain's new towns are based on less grandiose technologies
than those of the Soviet Union, and are workable models for many
economies. The long history of urbanization and urban problems,
dating back more than a century to the hey-day of the industrial
revolution has given Britain the kind of planning experience
that can now be turned to advantage.

Britain: New Towns
Britain entered the 20th century with 38 million people, almost
four times the 1800 population. London had 4.5 million, but the
industrial north and Midlands and parts of Scotland and Wales
showed the worst conditions, with most working people living in
houses hastily and shoddily built, overcrowded, and in a drab
and unhealthy environment. High birth rates plus the reduced
infant mortality that was the result of medical advances aggravated overcrowding.

Gradually public opinion accepted that only town planning could
prevent such conditions. Ebenezer Howard's first "garden city"
at Letchworth (1903) demonstrated that working people could have
good homes in attractive surroundings; and legislation permitted
local authorities to make plans controlling new housing, though
their powers were totally inadequate. That year Liverpool
University started a civic design department; and in 1914 the
Town Planning Institute was founded. Planning as a serious
professional activity had arrived.

After the 1914-18 war, the government made "Homes for Heroes"
its priority and provided subsidies. This produced many large
municipal housing estates, their houses well built and spacious,

to densities of 30 persons to the hectare and with generous
gardens. But they were monotonous and drab and often lacked
shops, pubs, churches and other amenities. Their failings
strengthened the Garden City Movement's plea for self-contained
new towns. In inner city districts, councils cleared 18th and
19th-century slums, replacing them with four and five storey
"walk-up" flats.

Alongside municipal housing, the private house market grew rapidly, making possible owner-occupation even by people of modest
means. Hampstead Garden Suburb (started 1905) and Welwyn Garden
City (1920) set high design standards; but expanding public
transportation and mortgage financing triggered a rash of spec-
ulative developments with lower standards than those of the
municipal estates.

The 1930s saw Britain's first attempts to control urban sprawl.
In 1938 the London Country Council took powers to establish a
"green belt" around London. Industry and commerce, however,
concentrated increasingly on city centre sites, producing traffic
congestion. Public transportation - first trams, then buses,
electrified suburban railways and, in London, the much extended
underground system - encouraged commuting from greater and greater distances. The inter-war period (1919-1939) also saw the
first tentative steps towards regional economic planning.

In 1943 the government set up a separate Ministry of Town and
Country Planning under a minister charged with securing consis-
tency and continuity in land use and development in England and
Wales.

The 1947 Town and Country Planning Act formed the keystone to
the post-war planning system and provided the statutory basis
for the next two decades of land-use planning.

A New Towns Act empowered the minister to designate land for a
new town after consulting local authorities and statutory boards
providing services. After a procedure which normally includes a
public inquiry, he appoints a "development corporation" - quite
separate from the elected local authorities - which buys the
land, prepares plans, builds houses and initiates other development. Central government exercises planning powers and provides
much of the finance.

The planners of new towns encountered many problems. Finding
suitable sites was not easy. Then development corporations
needed to provide shops and services for early residents to
persuade industry to move in so that jobs could be matched to
homes, and to cope with imbalances in the migrating populations,
whose dominant age groups were 20-30 and 0-5 years. By 1960 the
first 15 towns had provided more than 100,000 new homes. See
Fig. 11.1.

A typical British new town, aiming at an ultimate population of
100,000, consists of a series of village-like neighbourhoods

grouped around the town centre. Each has a primary school, community hall, clinic, local shops and pub within easy walking
distance of all houses; the road pattern excludes through
traffic; and there are separate road and footpath systems. Most
houses that are built for rent through successive governments
have sought to increase owner-occupation.

The latest generation of new towns aim at populations of
420,000, and are based on the expansion of existing settlements.

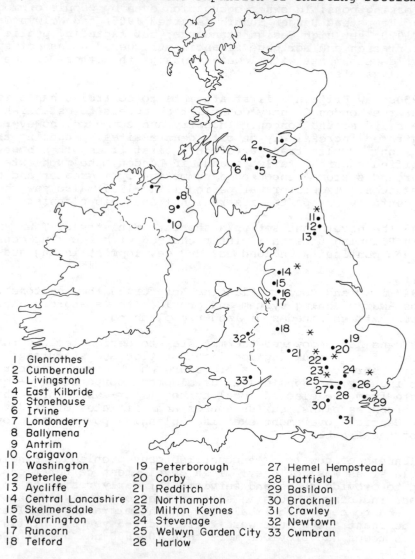

1	Glenrothes				
2	Cumbernauld				
3	Livingston				
4	East Kilbride				
5	Stonehouse				
6	Irvine				
7	Londonderry				
8	Ballymena				
9	Antrim				
10	Craigavon				
11	Washington	19	Peterborough	27	Hemel Hempstead
12	Peterlee	20	Corby	28	Hatfield
13	Aycliffe	21	Redditch	29	Basildon
14	Central Lancashire	22	Northampton	30	Bracknell
15	Skelmersdale	23	Milton Keynes	31	Crawley
16	Warrington	24	Stevenage	32	Newtown
17	Runcorn	25	Welwyn Garden City	33	Cwmbran
18	Telford	26	Harlow		

Fig. 11.1. British new towns

Netherlands: New Polder Planning
The history of planning in the Netherlands is interesting because it has frequently been carried out on brand new land with
no pre-existing settlements to interfere. It is interesting
too because of the long span of time involved, and the different
land use interests at different times.

The Netherlands is a small country lying at the mouth of three
great rivers: the Rhine, the Maas and the Scheldt. It is to a
large extent a delta area.

The land and climate are well suited to agriculture and animal
husbandry, and the estuaries of the great rivers provide a
strategic position for trade between the hinterland and
countries overseas.

Without human intervention, large tracts of the land would be
under water. The first inhabitants of the country had to con-
tend constantly with flooding and, in the beginning, knew no
other way of dealing with these occurrences than to build artificial mounds to which they could retreat with their livestock
in times of danger. When better social organization made it
possible, they adopted more elaborate means of defending their
lands against the water: they joined forces and built dikes,
earth walls which held back the water. They were thus able to
enclose tracts of land which remained permanently dry.

A network of ditches and canals opened when the outer water level
was low (low tide) to discharge the water. When the outer water
level was high (high tide), the sluices remained closed and no
water could enter. By this means, only those areas could be
drained which lay higher than the lowest level of the sea: the
process depended on gravity.

This was changed in the 16th century when, with the aid of wind
energy, converted by windmills into power which could drive
pumps, it became possible to move water from low-lying to higher
areas. Using this technique it also became possible to drain
lands which were permanently below sea level and to keep them
drained. In theory, it had become possible to drain large lakes.
But this required the investment of capital which the farming
population could not provide. It did however become practicable
when merchants, particularly from Amsterdam, had become so rich
from overseas trade that they went out in search of suitable
investments for their capital.

Between 1930 and 1970 four major polders were opened:
Wieringermeer, in the northwest in 1930; the northeast polder in
1942; East Flevoland in 1957; South Flevoland in 1967. See Fig.
11.2.

The primary aim of the first polder was to create a farming area
which would bring about an increase in agricultural land. Agriculture would be placed on as modern a footing as possible. The
same crops were to be grown as in other similar coastal areas of

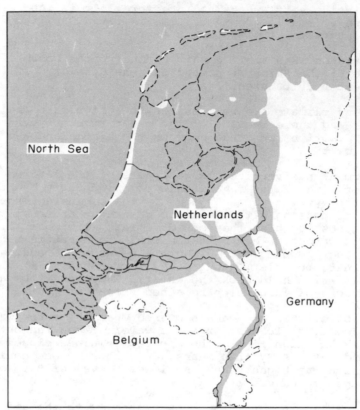

Holland, below water level

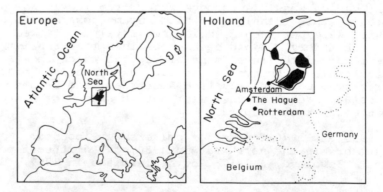

Fig. 11.2. Netherlands Polders

the country. Grazing land would be included on which cattle
could be kept.

The producers had to be farmers, who would rent the land from
the State and who would have self-contained holdings of an area
which had proved by experience on the old land to be the optimum
size and on which there was good scope for further modernization.
The areas envisaged were 40-60 hectares for arable holdings and
20-40 hectares for holdings based on pastures. In holdings of
the proposed type there was room, in addition to the farmer and
his family, for some employed manpower (farm labourers), often
in permanent employment on one holding, but also employed as
casual labour, mainly during the harvest.

The plan for the second polder was much less experimental than
the first. The technical, water control and soil technology
problems had been mastered and more attention could now be devoted to settlement patterns and the associated patterns of
roads and other servies.

A hierarchial pattern was finally developed with a regional
centre in the middle and a ring of ten villages in the surrounding area. It was expected that each village and the regional
centre would have an adequate plane of support for the servicing
and supply functions which had been assigned to them. Under
this system, the distance from the periphery of a village to the
nucleus would be about 5 km. Distances greater than this would
be a serious hindrance to the community life to which people had
become accustomed.

It soon became apparent that the plan took too little account of
a number of far-reaching changes which had overtaken the country.

Firstly, the rise in wages and the mechanization in agriculture
drastically reduced the population: not 50,000 now, but 30,000
inhabitants.

Secondly, the increase in levels of prosperity meant that the
villages could not produce the needed supplies and services
demanded, so people had to go elsewhere. Thirdly, the automobile made the 5 km distance meaningless.

When the third polder appeared, the primary objective was still
the development of new agricultural land, but this time it was
not only to increase agricultural production. There was a new
need to offset land lost elsewhere to urbanization.

By the time of the fourth polder an altogether new approach to
land use planning was in operation. Recreation, new towns,
forests, beaches, and native reserves - all vied with agriculture for the use of the new land.

A single agency overviews planning, development and management
under one roof. In this way it has been possible to introduce
new towns into the overall conception. The new towns have thus

evolved in a new environment in which both the pre-existing
environment and the towns are designed and developed as a totality.

When the Ijsselmeer Polder Project is presented as a successful
example of integral planning and development, the objection is
often raised that one is dealing here with an exceptional situation: there was after all nothing there before, there is not a
single historical obstacle, there is not even a population who
might have created difficulties in the early stages in exercise
of their democratic rights. There is thus nothing to stop it
going ahead as an exercise in technocracy. Such a situation as
this is encountered virtually nowhere else in the world, and the
experience gathered here is thus only of limited value to
others.

People who raise such objections overestimate the power of the
State, in this case the Development Authority, and they also
underestimate the difficulties which such an authority encounters
along its road.

In practice, especially in a country suffering from overcrowding,
any new territory immediately becomes a hunting ground for those
seeking space not available elsewhere or for purposes and activities which are prohibited elsewhere.

Dodoma
The world's newest capital city is rising in the highlands of
central Tanzania. It is designed to provide each family with
its own kitchen garden and easy and ample public transportation.

When, probably by 1990, all the central government's activities
have been moved to the new city, being built in and around the
existing town of Dodoma, the population is expected to be
400,000 people. Situated 1,300 metres above sea level, Dodoma
enjoys a more temperate climate than the present capital, Dar es
Salaam, a humid, tropical port on the Indian Ocean.

A basic principle of the master plan for the new city is complete integration between the built-up area and the land on
which it stands. Open space, both within the city and in
surrounding rural areas, is designed to form a comprehensive
system, ranging from small neighbourhood parks to farming areas
and large regional forest and wildlife reserves.

People in Africa have always done many village tasks together
and the master plan intends to promote this in the new city
through a self-help approach, whether in building classrooms,
starting an adult literacy class or simply arranging for joint
maize-pounding sessions.

Small-scale industrial development is planned within the
communities both to keep the distance between home and place of
work as short as possible and to avoid an over-concentration of
industrial activity in the old town of Dodoma and in the

planned heavy industry sites. The biggest of these sites lies
to the northwest where the prevailing southern winds will blow
pollutants away from the city.

Walking and bicycling are recognized as important means of
transportation and provision has been made for pedestrian and
bicycle paths, often passing through open spaces, within and
between the communities. Because Dodoma is expected to have
relatively few private cars in the foreseeable future, there is
little need for an expensive and elaborate road system and the
roads that are planned will be used primarily to carry goods and
public service vehicles.

Munich

Between 1965 and 1970 the proportion of users of public transportation in Munich dropped from 43 percent to 37 percent. This
reduction in public transportation corresponded to an ever increasing level of private car ownership in the community. In
1960 there was one car for every eight inhabitants in the city
of Munich and one for every ten inhabitants in the immediate
surroundings. In 1970 the figure was one car to every four inhabitants, with no difference between the city and the surrounding countryside.

Car ownership thus increased more quickly in the countryside, and
this corresponded to a reduction in traffic for suburban public
transportation in spite of an increase in the population of the
region. For this reason suburban services were reduced still
further on economic grounds.

The most important conditions for the attractiveness of public
transportation are the frequencies of services. Munich
authorities introduced an integrated transportation system in
which train intervals on the suburban routes were 20 minutes at
peak times and 40 minutes otherwise. The less heavily used
routes in the region had a 40 minute frequency at all times. On
the central section of the suburban network six separate routes
merge, giving a frequency of one train every 3 minutes at peak
times and one every 4 minutes at other times.

The underground operates in the rush-hour on a five-minute
interval system, at other times on a ten-minute interval system.
Where several routes operate on a single stretch of track this
gives a frequency of one train every 2½ minutes in the rush hour
and one train every 5 minutes otherwise. Even in the off-peak
times in the late evening a train frequency of one every 7½
minutes is attained on joint stretches.

The new service has led to a noticeable change in the use of
public transportation. Its share of traffic has risen once more
to 40 percent.

Questionnaires in 1973 and 1974 gave the following picture of
people using public transportation.

- 60 percent of those questioned hardly ever used any form of
  public transportation in the previous year.

- 23 percent now used public transportation on more than 14 days
  each month.

A study of air pollution in Munich is interesting. Between 1970
and 1973 - the years in which the new integrated transportation
system was introduced - there was a 25 percent drop in the concentration of harmful substances. The main reasons were the
better flow of traffic in the city area and the larger share of
total traffic taken by public transportation.

The Tetrahedronal City
Buckminster Fuller's ideas on planning are often considered too
grandiose and too impracticable to be of immediate use. While
it is true that some of Fuller's designs are futuristic, others
are very much an answer to immediate needs.

A tetrahedronal city was designed by Fuller a few years ago in
Toronto. See Fig. 11.3. It was accepted by planners as an
economic and efficient use of downtown city space. The fact
that it was never built is the result of a change in plans by
the city for a freeway network.

It was intended to house a million people. Each family of the
300,000 occupying the city would have apartments with each
measuring 200 m^2 of floor area plus a balcony.

Everything needed for the operation of the city is housed inside
the tetrahedron. The whole structure is so efficient structur-
ally, and therefore so light, relatively speaking, that it can
float.

Tetrahedronal floating cities measure 2 miles on each of the 3
base edges. The foundations are 60 metres deep - deep enough
to get below the turbulence level of the sea. It is earthquake
proof. It can be floated out and anchored anywhere. Base
edges serve as landing strips for jets and the interior harbour
provides refuge for the largest ships.

Withdrawal of materials from obsolete buildings on land will
provide enough to produce many tetrahedronal cities, spaced
across the oceans at convenient small boat distances from one
another. Additions can be made to any side without changing
the shape or stability of the whole. A new city could thus be
built with an initial population as low as 1,000.

Atomic power for the cities will generate enough heat to
desalinate ocean water and provide fresh water in abundance.
Access to ocean floor minerals will be much easier when major
urban centres are located over them.

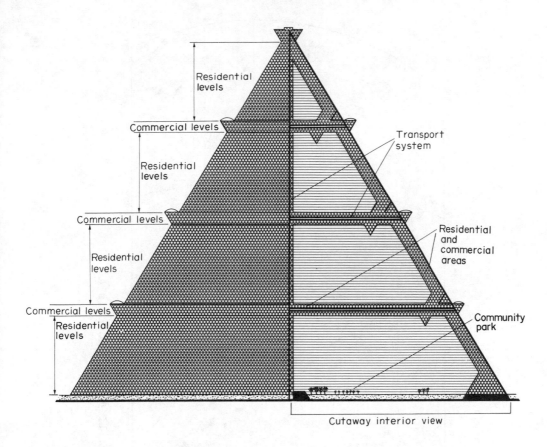

Fig. 11.3. Buckminster Fuller's tetrahedronal city

Ecumenopolis
In his idea of Ecumenopolis, Constantinos Doxiadis makes a contribution to planning that is quite different from that of Buckminster Fuller. Fuller designs for the present. Doxiadis looks far down the road - to the year 2100 - and considers the problems of settlement at that time. In his view we are moving, not only from the city to the metropolis and from the metropolis to the megalopolis, but also we are moving from the megalopolis to the universal city, where all the great cities of the world will be interconnected in one system, the Ecumenopolis. See Fig. 11.4.

Recent studies of the Great Lakes Area show that, by the year 2000, the Chicago and Detroit areas will be physically interconnected. A century from now we will have the universal system, a system which will have even more inhuman conditions within it than the present-day big cities.

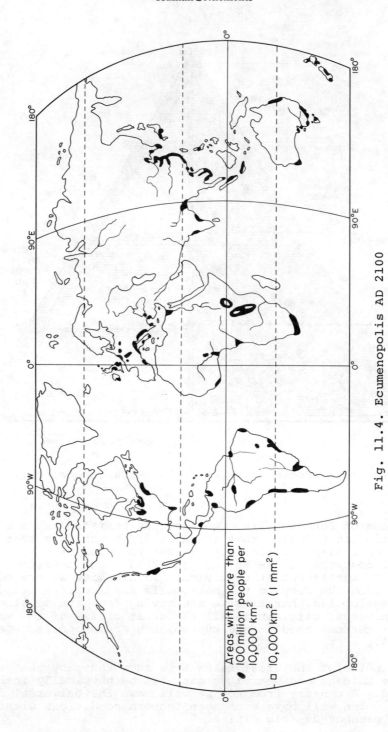

Areas with more than
100 million people per
10,000 km² (1 mm²)

□ 10,000 km² (1 mm²)

Fig. 11.4. Ecumenopolis AD 2100

The universal city will be so big that it will threaten man and
human values. At that time the world will have more than 12
billions of people, mostly urban dwellers.

Ecumenopolis will be hierarchial in structure. It will have
centres of different orders ranging from the highest to the very
small ones which serve people in their various neighbourhoods.
It will have facilities of different orders, from the world
highways and lines of communication down to small residential
roads.

Ecumenopolis will have to be built to different scales. The city
of man needs the car as its servant and not as its master, as at
present. In order to do this, a network of movements has to be
created for pedestrians which, while completely separate from
the network of cars, will nevertheless blend with the movements
of cars. The age-old notion of the city block will have to
change to the city sector. Such a sector should be called "the
human sector", for it will be dedicated to man and can have
dimensions of, say, one mile long. Within the sector, cars will
enter from all four sides, and reach the centre and serve it;
they will never, however, cross the sector.

Ecumenopolis will be a city built to a human scale, the city of
man. It will have one main goal: to serve man, to serve him for
a better way of life. This will be the city which, according to
the old definition of Aristotle, will give its inhabitants
security and happiness. This should be the main goal for
Ecumenopolis.

A number of forces will determine where high, medium or low
densities of habitation will develop on the globe. The highest
densities will be able to develop near large water bodies,
primarily ocean coasts, since desalination of sea water is expected to become economically accessible. In addition, the
growing economic, technological and environmental importance of
the ocean will increase the intensity of such coastal development. Some of the largest rivers and lakes may also permit the
development of high densities along their shores.

It seems that the location of settlements will continue to become less and less dependent upon the location of natural
resources. Other factors such as a particularly favourable
climate, are likely to exert a more powerful attraction upon
population. On the other hand, existing nuclei of population
concentrations are expected to continue to serve as focal points
in the distribution of Ecumenopolis densities. Other new
centres will have to be created, and many of these will become
the centres of gravity of large areas that have previously
remained uninhabited. As a result, a strongly interconnected
system of higher order settlements will develop on the habitable
areas of our planet.

Space Colonies
Most imaginative and far-reaching of all future planning projects

is that of Gerard O'Neill. In fact it is the only plan in
existence that claims to cope with an indefinitely growing human
population.

Gerard O'Neill is a physicist at Princeton University. Until
recently, O'Neill's research was focused on problems in high-
energy physics.

The idea of building man-made worlds in space occurred to
O'Neill by chance, he says, and initially almost as a joke. In
1969, as an exercise for some of his first-year physics students,
O'Neill asked the question: "Is a planetary surface really the
right place for an expanding technological civilization?" To
his surprise calculations showed that the answer was "no".

O'Neill then began to take the problem of man-made colonies
seriously. The more he examined the question, the more convinc-
ed he became that they were indeed possible within our lifetimes.

O'Neill's interest in space colonies was not taken very seriously by the scientific community. It was not until 1974, after
four years of submitting articles, that his proposals were
finally published. Since that first article in Physics Today,
O'Neill and his ideas have received much attention.

O'Neill proposed building colonies at certain points between
earth and our moon. These points are carefully chosen to ensure
that objects will stay where you put them. See Fig. 11.5.

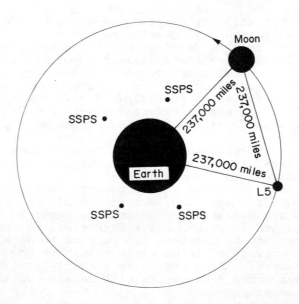

Fig. 11.5. Space colony location (L5)
(SSPS: Satellite Solar Power Station)

The first model colony would consist of a pair of 1 km-long cylinders and would support 10,000 inhabitants. The cylinders would rotate slowly; centrifugal force would hold soil, buildings and people to the inner surfaces and would simulate earth's gravity. Inside each cylinder would be a closed ecological system, an earth-like environment fed with sunlight reflected in by mirrors.

Each cylinder would weigh about a half million tonnes. If building materials came from earth, the amount of energy needed to lift such masses through earth's atmosphere and away from earth's gravity would make the project impossible.

Most of the materials needed, however, exist on the moon. O'Neill proposes establishing mines on the moon: he calculates that 90 percent of the materials needed to build the first colony could be obtained in this way.

O'Neill calls the process by which this first colony would be established "the boot-strap process". First, tools, equipment, people and a space station (a sort of "construction shack"), would be sent by rocket. An outpost would then be established on the moon, and lunar soils would be catapulted back to the "construction shack". The soils would be processed into the required materials - glass, soil, oxygen. A construction crew would build, with these processed materials, the first habitat for 10,000 people. O'Neill feels this construction effort would be comparable, in tonnes per man-year, to that of larger-scale bridge-building on earth.

The first colony would serve as a base for constructing successively larger colonies. The largest colony would have cylinders 32 km in length and 6.4 km in diameter: a large colony could be inhabited by several million people. Eventually materials would be mined from the asteroid belt; this supply, O'Neill calculates, would last 500 years.

O'Neill describes the environment in one of the large cylinders (32 km in length) as being quite like that of earth. There would be natural sunlight, days, nights, and seasons as on earth, and a controlled climate. Solar energy would be used to sustain a closed ecological system with forests, lakes, rivers and mammals.

One of the most attractive possibilities of O'Neill's scheme is that of establishing satellite solar power stations to beam power back to earth. O'Neill asks, first, for a one-million dollar research grant. When we know more about the possibilities of space colonies and SSPS, O'Neill contends, we will better be able to decide which route to choose in searching for new energy sources. O'Neill has estimated that the cost of establishing Model 1 would be about $120 billion. But that amount represents only 1/5 the estimated cost of Project Independence, the $600 billion U.S. attempt to be independent of foreign energy supplies by the year 2000. And it is well known that the

U.S. is investing heavily in nuclear technology in its attempts to solve the energy problem.

In a series of graphs and calculations, O'Neill has "proven" that, even given the present rates of increase, it is technically possible to reverse the rise in Earth's population by the year 2050. O'Neill's optimism lies in his belief in technology; if projects such as the U.S. space shuttle program are successful in the 1980's, a fleet of fully-reusable composite-engine shuttles might be developed, comparable in size to the present fleet of commercial jets on Earth. Once in orbit, the shuttles would rendezvous with large ships whose engines would be fueled by lunar materials.

Identify the Issues

1. In the Netherlands, settlement on the new land reclaimed from the sea (the Ijsselmeer polders) can be organized without reference to existing settlements. What elements prevent the creation of ideal designs for settlements on these polders?

2. Is small scale technology something for developing countries only? Does it have any application in developed, urbanized areas?

3. Find out all you can about the tetrahedronal city. Look up the name Buckminster Fuller in your local library and see if there is a detailed description of the triangular city there.

CHAPTER TWELVE

The First Step

A major innovation was introduced into United Nations
activities at Stockholm in 1972 at the Conference on the
Environment. Non-government agencies were allowed to
participate though separate from the plenary sessions of the
official delegations. The same practice was continued at the
Vancouver Habitat Conference and all kinds of non-government
agencies took advantage of the opportunity to mount a major
parallel series of meetings.

One organization dominated this parallel scene. It was the
Vancouver Symposium, a joint project of the International
Institute for Environment and Development, The National Audubon
Society, and the Population Institute. And in the forefront of
the organization was Barbara Ward (Lady Jackson) who had worked
long and hard on the preparations for the Habitat Conference.
She was given the rare privilege of addressing the official
delegations. The following is the complete text of the speech
she delivered on June 1, 1976.

One of the most hopeful developments of the Seventies is the
degree to which world society has begun to examine, seriously
and together, what one might call the basic facts of "planetary
housekeeping". The U.N. Conference on the Human Environment
at Stockholm in 1972 set the trend. Since then, we have seen
the consideration of world population at Bucharest, of world
food at Rome, of the role and status of women at Mexico City
and at repeated sessions of the U.N. General Assembly - and most
recently at UNCTAD's deliberations at Nairobi - an urgent
discussion of the new economic order, in other words of the
overall calculus of interest and advantage in the global economy
and, with it, a deepening sense of the need to put an end to old
colonial injustices and distortions and create some kind of new,
more just and more balanced economic order.

But at no conference have all the aspects of man's daily living
been brought together more comprehensively than here at Habitat,
the U.N. Conference on Human Settlements. Nearly everything
that happens to the human race happens in its settlements and
although the task of considering everything on a global basis
may seen an impossible one, there is the counter-argument, felt
more and more strongly as people reflect more rationally on
their ways of life, that most human activities are profoundly
interconnected. Take food or population or science and
technology or women's status or whatever other vital issue out
of the context in which they are actually experienced and we may
need from time to time to correct our vision by fitting them

back into the continuum of daily life which is where their real
impact is experienced. The Stockholm Conference had an
important element of this sense of interconnexion. Vancouver is
host to the next great effort to examine global human experience
not in all its "minute particulars" but in the close web of
inter-dependence which holds it all together and largely
determines the impact of each separate part.

Admittedly to study a whole context is forbiddingly difficult
and the danger of looking at everything is that one can end up
by seeing nothing. But the risk must be taken from time to
time. Man is more than his brain or his liver or his heart. A
society is more than its population problem, its food problem,
its energy problem and so forth: they all come together in the
human settlement. It is only by examining them there that we
can avoid the fate of the man in the Bible who first looked in
the mirror and then went away and "forgot what manner of man he
was".

So let us look in the mirror. Where are we in our settlements?
What is happening to us? Where are we tending in our planetary
existance? These are questions we cannot answer unless we stand
off a little from the daily turmoil and try to see ourselves in
some sort of historical perspective. Of course, some will say,
with Henry Ford, that history is "bunk", in other words, what
is going on now is much too different from anything that has
already happened that comparisons are not only odious but simply
useless. But is is not unreasonable to suspect that Santayana
was nearer the truth when he said that those who will not learn
from history are destined to repeat it. Modern man has a long
history to learn from and a great deal of it should not, at all
costs, be repeated. So it is surely safer to see what the
historical perspective can tell us about our present plight.

Broadly speaking, we can say that the human race is just about
half way through its entry into the technological and urban
order. The changes are on an even more vast and radical a
scale than any previous fundamental change in the human
condition. The last two upheavals in man's total way of life -
the invention of settled agriculture some 20,000 years ago, the
invention of the city about 5,000 years ago - changed much and
laid the groundwork for modernity. But they were slow and
scattered and did not involve simultaneously the entire planet.
Our new transformation - to the science-based high technology,
urban society - began to gather momentum between the 16th and
18th Century with the steady development of accurate measure-
ment, scientific observation and practical inventions which,
applying mechanical energy and a deepening grasp of the nature
of chemical elements to man's daily work, brought the bulk of
economic activity out of the fields to the cities, sucked in
the manpower to work the new power-driven machinery in the
factories and set in motion an urbanizing process which in the
most developed societies has by now reduced the numbers working
directly in agriculture to under 10 percent of the workforce
and consigned nearly 80 percent of the people to settlements of

over 20,000 inhabitants.

For the quarter of humanity that are more or less through to
this urban condition, the process has taken a couple of
centuries. But everything is speeding up in the 20th Century.
For the two-thirds of humanity who still have over 70 percent
of their people on the farms, the percentage of people in the
countryside may have dropped to about half in the next three
decades. A predominantly "urban planet" could be not much more
than fifty or sixty years ahead.

If for a moment we disregard the speeding up of the process, it
is not altogether irrational to look back at the past history of
already developed countries and see how matters stood when they,
like the whole planet today, were roughly halfway along towards
fullscale industrialization and urbanization. If we take the
pioneer Britain - coming up to the middle of the 19th Century,
we may find some useful analogies. The fact that they are not
very reassuring should not deter us. The present condition of
our planet is not very reassuring either. And at least on
some critical issues Britain has done rather better since. So
it offers not only a warning. There are also some small
prospects of hope.

In the 1840s, a prime factor in Britain was an astonishing skew
in the distribution of wealth - the vast new resources poured
out by the new machines went overwhelmingly to the owners and
managers. It seems probable that between 1800 and 1850 the
share of the labourers and mechanics did not increase at all
while dukes and earls lucky enough to have coal under their
properties or cities advancing on their farms were able, as the
Earl of Durham put it, to "jog along" on the modern equivalent
of untaxed income of two to three million dollars a year.
Disraeli called Britain "two nations - the nation of the rich
and the nation of the poor" and the disparities showed up in
very vital statistics. The better-off in Manchester, for
instance, lived, on average, twice as long as the labourers -
although, in that noisome city, even the wealthy average was
under forty years. Infantile mortality was as high as in any
modern favela and, at five or six, the children were packed off -
manacled if they were paupers - to work at the looms and as
often as not fall into them. The first legislation passed to
remedy their plight can still leave us a little stunned. Their
hours were reduced to twelve hours a day in stupefying heat,
noise and danger. It took a strong ten-year-old to survive such
exposure.

The dirt and pollution of these early industrial centers would
give any modern environmentalist cardiac arrest. Here is a
description of Manchester's main river in the 1840s:

    "A narrow, coal-black, foul-smelling stream full of
    debris and refuse which it deposits on the shallow
    right bank. In dry weather, a long string of the
    most disgusting blackish, green slime pools are left

> standing on the bank, from the depths of which
> bubbles of miasmatic gas constantly rise and
> give forth a stench unendurable even on the
> bridge forty or fifty feet above the surface of
> the stream."

Interestingly enough the writer is Friedrich Engels and he is
sending his account to a friend called Karl Marx.

And over all the poor hung the old fear of recurrent hunger.
Cobbet tells us that the Lancashire textile workers survived on
oatmeal and water. When the looms were mechanized, Europe's
weavers literally starved to death. Then the bad harvests of
the Forties - the Hungry Forties - plus the potato blight
produced famine in Ireland and stringency all over industrial-
izing Europe. If anyone wants to read about the settlements of
this early industrial age, there they are in all their raw and
ruthless misery in the pages of Dickens' novels - Hard Times,
Bleak House - or, less poetically but even more painfully in
such offical documents as Britain's Report on the Sanitary
Conditions of the Labouring Population, an unrelieved report of
misery, foul water, filthy tenements, endless labour and early
death.

No-one can deny that conditions today in many parts of our
planetary economy are uncomfortably close to the Dickensian
horrow stories. The skew in world income is as great. The
already developed peoples - North America, Europe, the Soviet
Union, Japan - are the latter-day dukes, commanding over 70
percent of the planet's wealth for less than a quarter of the
population. And in all too many developing countries the
economic growth of the last two decades has been almost entirely
appropriated by the wealthiest ten percent of the people. The
comparisons in health, length of life, diet, literacy all work
out on the old Victorian patterns of unbelievable injustice.
Between the 1900 pounds of grain, all but 150 pounds eaten in
the form of wastefully processed animal products (and alcohol)
of the rich American or Russian and the average Indian's 400
pounds direct consumption of grain, the gap is as great as the
one between Cobbet's labourer and Charles Dickens' descriptions
of Mr. Merdle's ten-course London dinners. To the old
environmental degradations of stinking sewers and foul water are
now added the more refined effluents of chemical industries
warmed up with waste heat from power stations. Indeed, in many
ways the picture is more bleak. In the 19th Century, this productivity of agriculture was rising and the vast temperate lands
of North and South America, Southern Russia and Australia were
about to be brought under the plough. The shadow of hunger
passed after the 1840s. But it hangs over the world like a vast
thunder-head today with grain reserves down to 20 days
consumption and all of the surplus provided by a sometimes
drought-prone North America. Nor, in many areas, is productivity in farming on the increase. Or if it is, it is by capital
intensive methods which drive still more of the increasing rural
population away to the cities, to casual and uncertain employ-

ment, to polluted air and water and to all the indignities of
desperate poverty beside the shining skyscrapers of the new rich.

Again in the 19th Century, the workforce was only rising by
about 0.7 percent a year and what the new industries needed was
still unskilled labour - "hands" - even the hands of ten-year-
olds. By the time machines and processes demanded better
skills, the workers had become settled town-dwellers with
literacy, experience, greater confidence, working wives, smaller
families, more organization and trade. By historical good luck,
the cities were not swamped. There was a measure of balance
between in-migration and employment. Today, the workforce
grows by 2 percent a year. Yet, to an increasing degree,
industry wants skills, not hands. The classic example of a
plastic sandals factory in Latin America knocking out 15,000
artisans and providing work for 40 machinists is not unhappily
apocryphal. So when the rural poor arrive in the urban areas,
it is the push off the farms, not the pull into industrial jobs,
that all too often determines their movement and leaves 25 percent of them without regular work. Cities grow beyond the 3
million mark while under 10 percent of the workforce are in
industry - an almost exact reversal of the normal 19th Century
pattern and a reversal which spells unrelieved pressure and
continuing and desperate poverty for a majority of the new
urban dwellers.

Add the fact that over 40 million migrants could leave Europe
for the New World in the 19th Century while, today, the largest
"wandering of the peoples" in history is taking place within
the nations internally, from rural destitution to urban poverty
all inside the same developing land and we can add up a picture
which, while in its broad outlines resembles the earlier
experience of now developed societies when they heaved themselves
into the industrial urban order, in every case offers greater
obstacles, greater difficulties, greater incoherences, blockages
and dangers than any of the nations, now developed and urbanized,
ever experienced in their own transition. We are seeing the
same process - yes. But it is taking place in a wholly new
context of misfortune and hair-raising risk.

So, perhaps the differences are too great for the past to be
relevant. Perhaps we have nothing to learn, no guidance to
receive, no hints for hope and survival. But since we have
nowhere else to look, let us struggle all the same with the
angel of history and try to find some answers in past human
behaviour and past human experience to the fearful dilemmas of
our own day.

We must begin by accepting the element of chance and luck in
history. Those of us who are rich, white, developed and barely
post-imperialist must be specially careful to recognise that the
people of European stock and their descendants - Anglo-Saxons,
Iberians, Teutons, Franks, Slavs - by conquest and settlement
took over all the best land in the planet in the last four
hundred years and this vast takeover, which they still command,

enormously cushioned their transition to the industrial economy.
To give one example - but the most critical - the opening up of
the world's temperate grain lands by European settlers flooded
the late 19th Century system with cheap food. And this colossal
defeat of the old eternal enemy of mankind - malnutrition and
recurrent local famine - coupled with the accompanying sanitary
revolution of clean water and reliable drains, proved a point
about human development whose importance it is hard to overestimate. Steady food and clean water began to end the horrible
levels of infantile mortality in the earlier cities and as
parents came to see their first three children survive, they
began to doubt the need to have ten more as insurance for their
old age. By the end of the 19th Century, in developed lands,
Thomas Malthus had been proved wrong. Population does not
necessarily rise to consume the resources made available to it.
At a certain level of nutrition, security, income and - one
should add - literacy and opportunity, family size begins to
stabilize.

But we should notice more than the good fortune of abundant
harvests in all this. The other critical element - clean water
and the heroic achievements of late Victorian society in
sanitation and sewage - were not acts of fortune, like occupying
empty, supremely fertile farm land. They were acts of policy.
And here we have a lot to learn from our forefathers about
effective or disastrous routes into the urban order. Do not
think that the sanitary revolution, the beginnings of housing
for the poor, the introduction of universal education, the
beginnings of social insurance and a concern for unemployment
came in on a great tide of popular approval. They had to be
fought for step by step by a coalition of generous-minded
reformers among the fortunate and of tough, hard bargaining
leaders among the increasingly self-conscious and impatient
poor. The Disraeli who defined Britain in terms of a total
division based on wealth and poverty was also the Disraeli who
saw the implications of extending the franchise to all adult
males (of course) and who called one of his chief aims "sanitas,
omne sanitatum" and introduced the first housing acts. His was
the type of genius of conservative leadership that simply saw
the gap between fortune and misery would tear society apart
unless the fortunate themselves were prepared for the transfer
of resources and the openness for reform needed to lessen the
gap and create a social order in which every citizen had some
share. True, in Britain, it was an old aspiration. The cry of
Cromwell's man, John Lilburne, "the poorest he that is in
England hath a right to live as the richest he" went on echoing
through generous hearts and consciences and ensured that, at
every turning point of strain and storm, there was enough sense
of justice and compassion among the fortunate to maintain the
momentum of essential reform.

But at the same time, the pressures increased from the side of
the poor and exploited. With literacy, with growing trade union
organization, later with the vote and the growth of every
variant of socialism and social democracy, the determination of

three-quarters of the citizens to have a greater share in the
wealth their labours helped to produce, began in the late 19th
Century to push society towards a rather less skewed and in-
defensible distribution of rewards - and the pressures have
continued ever since. In fact, we can come here to something of
an historical conclusion. Where the conjunction of a far-
sighted sense of justice among the fortunate and urgent pressure
for fairer shares among the mass of the people have produced a
steadily maintained movement of reform, a readiness to
reconsider institutional blockages, an ability to sit down
together and argue about the realities of daily bread and about
the rights of the "poorest he", then that society, with all its
difficulties and disturbances, has made not too painful and
violent a transition to the new industrial urban order. Where
these have been lacking, there has been social convulsion,
violent revolution and an impetus to merciless world-wide war
and conquest. A period which includes two world wars, ever-
renewed depressions and a thousand colonial expeditions can
hardly be counted a model of good order. But the states which
within this unhappy phase of history contrived to develop
freedom, open institutions, greater justice, a more equal
citizenship and minds open to the ever renewed need for further
reform were those where the dialogue of fortunate and miserable,
of elite and masses, of rich and poor led not to deadly
confrontation and breakdown but to a progressive search for
better answers, better policies and better results.

Let us apply this analogy to our present phase of world development. What we have to do is adopt Disraeli's analogy, we have
"two planets - a planet of the rich and the planet of the poor"
and I would suggest that, among all the priorities that we have
to consider in a Conference that includes all of human life and
hope - or despair and violence - the three priorities that
determined peace or revolt in the 19th Century are those which
should occupy us now.

The first is not so much a program as an attitude - to achieve
a balance of openness and generosity among the fortunate and
of pressure and realism among the vast majority who are not.
Here, at Habitat, let this be the mood in all the debates and
all the discussions. Hard liners, gross misunderstandings,
closed minds, closed hearts - that is the route to planetary
disaster here or in any other international conference.

The second is a concrete strategy. We cannot reinvent the good
fortune of 19th Century food supplies. The world of a billion
has grown to four billion. The temperate lands are all ploughed
up. The entire grain reserve is in the hands of the fortunate
North Americans and for their food, the poorer lands paid 11
billion dollars more between 1973 and 1975. This, coupled with
rising energy prices, threatens to cripple the economies of the
poorest peoples. Worse still, it threatens them with famine.
But let us use our cooperation and inventiveness to make good
with hard thought, hard work and hard resources the fabulous
good luck of earlier days. Let a high priority of Habitat be to

send to the meeting of the World Food Council which immediately
follows this conference a double message - support for the Rome
Food Conference's aim of $25-30 billion a year invested in
Third World agriculture, of which $5 billion should come from
the old rich of the industrialized world and the new rich of
the oil fields. So far, about a billion of this external
commitment is firmly pledged. Let us move along to the full
sum required.

Within Habitat itself, let us look at the overwhelming need to
give farming the infrastructure of settlements - the intermediate markets, agro-industries, market roads, regional urban
centers - without which the aim of an annual 5 percent increase
in developing farm output will simply not take place. If we can
together give Third World agriculture the stimulus it needs -
and this requires a national policy for regional and local
distribution of population, settlements, investment and
opportunity - then we can, as it were, invent by good planning
the equivalent of the good luck which fell into the laps of the
19th Century settlers. And in doing so, we can banish that dark
cloud of the risk of famine hanging over the world and at the
same time begin to ensure the survival of children and hence
the stabilization of family size.

And this agricultural strategy can help to lessen the lemming-
like surges of peasant to city which threatens to overwhelm
even the bravest urban plans. With world population possibly
doubling to nearly 7 billion by the year 2000, with nearly half
still on the land in developing countries, there is a vast
overhang waiting to be dislodged at the least disturbance - soil
eroding, monsoons failing, mechanization pushing ahead. The
first need in taking the strain off cities is not to allow the
megalopoles to grow still further but build up the intermediate centers - as in France or Romania or China - which both
save a flourishing farming system and provide other outlets for
urban movement.

And now for the third priority, within the settlements themselves, let us begin and carry through the nineteenth century
reforms of urban sanitation, public housing, education and
communal services. There are, of course, a thousand other
needs. Water and sewage plans cannot be carried out without
control of land use, an end of land speculation, securing the
unearned increment for community investment and planning and
siting cities in such a way that they can be clean, healthy and
safe. But since priorities there must be, let them be
sanitation and clean water. The World Bank has published the
outline of a package for basic infrastructure in settlements -
sites and services, self-help housing, urban public transport,
health services, clean water. The whole program is about $30
billion a year, the share of water $3 billion. If this plan
could be adopted, the world in every sense would be a sweeter
place.

But here, I fear, we hear the voices of the selfish rich

exclaiming that no such thing is possible. The developed world,
they say, is in such disarray, in such danger of inflation, in
such precarious economic health that transfers of this sort are
inconceivable. We have just been told at UNCTAD by a
responsible Western government that $6 billions for commodity
agreements might restart inflation among the wealthy. I confess
my answer here, in the immortal phrase of Morecombe and Wise,
is simply "rubbish"! The developed world is inflated because
it systematically tries to take out more than it puts in. Take
two chief examples. The first is waste. We operate our
electricity systems at about 35 percent capacity. We have
private transport systems which waste up to 40 percent of the
petroleum they use. We have a B1 bomber which in a year uses
the equivalent of all America's buses. We have 80 storey
zigguruts which need simultaneous heating and cooling. We stock
invaluable organic wastes to pollute our water courses. We
throw away billions of cans and bottles and buy new ones
manufactured at higher cost in energy. On a sober calculus,
North America could save 50 percent of the energy it buys and
still achieve much the same standard of living. The whole
program for agricultural development and urban renewal, could be
financed either from what we waste or by a cut of, say, a third
in our consumption of alcohol.

The second appalling desperate and continuous cause of inflation
is our arms spending. Since 1973 it has increased by $60
billions a year. It now tops $300 billions. Since no goods
are made by arms industries to mop up the wages they create,
arms spending is by definition the most inflationary of all
expenditure. And what do we get? The ability to blow up the
planet twenty times over? Once is enough. Plutonium bombs
which can give the whole world cancer? Plutonium wastes that
after twenty years are beginning to burst their containers on
the oceanbeds to release poisons with a half life of 25,000
years? Just how rational can we be? We spend $300 billions on
the weapons of death, we boggle at $30 billions for the means of
life.

But is there a hope here? The disproportions have become so
tragi-comic that perhaps here at Habitat a stand can be made
and a reversal begun. Three years ago, the Soviet Union
proposed and the U.N. General Assembly approved a proposal to
cut arms spending by 10 percent and devote a little of it - only
10 percent, alas - to development. The resolution stands but
nothing, nothing at all, has been done about it. Why not then
propose that arms spending, the prime source of world inflation,
be now cut by 10 percent and the $30 billions devoted to basic
agricultural and urban development? The mechanics of the
process can be worked out. What is needed now is the commitment
and the funds. And if it is not possible to change the original
Resolution 3093 (XXVII) from the 2194th Plenary Meeting of the
General Assembly, 7th December 1973 (in case anyone, including
the Soviet delegates, are interested), could we not stick at
least to the 10 percent of the 10 percent which gives us just
what we need for safe world water supplies in every settlement -

$3 billions a year for ten years. With it could come good
health, surviving babies, stabilizing families and a vast
increase in human dignity and human happiness. In fact it may
well be the fastest, surest route we have to a planet beginning
to grow away from enmity and death and look towards the works of
life.

It is simply not possible to underline sufficiently the
appalling state of our collective imagination when $300 billions
for arms seems normal and $3 billions for water exceptional.
But Habitat can perhaps show that the beginning of a vast
reversal of values is taking place. The city of man is turning
its face against the image of necropolis. The model of sure
and shared supplies of food and water, of the extension of
literacy and health and justice to all the people is the model
we have to learn from the first phase of the technological
order. Can we in the turmoils ahead, show that as a small
species on our fragile planet we can collectively "choose life"
and by that creative process of generosity among the fortunate
elites and determined pressure from the mass of the people,
build an order in our settlements which gives us some reasonable
hope of living in peace ourselves and leaving a peaceful planet
to our children? We shall not get it by chance or luck. We
shall not secure it by the present divisions and conflicts of
"our proud and angry dust". But we could begin to build it by
working to make decent settlements our first priority and
giving them the dedication and resources we have too often
reserved only for fear and war. If we can begin to accept the
priority at Habitat, what a turning point in human destiny this
encounter could prove to be! To overcome the vast obstructions
of the next decades is indeed "a journey of a thousand days".
But let us, here in Vancouver, take the first step.

Identify The Issues

1.   What is the first step that Barbara Ward is proposing?
     How much will it cost?

2.   Is this first step something that the nations of the world
     can afford? What other needs might be more urgent?

3.   Compare factory conditions in 18th century England with
     the situations in today's third world countries. List 3
     bad social conditions from England that were worse than
     anything you could find today.

Some Facts and Figures

Country	Area sq.mi.	in km^2	Latitude from	to
Australia	2,968,000	7,687,000	11°S	43°S
Bangladesh	55,126	142,776	22°N	26°N
Brazil	3,286,486	8,511,965	34°S	5°N
Canada	3,851,809	9,976,139	42°N	83°N
Chile	292,257	756,946	17°S	56°S
Cuba	43,000	111,000	20°N	23°N
Egypt	386,900	1,002,000	22°N	32°N
France	212,742	551,000	43°N	51°N
Finland	130,000	337,000	60°N	70°N
Honduras	43,000	112,000	13°N	16°N
India	1,262,000	3,268,000	8°N	33°N
Indonesia	782,663	2,027,087	4°N	10°S
Iran	636,000	1,648,000	25°N	40°N
Israel	7,992	20,700	29°N	33°N
Italy	116,314	301,253	36°N	46°N
Japan	144,000	372,000	30°N	46°N
Kenya	225,000	583,000	5°N	5°S
Malaysia	127,316	329,736	6°N	1°N
Mexico	762,000	1,973,000	15°N	32°N
Netherlands	15,892	41,160	51°N	54°N
New Zealand	103,736	268,676	34°S	48°S
Nigeria	356,669	923,773	14°N	6°N
Pakistan	307,374	796,095	24°N	37°N
Peru	496,000	1,285,000	0°	18°S
Philippines	115,830	300,000	5°N	20°N
Saudi Arabia	865,000	2,240,000	17°N	32°N
Senegal	79,000	204,000	12°N	17°N
Singapore	226	586	2°N	2°N
Somalia	246,154	637,541	12°N	1°S
Soviet Union	8,649,500	22,402,200	37°N	80°N
Sudan	967,491	2,505,805	4°N	23°N
Swaziland	6,704	17,364	26°S	27°S
Sweden	173,649	449,750	55°N	69°N
Tanzania	365,000	945,000	1°S	12°S
Turkey	301,380	780,576	36°N	42°N
United Kingdom	94,512	244,785	50°N	59°N
United States	3,615,122	9,363,123	25°N	49°N

SOME FACTS AND FIGURES

Country	Rate per 1000 of pop:		% of pop:		% of pop: literate
	Births	Deaths	Under 15	Over 60	
Australia	20.6	9.1	29	12.4	N/A
Bangladesh	50.9	18.4	46.1	5.2	21.5
Brazil	37.8	9.5	41.7	5.3	68.0
Canada	17.1	7.3	29.6	12.2	94.8
Chile	26.6	9.0	39	7.1	87.1
Cuba	28.6	6.5	36.7	7.0	N/A
Egypt	34.9	15.0	42.8	6.0	26.3
France	17.2	10.8	24.8	18.1	100
Finland	13.3	9.9	24.3	14.3	100
Honduras	43	9	46.8	3.9	45
India	38.6	14	41.6	5.2	29
Indonesia	48.3	19.4	44.1	4.4	39
Iran	44	18	46.1	6.5	28
Israel	27.3	7.2	33	10.8	91
Italy	16.5	9.5	24.4	15.2	98
Japan	18.6	6.9	24	10.7	100
Kenya	50	17	48.4	5.4	60
Malaysia	35.2	7.6	43.8	6.0	58.5
Mexico	43.4	9.9	46.2	5.6	76.2
Netherlands	18.3	8.4	27.2	14.6	100
New Zealand	22.1	8.8	31.6	12.4	100
Nigeria	49.6	24.9	43	3.5	25
Pakistan	50.9	18.4	42.4	6.9	16.3
Peru	43.5	12.3	45	4.9	61
Philippines	44.7	12.0	47	4.2	83.4
Saudi Arabia	50.0	22.7	N/A	N/A	10
Senegal	46.3	22.8	42.5	5.6	6
Singapore	22.3	5.4	38.8	5.7	70
Somalia	45.9	24.0	37.2	4.8	15
Soviet Union	17.4	8.2	27.6	11.8	99.7
Sudan	48.9	18.4	47.3	3.6	19.4
Swaziland	48	22	47.8	4.4	29.2
Sweden	14.1	10.2	20.6	19.9	100
Tanzania	47	22	43.9	7.4	12.5
Turkey	39.6	14.6	41.5	7.2	55.4
United Kingdom	16.2	11.6	24.3	18.7	100
United States	15.6	9.4	27.8	14.2	99

N/A: Not Available

SOME FACTS AND FIGURES

Country	Capital City	Monetary Unit	Main Language(s)
Australia	Canberra	Dollar	English
Bangladesh	Dacca	Taka	Bengali
Brazil	Brasilia	Cruzeiro	Portuguese
Canada	Ottawa	Dollar	English & French
Chile	Santiago	Escudo	Spanish
Cuba	Havana	Peso	Spanish
Egypt	Cairo	Pound	Arabic
France	Paris	Franc	French
Finland	Helsinki	Markka	Finnish & Swedish
Honduras	Teguicigalpa	Lempira	Spanish
India	New Delhi	Rupee	Hindi & English
Indonesia	Jakarta	Rupiah	Bahasa Indonesian
Iran	Teheran	Rial	Persian
Israel	Jerusalem	Pound	Hebrew & Arabic
Italy	Rome	Lira	Italian
Japan	Tokyo	Yen	Japanese
Kenya	Nairobi	Shilling	Swahili & English
Malaysia	Kuala Lumpur	Dollar	Malay
Mexico	Mexico City	Peso	Spanish
Netherlands	Amsterdam; The Hague	Ruilder	Dutch
New Zealand	Wellington	Dollar	English
Nigeria	Lagos	Pound	English
Pakistan	Islamabad	Rupee	Bengali,Urdu,English
Peru	Lima	Sol	Spanish
Philippines	Quezon City	Peso	Philipino & English
Saudi Arabia	Riyadh	Riyal	Arabic
Senegal	Dakar	Franc	French
Singapore	Singapore	Dollar	Chinese & English Malay & Tamil
Somalia	Mogadiscio	Shilling	Somali
Soviet Union	Moscow	Ruble	Russian
Sudan	Khartoum	Pound	Arabic
Swaziland	Mbabane	Rand	Siswati & English
Sweden	Stockholm	Krona	Swedish
Tanzania	Dar es Salaam	Shilling	Swahili & English
Turkey	Ankara	Lira	Turkish
United Kingdom	London	Pound	English
United States	Washington	Dollar	English

SOME FACTS AND FIGURES

Country	% of land arable	Density of population per sq.mi.	per km^2
Australia	6	4.3	1.7
Bangladesh	63.7	1,325	511.8
Brazil	3.5	30.0	11.8
Canada	4.7	6.1	2.4
Chile	6	30.2	11.7
Cuba	50	202	78
Egypt	2.8	97	37
France	35.4	245.1	94.6
Finland	8.8	39.3	15.2
Honduras	7.3	58	22.4
India	50	433.8	167.5
Indonesia	6.7	158.5	61.2
Iran	11	47.4	18.3
Israel	20.2	399.5	154.2
Italy	49.6	482.3	178.5
Japan	15.2	736.8	284.5
Kenya	2.9	53.2	20.5
Malaysia	20.7	82.1	31.7
Mexico	12.1	66.9	25.8
Netherlands	25.7	901.4	348
New Zealand	3.5	27.6	10.7
Nigeria	23.6	154.4	59.6
Pakistan	24	211.1	81.5
Peru	2	27.4	10.6
Philippines	29.9	316.7	122.3
Saudi Arabia	0.4	8.9	3.5
Senegal	29	47.7	18.4
Singapore	24.5	9,422	3,634
Somalia	1.5	11.6	4.5
Soviet Union	10.4	28.4	10.9
Sudan	3.0	17	6.6
Swaziland	14.8	66.5	25.7
Sweden	2.4	51.2	19.8
Tanzania	13	38.4	14.8
Turkey	35.1	121.4	46.9
United Kingdom	30.1	595	229.7
United States	19.2	59	22.8

SOME FACTS AND FIGURES

Country	Population 1975 Urban (in millions)	Rural	Population 2000 est. Urban (in millions)	Rural
Australia	11.9	1.9	18.6	1.7
Bangladesh	5	68.7	17.3	127
Brazil	66.3	44.5	162.2	50.3
Canada	17.9	4.9	28	3.7
Chile	8.5	1.7	14.1	1.2
Cuba	5.8	3.6	11.4	3.8
Egypt	17.9	19.6	41.5	23.1
France	40.2	12.7	54.2	8
Finland	2.6	2.1	3.5	1.3
Honduras	.9	2.2	2.7	4.2
India	131.8	481.7	342.2	717.6
Indonesia	26.2	109.8	74.7	162.8
Iran	14.6	18.3	40.8	25.8
Israel	2.9	.6	5	.5
Italy	36.7	18.3	48.1	12.8
Japan	80.6	27.5	116.1	16.8
Kenya	1.5	11.8	6.4	24.6
Malaysia	3.7	8.4	9.9	12.1
Mexico	37.4	21.8	103.6	28.7
Netherlands	10.8	2.8	14	2
New Zealand	2.5	.5	3.9	.4
Nigeria	11.4	51.5	40.9	94
Pakistan	19	51.6	62.3	84.6
Peru	8.7	6.6	22.1	8.5
Philippines	16	28.5	45.6	44.1
Saudi Arabia	1.9	7.1	7	11.6
Senegal	1.3	3.2	3.5	4.7
Singapore	2	.2	3	.1
Somalia	.9	2.3	2.9	3.7
Soviet Union	154.3	100.7	240.5	74.5
Sudan	2.4	15.9	8.9	30
Swaziland	.07	.4	.3	.6
Sweden	6.9	1.3	8.6	.8
Tanzania	1	14.4	4.3	29.8
Turkey	17.2	22.7	45.5	27.1
United Kingdom	44.1	12.3	53.3	9.5
United States	163.3	50.7	227.8	36.6

Introductory Bibliography

Ekistics, Science of Human Settlements, Vol. 41, No. 247, June 1976, 100pp

Environmental Handbook, (ed) G. De Bell, Ballantine Books, 1970, 367pp

Environment of Human Settlements, (ed) P. Laconte et al, Pergamon Press, 1976, 322pp

Finite Resources and the Human Future, (ed) Ian G. Barbour, Augsburg, 1976, 192pp

Geography of Population, (ed) P.F. Griffin, Fearon, 1969, NCGE Yearbook, 370pp

Global History, G. Walsh, McClelland and Stewart, 1975, 144pp

Global Review of Human Settlements and Statistical Index, Pergamon Press, 1976, 576pp

Habitat, (Bimonthly Journal), Pergamon Press, 1976 –

Home of Man, B. Ward, McCelland and Stewart, 1976, 297pp

Human Settlements: Annotated Bibliography, Pergamon Press, 1976, 228pp

Human Settlements: National Reports Summaries: Pergamon Press, 1976, 136pp

Improving Human Settlements, (ed) H. Peter Oberlander, University of British Columbia Press, 1977, 200pp

People: an International Choice, Rafael M. Salas, Pergamon Press, 1976, 150pp

Taming the Megalopolis, Lauchlin Currie, Pergamon Press, 1976, 185pp

Utopia or Oblivion, R. Buckminster Fuller, Bantam Books, 1969, 366pp

Index